Where Christianity Errs

Where Christianity Errs

A Fair and Clear Philosophical Assessment

Richard Schoenig

WIPF & STOCK · Eugene, Oregon

WHERE CHRISTIANITY ERRS
A Fair and Clear Philosophical Assessment

Copyright © 2024 Richard Schoenig. All rights reserved. Except for brief quotations in critical publications or reviews, no part of this book may be reproduced in any manner without prior written permission from the publisher. Write: Permissions, Wipf and Stock Publishers, 199 W. 8th Ave., Suite 3, Eugene, OR 97401.

Wipf & Stock
An Imprint of Wipf and Stock Publishers
199 W. 8th Ave., Suite 3
Eugene, OR 97401

www.wipfandstock.com

PAPERBACK ISBN: 979-8-3852-0592-9
HARDCOVER ISBN: 979-8-3852-0593-6
EBOOK ISBN: 979-8-3852-0594-3

VERSION NUMBER 04/03/24

Scripture quotations marked (GNT) are from the Good News Translation in Today's English Version—Second Edition Copyright © 1992 by American Bible Society. Used by Permission.

Scripture quotations marked (KJV) are from The Authorized (King James) Version. Rights in the Authorized Version in the United Kingdom are vested in the Crown. Reproduced by permission of the Crown's patentee, Cambridge University Press.

Scripture quotations marked (NIV) are taken from the Holy Bible, New International Version®, NIV®. Copyright © 1973, 1978, 1984, 2011 by Biblica, Inc.™ Used by permission of Zondervan. All rights reserved worldwide. www.zondervan.com The "NIV" and "New International Version" are trademarks registered in the United States Patent and Trademark Office by Biblica, Inc.™

Scripture quotations marked (ESV) are from the ESV® Bible (The Holy Bible, English Standard Version®), © 2001 by Crossway, a publishing ministry of Good News Publishers. Used by permission. All rights reserved. The ESV text may not be quoted in any publication made available to the public by a Creative Commons license. The ESV may not be translated in whole or in part into any other language.

For Neddy: many thanks for your invaluable help and encouragement.

Truth makes you free. (John 8:32)

Reason brings you truth.

Contents

Preface | xix
Acknowledgements | xxv

Part I: Critiques of Select Aspects of Christian Beliefs

Chapter 1: Original Sin: Can't Live With It; Can't Live Without It | 3
    Preview   3
    Creation, Garden of Eden Story, and the Doctrine of Original Sin   3
  Can't Live With the Doctrine of Original Sin   4
    Doctrine of Original Sin's History and Science Problems   4
      Faith-Based Support to the Rescue?   6
    Doctrine of Original Sin's Moral Problems   6
      Evaluation of Three Christian Retorts to the Claim That the Doctrine of Original Sin Has a Moral Problem   9
        Preternatural Gifts Retort to the Claim That the Doctrine of Original Sin Has a Moral Problem   9
        Important Relevant Data About Prenatal Mortality   11
        Representation Retort Against the Claim That the Doctrine of Original Sin Has a Moral Problem   15
        Creator Retort Against the Claim That the Doctrine of Original Sin Has a Moral Problem   16
    Doctrine of Original Sin's Knowledge Problem   17

CONTENTS

    Can't Live Without the Doctrine of Original Sin   18

        Summary of the Christian Rationale for the Historical Truth of the Doctrine of Original Sin   21

        Two Mistakes Involving the Christian Rationale for the Truth of the Doctrine of Original Sin   21

            First Mistake Involving the Rationale for the Truth of the Doctrine of Original Sin   21

            Second Mistake Involving the Rationale for the Truth of the Doctrine of Original Sin   25

    Conclusion   26

Chapter 2: Petitionary and Thanksgiving Prayer: Innocuous but Pointless | 27

        Preview   27

    Introduction   27

    Reasons Why Petitionary Prayer (PP) Is Not a Cogent Practice   28

        PP Lacks Adequate Evidence Supporting Its Efficacy   28

        Christians Never Hold God Responsible for Not Answering PP   28

        Christian Defenses of PP Are Weak.   28

            Let-God-Know Defense of PP   28

            Just-Ask Defense of PP   29

            Character Enhancement Defense of PP   31

    PP Assessment Conclusion   33

    Reasons Why Thanksgiving Prayer (TP) Is Not a Cogent Practice   34

        TP Is Incoherent   34

    Conclusion   35

Chapter 3: Religious Faith: A Peek Behind the Curtain | 36

        Preview   36

    Introduction   36

    Faith   37

    Reason   39

CONTENTS

    Problems Associated With Faith   39

    Faith Contradicts Reason   39

    Faith Is Not a Path to Knowledge   40

    Faith Cannot Objectively Judge Competing Faith-Based Claims   42

    Faith Cannot Be Justified by Strength of Conviction   43

    Faith Is Not Found in Everyone   44

Chapter Summary   45

Chapter 4: Does God Send People to Hell? | 46

    Preview   46

Introduction   46

Debunking the Claim That God Does Not Send People to Hell   47

Chapter 5: How to Assure Christian Salvation through Murder! | 52

    Preview   52

Introduction   52

General Christian Soteriology   53

Christian-Assured-Salvation Strategy   53

Objections to the Christian-Assured-Salvation Strategy and My Responses   55

Conclusions   59

Summary   60

Chapter 6: Christianity and the Meaning of Life | 61

    Preview   61

Introduction   61

    Q = What Is the Meaning of Life?   62

Clarification of "Meaning Of"   62

Examination of Reformulations of Q (R1–R4)   64

    R1: Meaning-in-Significance: What Gives My Life Significance?   64

    Christian Interpretation of the Meaning of Life   65

    R2: Meaning-in-Purpose: What Is the Purpose of My Life?   67

CONTENTS

    R3: Meaning-in-Effect: Does It Really Matter That I Live and Will Die? 68

    R4: Meaning-in-Cause: Why Am I Living? 68

  My Proposed Interpretation And Answer To Q 69

    R5: Meaning-in-Prescription: What Procedures, Standards, Virtues Should Guide Human Life to Satisfaction? 70

  Meaning Of Life—Proposed 72

Chapter 7: Christian Apologists: Why Do They Even Bother? | 73

    Preview 73

  Christian Apologetics Is Unchristian! 73

  Christian Apologetics Is Dangerous 75

  So, Why Do Christian Apologists Even Bother Then? 76

    Fame and Fortune 76

    Half a Loaf Is Better Than None 77

    It's the Faith, Stupid! 77

  Conclusion 78

Chapter 8: Critiques of Three Miscellaneous Christian Topics | 79

    Preview 79

  (1) Why Do Atheists Always Blame God for the Suffering in the World? 79

  (2) Why Do Atheists Always Seem So Angry At Religion, Especially Christianity? 80

  (3) What's Up With God and Glory Anyway? 81

    Glory Defined 81

    God Likes Glory 81

    John Piper's Comments on God and His Glory 81

    My Comments 84

Part II: Christianity and Ethics

Chapter 9: By Their Fruits Ye Shall Know Them | 89

    Preview 89

  Atheist Atrocities Argument 89

CONTENTS

Response to the Atheist Atrocities Argument   90
    Fatalities from the Old Testament Era   91
    Fatalities from the New Testament Era   91
        Fatalities Caused by Christian Ideology   91
        Fatalities carried out by Christians for Nonreligious Reasons   94
    Tale of the Tape   94
Claim GA: God Is Morally Responsible for Causing Four Thousand Eight Hundred Times More Deaths Than Were Caused by SPHM   95
    Argument in Support of Claim GA   95
    Christian Retorts to Claim GA and My Responses   96
        Devil-Is-Responsible Retort to Claim GA   96
        Soul-Making Retort to Claim GA   96
        Summum Bonum Retort to Claim GA   97
Conclusions   97

Chapter 10: Jesus Christ: Ethical Sage? | 99
    Preview   99
    Section I: Assessment of Four Moral Prescriptions from the Sermon on the Mount   99
        JEP: (1) Love, (2) Don't Resist, (3) Turn the Other Cheek to, (4) Do Good to Your Enemies.   99
        Counterexample to JEP   100
    Christian Defenses of JEP Evaluated   101
        JEP Is Cogent Because It Prevents Resisters from Becoming Harm-Doers   101
        JEP Embodies a More Elevated Morality than Previously Practiced.   101
        JEP Is Cogent Because It's Actually Hyperbole   103
        JEP Is Cogent Because It Rules Out Only Retaliatory or Vengeful Resistance.   104
        JEP Is Cogent Because It Should Not Be Understood Literally   106

JEP Is Cogent Because It Should Be Understood More as Suggestions   107

JEP Is Cogent Because It Permits One to Resist Evil, But Only Nonviolently.   108

JEP Is Cogent Because Its Prescriptions Were Meant as Divinely Sourced Moral Ideals   110

Conclusions About Section I   110

Section II: Assessment of Christianity's Two Greatest Commandments   111

Section III: Assessment of "Do Not Judge, Lest You Also Be Judged"   112

Face Value Interpretation of A1   112

Be Not Hypocritical Interpretation of A1   112

Section IV: Assessment of "Hate the Sin; Love the Sinner"   113

Coda: What Jesus Should Have Said   114

Chapter 11: Two Inconsistencies in the Christian Antiabortion Stance | 116

Preview

Violence against Abortion Providers   116

Abortion and the Fate of Frozen Fertilized Human Eggs   118

Evaluation of Two Christian Retorts to the Claim That Rescuing Unwanted Frozen Zygotes Is Morally Required   119

Chapter Summary   121

Chapter 12: American Christianity and Political Conservatism | 122

Preview   122

Introduction   122

Birds of a Feather   123

Those Were the Days My Friend . . .   123

The Enemy of My Enemy Is My Friend   124

You Scratch My Back And . . .   125

Religion Bakes No Bread   125

Onward Christian Soldiers!   127

A "Heads Up" 128
Chapter Summary 128

Chapter 13: A Novel Defense of Objective Ethics Without Christianity or Any Religion | 130

    Preview 130

    Introduction 130

    Argument for God's Existence from the Objectivity of Ethics 131

    Ethical Rationalism 131

        Starting Point: A Fulfilling Life 131

        Connection between a Fulfilling Life and a Universally Correct Moral Code 132

        Ethical Rationalism's Two Principles 133

            No Harm Principle 133

            Principle of Assistance 133

        Additional Comments on Ethical Rationalism's Moral Code 134

        Justification of Ethical Rationalism 136

            Following Ethical Rationalism's Two Principles Is Necessary for Living a Fulfilling Life 136

            Following Ethical Rationalism's Two Principles Is Sufficient for Living a Fulfilling Life 138

        Justification Argument for Ethical Rationalism 139

        Beyond Ethical Rationalism's Moral Code 140

    Conclusion 142

Part III: Christianity and Atheism

Chapter 14: The Christian God Doesn't Exist Because Of Unfair Human Experiences | 145

    Preview 145

    Introduction 145

    Definition of Unfairness 146

    Argument for God's Nonexistence from the Existence of Unfair Human Experiences 147

CONTENTS

Thought Experiment TE   147

Argument for God's Nonexistence from the Existence of Unfair Human Experiences Formatted   148

Retorts to Objections to the Argument for God's Nonexistence from the Existence of Unfair Human Experiences   149

Chapter 15: Christian God Doesn't Exist Because of Unfair Salvific Opportunities | 153

Preview   153

Definition of Unfairness   154

General Christian Doctrine of Salvation   154

Argument For God's Nonexistence from the Existence of Unfair Salvific Opportunities   155

Argument for God's Nonexistence from Existence of Unfair Salvific Opportunities Formatted   156

Defense of Premise 3 That It's Likely That God Acts Unfairly   155

"Unables" and "Ables" Groups of Humans   156

Unables Vis-à-Vis Ables Intergroup Unfairness Described and Evaluated   159

Evaluation of Five Christian Retorts to the Conclusion That the Correct Doctrine of Salvation Involves Invidious Discrimination against Unables   160

First Christian Retort: Class III and IV Unables Have Sufficient Salvific Knowledge; The General Revelation Defense.   160

Second Christian Retort to the Claim of Invidious Discrimination against the Unables Vis-à-Vis the Ables: The Salvation-for-All-Unables Defense.   165

Third Christian Retort to the Claim of Divine Invidious Discrimination against the Unables Vis-à-Vis the Ables: The Salvific Universalism Defense   166

Fourth Christian Retort to the Claim of Divine Invidious Discrimination against the Unables Vis-à-Vis the Ables: The Middle Knowledge Defense   167

Fifth Christian Retort to the Claim of Invidious Discrimination against the Unables Vis-à-Vis the Ables: All Unables Are Lost to Hell Because of Their "Transworld Damnation." 170

Sixth Christian Retort to the Claim of Invidious Discrimination Against the Unables Vis-à-Vis the Ables: The Postmortem Opportunity Defense 171

Ables Intragroup Unfairness Evaluated 174

Evaluation of the Skeptical Theism Challenge to Premise 3 of the Argument for God's Existence from the Existence of Unfair Salvific Opportunities 175

Summary and Conclusion 177

Chapter 16: Christian God Doesn't Exist Because If He Did, He'd Be An Absentee Father | 178

Preview 178

Argument for God's Nonexistence from the Existence of a Divine Temporal Gap 178

Defense of the Soundness of the Argument For God's Nonexistence from the Existence of a Divine Temporal Gap 180

The Gap 180

Young Earth Defense of the Gap 182

Skeptical Theism Defense of the Gap 182

Paul of Tarsus Defense: There Was No Gap 183

Conclusion 183

Coda: William Lane Craig on the Historicity of Adam and Eve 183

Chapter 17: The Christian God Doesn't Exist Because Of The Quantity Of Apparently Unjustified Suffering | 185

Preview 185

Introduction 185

Formatted Argument for God's Nonexistence from the Quantity of Apparently Unjustified Suffering 186

Argument for God's Nonexistence from the Quantity of Apparently Unjustified Suffering Defended 187

Defense of the Truth of Premise (1) 187
    Estimation of the Quantity of AUS Experienced by Humans 187
    Estimation of Quantity of AUS Experienced by Sentient Animals 188
    Total Amount of Animal and Human AUS 188
Defense of the Truth of Premise (2) 188
Response to the Skeptical Theism Challenge to Premise (2) 189
Bayesian Calculations Defending the Truth of Premise (2) 191
Defense of the Truth of Premise (4) 194
Chapter Conclusion 195

Chapter 18: Christian God Doesn't Exist Because This World Does | 196

Preview 196

Introduction 196

Heaven World (HW) 197

HW Argument For the Nonexistence of God 199

Heaven World Argument for the Nonexistence of God Formatted 199

Heaven World Argument for the Nonexistence of God Evaluated 200

Response to Christian Challenges to the HW Argument for the Nonexistence of God 203

    First Challenge to the HW Argument: In HW Humans Would Have to Forego the Great Good of Having a Conscious, Embodied Earthly Life 203

    Second Challenge to the HW Argument: In HW Humans Would Have to Forego the Value Associated with God's Keeping His Epistemic (Knowledge of Him) Distance from Them. 204

    Third Challenge to the HW Argument: In HW Humans Would Not Experience the Value of Soul-Making 205

    Fourth Challenge to the HW Argument: Actualizing TW Involved No Moral Deficiencies on God's Part 209

CONTENTS

    Christian "No Best World" Retort   211

    Fifth Challenge to the HW Argument: God's Reasons for Actualizing TW Rather Than HW May Be Impossible to Understand (Skeptical Theism—Yet Again!).   213

    Sixth Challenge to the HW Argument: More Skeptical Theism   214

Chapter Summary and Conclusion   215

Coda For Part III   215

Bibliography | 217
About the Author | 225
Index | 227

Preface

MOTIVATION FOR THE BOOK

Dr. William Lane Craig is arguably the most visible, credentialed, and celebrated Christian apologist (defender of the faith) in the world today. His master apologetic work is a book entitled *Reasonable Faith, Christian Truth and Apologetics*. In the early part of that book Craig says the following.

> Therefore, when a person refuses to come to Christ, it is never just because of lack of evidence or because of intellectual difficulties: at root, he refuses to come because he willingly ignores and rejects the drawing of God's Spirit on his heart. No one in the final analysis really fails to become a Christian because of lack of arguments; he fails to become a Christian because he loves darkness rather than light and wants nothing to do with God. But anyone who responds to the drawing of God's Spirit with an open mind and an open heart can know with assurance that Christianity is true, because God's Spirit will convict him that it is.[1]

With all due respect to Dr. Craig, I believe that he is mistaken in holding that those who reject Christianity do so because they love "darkness rather than light" or want "nothing to do with God." In *Where Christianity Errs* I aim to show in a fair-minded way that, based on Christianity's "lack of evidence," "intellectual difficulties," and "lack of [sound] arguments," there are, in fact, compelling reasons for anyone with an "open mind and an open heart" to doubt that Christianity is true.

---

1. Craig, *Reasonable Faith*, 47.

PREFACE

CONTENT AND FORMAT

The eighteen essays in this book are sorted into three parts. Note that the chapters can be read in any order.

Part I comprises eight chapters which evaluate certain common and important Christian beliefs and practices.

Chapter 1 highlights the many shortcomings with the central Christian doctrine of original sin, which leads to the conclusion that Christianity can't live with it and can't live without it.

Chapter 2 critiques petitionary and thanksgiving prayer. The conclusion is that both types of praying are innocuous but pointless.

Chapter 3 explains why Christianity's indispensable doctrine of faith is irremediably defective.

Chapter 4 rebuts the contention, held by many Christians, that God doesn't send people to hell. Rather, people choose to be there.

Chapter 5 shows how Christian salvation is flawed because it can be guaranteed by murder! Stay tuned for that.

Chapter 6 analyzes the notion of the meaning of life within a Christian worldview and within a nonreligious worldview.

Chapter 7 shows that the phrase "Christian apologetics" (arguments to justify Christianity) is actually an oxymoron, which is to say, it involves an implicit contradiction.

Chapter 8 responds to two common Christian complaints about atheists. Why do atheists always blame every evil in this world on God, and why are atheists always so angry with religion, especially with Christianity? It also examines God's peculiar attraction to glory for himself.

Part II comprises five chapters which deal with issues of Christianity and ethics.

Chapter 9 rebuts the Christian implication that atheism leads to extremely immoral behavior as evidenced in the policies and practices of atheists Joseph Stalin, Pol Pot, Adolph Hitler, and Mao Zedong.

Chapter 10 points out serious problems with important Christian ethical prescriptions given or endorsed by Jesus.

Chapter 11 describes several important inconsistencies between the Christian condemnation of abortion and other widely shared Christian beliefs.

PREFACE

Chapter 12 explains and critiques what I argue is an unsavory alliance between a large segment of American Christianity and political conservatism.

Chapter 13 explains how one could defend an objective view of ethics that doesn't involve justification from any religious tradition, including Christianity.

Part III comprises five essays which address what I consider to be Christianity's most important error, namely, that God exists. In this part I set out five novel arguments to show that it's very likely that God does not exist. Their general theme is that the world we experience isn't what we would have expected if the Christian God existed. Such instances of what-we-wouldn't-have-expected-in-our-experience-of-the-world-if-the-Christian-God-existed constitute the main evidence for the atheistic conclusion of each of the five arguments in the following five chapters of Part III.

Chapter 14 presents the argument for God's nonexistence from unfair human experiences. The what-we-wouldn't-have-expected-in-our-experience-of-the-world-if-the-Christian-God-existed is the existence of divinely sanctioned invidious discrimination against certain innocent humans.

Chapter 15 presents the argument for God's nonexistence from unfair salvific opportunities. The what-we-wouldn't-have-expected-in-our-experience-of-the-world-if-the-Christian-God-existed is the inherent unfairness in the opportunities available to humans for experiencing their *summum bonum* or highest good, namely, eternal salvation in heaven.

Chapter 16 presents the argument for God's nonexistence from the existence of a divine temporal gap. The what-we-wouldn't-have-expected-in-our-experience-of-the-world-if-the-Christian-God-existed is the existence of a divine temporal gap of at least some 296,000 years during which God was, in effect, an absentee Father to his human children.

Chapter 17 presents the Argument for God's nonexistence from the quantity of apparently unjustified suffering. The what-we-wouldn't-have-expected-in-our-experience-of-the-world-if-the-Christian-God-existed is the existence of an ungodly (see what I did there?) amount of apparently unjustified suffering, much of it horrendous, of sentient animals during the last five hundred million years and of humans during the last three hundred thousand years.

Chapter 18 presents the heaven world argument for the nonexistence of God. The what-we-wouldn't-have-expected-in-our-experience-of-the-world-if-the-Christian-God-existed is the very existence of this world itself! In effect, this chapter is my answer to the often posed question to atheists: What evidence would convince you that God exists?

METHODOLOGY

Many other books have well-critiqued, diverse Christian topics. I sought not to reiterate their criticisms. Rather, I strove to critique elements of Christianity that, to my knowledge, have not received appropriate scrutiny, or to critique elements that have been scrutinized, but to do so in novel, fair, and incisive ways.

It's important to recognize at the outset that the Christian tradition comprises a very diverse set of theological practices and beliefs. For example, consider the deep theological and liturgical differences between Eastern Orthodox Christianity and Appalachian snake-handler Christianity. So, the eighteen essays in this book are not claimed to comprise an exhaustive list of all the ways in which Christianity errs. What I aim to show is that the select and important Christian beliefs and practices evaluated in the book have fatal flaws.

STYLE

I've striven to make my critiques as accessible as possible to nonspecialist readers without sacrificing accuracy or completeness. At the same time, I think the essays are rigorous and novel enough to be attractive to those who have some background or interest in religion, atheism, Christianity, apologetics, philosophy, or philosophy of religion.

My interest in religion and the philosophy of religion has been honed by my own background as a former serious Christian (Roman Catholic) as well as by many decades of teaching these topics to undergraduate college students. Their questions and comments made me aware of the sorts of concerns that nonprofessional thinkers have with religion, especially Christianity. I like to think that answering their questions and listening to their ideas and concerns helped me to effectively explain where I contend Christianity indeed errs.

I've set out the arguments in the book without rancor and as clearly, succinctly, and impartially as I could, dispensing with as much technical jargon as pertinence allowed. The essays are not an effort to ridicule any reader's beliefs. I seek to reason with readers, not offend them. After all, the proper goal of philosophy, including, of course, the philosophy of religion, is to "get it right," not to score points or embarrass anyone. My aim is to explain and defend, in as fair and openminded a manner as I can, arguments that show that Christianity has indeed significantly erred in places. However, I'm keenly aware that in some instances it may be I who has erred. If so, I'd be more than willing to be set straight. Fortunately, truth is unlimitedly shareable. If you have it on a particular issue and I don't, you can give it to me and still retain it for yourself as well. If I have some of it in this book, I am more than happy to share it with you, dear reader. All in all, I hope you'll find the book to be clear, edifying, and thought-provoking.

CONVENTIONS

Definition of "God": I accept the most prevalent Christian understanding of God as a supernatural, spiritual person who is omniscient (all-knowing), omnipotent (all-powerful), and omnibenevolent (all-good). As such, he is the creator and sustainer of this world who maximally loves his human creations. In short, he is the most perfect being possible.

Pronouns: Speaking of "he," throughout the book I use male personal pronouns to refer to God. Theologically, this makes no sense, since God, by definition, has no gender. However, it is expedient and follows the commonly accepted convention of God-talk.

Acknowledgements

In a letter to Robert Hooke in 1675, Sir Isaac Newton made his famous statement: "If I have seen further it is by standing on the shoulders of Giants."[1] By no means do I presume to compare myself with Sir Isaac Newton. However, the most notable shoulders that have supported my seeing include those of David Hume, Michael Martin, Richard Carrier, and Jim McCarthy.

---

1. Turnbull, *Correspondence*, 416.

Part I: Critiques of Select Aspects of Christian Beliefs

Chapter 1: Original Sin: Can't Live With It; Can't Live Without It

Chapter 2: Petitionary and Thanksgiving Prayer: Innocuous but Pointless

Chapter 3: Religious Faith: A Peek Behind the Curtain

Chapter 4: Does God Send People to Hell?

Chapter 5: How to Assure Christian Salvation through Murder!

Chapter 6: Christianity and the Meaning of Life

Chapter 7: Christian Apologists: Why Do They Even Bother?

Chapter 8: Critiques of Three Miscellaneous Christian Topics

Chapter 1: **Original Sin: Can't Live With It; Can't Live Without It**

Preview

Christianity has a big problem with its doctrine of original sin. This problem falls under the rubric of "can't live with it; can't live without it." I argue that Christianity "can't live *with*" its doctrine of original sin because the latter is historically, scientifically, and morally implausible. I argue that Christianity "can't live *without*" its doctrine of original sin because in the course of over two thousand years it has become so insinuated into the vitals of the body of Christian doctrine that removing it at this stage could be fatal to the host.

Creation, Garden of Eden Story, and the Doctrine of Original Sin

The Doctrine of Original Sin is extracted from the larger Genesis creation and garden of Eden story (Gen 1–3), which I will refer to simply as the garden of Eden story. That story describes how God created the world and the primal human pair, Adam and Eve, and placed them in a garden of delights, Eden, filled with pleasing flora and fauna.[1] At this point Adam and Eve were immortal and immune to pain and suffering, as presumably were the fauna in the garden. Though they were invited to enjoy the

---

1. Lest one think that criticism of the real existence of Adam and Eve is beating a dead horse, consider that, according to a study sponsored by the BioLogos Foundation and conducted by Calvin College sociologist Jonathan Hill in 2014, 56 percent of American adults believe that Adam and Eve *were* real persons. Saletan, "God's Work?"

garden, God commanded them not to eat the fruit of one tree, the tree of the knowledge of good and evil, lest they die that very day. Nevertheless, they succumbed to the wiles of a talking snake[2] and ate from the tree. Most Christians refer to this first human moral transgression as the original sin, which resulted in the fall of man from God's grace/favor. As punishment, God exiled the pair from the garden and sentenced them to an existence replete with pain, suffering, hardship, and eventual death. Their punishment also included God altering their originally created perfected natures to ones that were now corrupted in a way that rendered them inclined to sin. Moreover, they were rendered unable to rehabilitate or redeem themselves by their own efforts from their fallen state. In addition, God decreed that their fallen status be passed on to all their descendants and shared as well, where applicable, by the members of the animal kingdom.

CAN'T LIVE WITH THE DOCTRINE OF ORIGINAL SIN

In order to show that Christianity can't live with the Doctrine of Original Sin I'll show three things.

1. The doctrine of original sin has a serious problem with history and science.
2. The doctrine of original sin has a number of challenging moral problems.
3. The doctrine of original sin has epistemic (that is, knowledge) problems.

Doctrine of Original Sin's History and Science Problems

As mentioned earlier, the doctrine of original sin is part of the garden of Eden story. If the garden of Eden story is not historically factual, then original sin is not historically factual either. This explains, in part, why fundamentalists,

---

2. The serpent is often interpreted to be Satan, although it is never explicitly described as such in Genesis itself. Fun fact: according to some, the "snake" was actually considered a dragon. Said dragon was cursed to become a snake by losing its legs and maybe even wings, if it was imagined to have any, as a punishment for its role in bringing about the original sin. This would explain why only *after* Adam and Eve's transgression did it have to "crawl on its belly" (Gen 3:14 GNT). What was it doing before then? Clearly, it wasn't a creature without legs until it was cursed by God.

ORIGINAL SIN: CAN'T LIVE WITH IT; CAN'T LIVE WITHOUT IT

for whom the doctrine of original sin is so integral to many of their other Christian beliefs, such as the incarnation, passion, death, and resurrection of Jesus, are very insistent on affirming the literal truth of the garden of Eden story. They have not been alone in this insistence. For nearly two millennia virtually all major Christian sources, including such luminaries as the apostle Paul and church father Augustine, held that the garden of Eden story describes a literal set of historical events which actually transpired.[3] As Bart Klink points out, such sources even include Jesus himself.

> In the . . . Bible, Adam is consistently treated as a single historical person. . . . This is why various biblical genealogies trace back to Adam. Genesis 4–5 lists Adam's descendants and their ages. The first chapter of 1 Chronicles mentions Adam and his pedigree as a historical person, too. Jesus is considered a descendant of Adam by the author of the Gospel according to Luke. "Jesus was about thirty years old when he began his work. He was the son (as was thought) of Joseph son of Heli, . . . son of Enos, son of Seth, son of Adam, son of God." (Luke 3:23–38) According to the Gospel of Matthew, even Jesus himself seems to speak about Adam and Eve as historical persons: "He answered, 'Have you not read that the one who made them at the beginning made them male and female.'" (Matt 19:4)[4]

The problem with all the claims of the historical facticity of the garden of Eden story is that the story is clearly inconsistent with numerous important tenets of virtually universally accepted history and science. Among other things, there's no evidence that the universe or *Homo sapiens* arose as described in Genesis, or that there was ever a tree the eating of whose fruit would impart a knowledge of good and evil, or that there were ever snakes capable of talking, or that there was ever a time when humans or animals were immortal or incapable of suffering or feeling pain. Not only is there no significant evidence *for* these elements of the garden of Eden Story, there is a great deal of compelling scientific evidence *against* these claims. Thus, the history and science regarding the garden of Eden story, and, therefore, also regarding the doctrine of original sin is made implausible by an avalanche of well-attested facts.

---

3. Ortlund, "Augustine."
4. Klink, "Untenability," 6.

Faith-Based Support to the Rescue?

Some Christians have attempted to defend the truth of the garden of Eden story by ultimately appealing to faith rather than historical or scientific evidence. The following excerpt from the organization Catholic Answers on the proper understanding of the fall of man in the garden of Eden story is a good example of this approach.

> The story of the creation and fall of man is a true one, even if not written entirely according to modern literary techniques. The *Catechism* [of the Catholic Church] states, "The account of the fall in Genesis 3 uses figurative language, but affirms a primeval event, a deed that took place at the beginning of the history of man. Revelation gives us the certainty of faith that the whole of human history is marked by the original fault freely committed by our first parents." (*Catechism of the Catholic Church*, 390).[5]

The Catechism starts out by claiming the historical facticity of the garden of Eden story in Gen 3. "*The account of the fall in Genesis 3 uses figurative language, but affirms a primeval event, a deed that took place at the beginning of the history of man.*" But then in the next sentence the Catechism's proposed claim that the "*deed that took place at the beginning of the history of man*" is not elucidated or supported by any fact-based evidence. Instead, defense of the garden of Eden Story is given in terms of a faith-based explanation. "*Revelation gives us the certainty of faith that the whole of human history is marked by the original fault freely committed by our first parents*" (emphasis added).

This retreat to a vague faith-based defense of the garden of Eden story obviously does nothing to answer the barrage of scientific and historical facts that are at odds with the biblical description of the original sin event. Thus, I conclude from this first section that the doctrine of original sin is implausible because the story from which it is derived, the garden of Eden story, is scientifically and historically deficient.

Doctrine of Original Sin's Moral Problems

There are serious moral problems for the doctrine of original sin with respect to the punishment that God is said to have meted out for it. Recall that the punishment included that Adam and Eve, their now more than

---

5. "Adam, Eve, and Evolution."

117 billion descendants,[6] and all the animals would thenceforth be subject to pain, suffering, deprivation, and death, often of the most excruciating varieties. (For an approximate numerical estimate of the amount of human and animal suffering over the past five hundred million years, see material in chapter 17 in the section entitled "Defense of the Truth of Premise 1"). Among the factors indicating that these punishments are morally questionable are the following.

First, it's not clear that immorality can be justly imputed to Adam and Eve's actions since the pair apparently lacked a sufficient understanding of morality before they ate from the tree of the knowledge of good and evil. True, they *did* get one piece of knowledge before eating the fruit, namely, God told them the consequences of such eating. If so, then one might argue that the pair were morally culpable since knowledge of consequences is sufficient under the law to convict.

However, what's problematic here is that they ate only because they were lied to. They were, in effect, conned by the serpent. Was such gullibility sufficient to charge Adam and Eve with being morally culpable? Consider that they didn't think to go and ask God first about what the serpent told them. This negligence indicates stupidity rather than guilt. Indeed, what the serpent did to them is literally called entrapment, and is a defense under the law in most penal systems. In fact it's worse than entrapment because they were deceived into thinking that what they were doing wasn't even wrong, which is an absolute defense under law. They lacked criminal intent. Imagine a police officer telling someone that speeding was legal, and then they get ticketed by another officer for speeding. They would have a valid defense, as they were deceived into believing they weren't breaking the law. Perhaps a more direct example would be if someone, unbeknownst to them, swapped speed limit signs on a stretch of road. The entrapment defense for Adam and Eve applies because God had knowledge and intent, given that he is omniscient. He knew that the serpent was going to con them, and didn't intervene to prevent it or correctly advise the pair. This entailed collusion, a conspiracy (with the serpent) to entrap.

Second, related to the first factor just discussed, a just punishment should have taken as a legitimate mitigating circumstance the fact that the recently created, perhaps childishly innocent, primal pair was no match for the wiles of the talking serpent who, according to Christian tradition, is identified with the devil, that is, Lucifer/Satan. According to that tradition,

---

6. Routley, "How Many Humans," para. 10.

Lucifer ("the shining one") is the most powerful and brilliant creation of God. The fact that Adam and Eve succumbed to such an extraordinarily resourceful and clever tempter should have been a morally relevant extenuating factor, at least in assigning the punishment in their case.

Third, it would be immoral to collectively punish all subsequent human beings (and animals) by giving them corrupted natures, pain, suffering, and death for an action for which they (subsequent human beings) could have had no conceivable responsibility.

Fourth, a life of pain, suffering, deprivation, and death for Adam and Eve as punishment for a simple act of mild disobedience was unjust because it was too severe, not proportionate to the act of disobedience. After all, Adam and Eve were apparently motivated to eat from the tree in large measure by their desire to be like the God they were in awe of and perhaps loved. Their transgression might be said to be analogous to that of an impressionable youngster who disobeys his parents by stuffing himself with Wheaties breakfast cereal so that he could be like the sports hero he idolizes on the front of the cereal box. A moral transgression? Perhaps. But if so, surely a very minor one and understandable in light of the star power of the sports hero and the persuasive power of advertising. The youngster's transgression was certainly not one that would deserve the death penalty. Analogously, eating the fruit, a moral transgression? Perhaps. But if so, surely a very minor one and understandable in light of the star power of God and the persuasive power of Lucifer. It was certainly not an act that deserved the death penalty.[7] In effect, no one was harmed by the eating of the fruit, certainly not God, a being so perfect as to be beyond harm. Also, since God is the most perfect being possible, any harms to Adam and Eve (such as, for example, guilt and shame, etc.) could have easily been revoked by God. He could have just erased those harms, like a doctor removing a toxin from the blood acquired by eating poisoned fruit. Consider that, if someone is tricked by a con artist into giving their savings away, it would not be moral to punish the victims with

---

7. Much less a genocidal punishment. Yet, that is the *actual* penalty God prescribes. He kills *all* humans in consequence of Adam and Eve eating the fruit. Note that the crime of genocide doesn't require success. You are not acquitted just because you failed to wipe out your target race. Merely engaging in targeted killing of a whole race en masse is the crime of genocide. In fact, if you look up the international crime statute for genocide ("Legal Definition of Genocide"), practically God's entire punishment qualifies, for example, the intentional infliction of suffering and hardship on a race can count as genocide as well.

death, or any punishment at all, especially if you could get the money back and restore the victim's savings and then punish the grifter who stole it. To punish a victim rather than recover them from harm makes no sense, especially when you can easily do the latter. If so, then there would be no moral purpose in punishing the victim. Denis Diderot, a French thinker and critic of religion, wrote mordantly in 1762 in *Addition aux Pensées philosphiques*, "The God of the Christians is a father who is a great deal more concerned about his apples than he is about his children."[8] Amen.

Evaluation of Three Christian Retorts to the Claim That the Doctrine of Original Sin Has a Moral Problem

Preternatural Gifts Retort to the Claim That the Doctrine of Original Sin Has a Moral Problem

Some Christians have advocated what I call the preternatural (beyond what is normal or natural) gifts retort. According to this retort, Adam and Eve were created with a particular nature to which God added some preternatural properties such as immortality, impassibility (incapacity for suffering), possession of sanctifying grace, and the ability to talk directly with God. After they committed the original sin, God punished them by revoking their preternatural properties, thus leaving them with just a "standard" human nature. It's this nature which has been passed on to all their descendants.

According to this preternatural gifts retort there is no divine immorality in any of this.

First, God's response toward Adam and Eve was not immoral since all it amounted to was the revocation of the gift of *preternatural* properties to which Adam and Eve had no moral claim in the first place, and certainly not after they disobeyed God.

Second, God did not act immorally toward Adam and Eve's descendants because they also had no moral claim to the preternatural properties that God had given to Adam and Eve. The following excerpt from *The Catholic Encyclopedia* expresses the preternatural gifts retort.

> But according to Catholic theology man has not lost his natural faculties: by the sin of Adam he has been deprived only of the Divine gifts to which his nature had no strict right, the complete

8. Diderot, *Oeuvres Complètes*.

mastery of his passions, exemption from death, sanctifying grace, the vision of God in the next life. The Creator, whose gifts were not due to the human race, had the right to bestow them on such conditions as He wished and to make their conservation depend on the fidelity of the head of the family. A prince can confer a hereditary dignity on condition that the recipient remains loyal, and that, in case of his rebelling, this dignity shall be taken from him and, in consequence, from his descendants. It is not, however, intelligible that the prince, on account of a fault committed by a father, should order the hands and feet of all the descendants of the guilty man to be cut off immediately after their birth. This comparison represents the doctrine of Luther which we in no way defend. The doctrine of the Church supposes no sensible or afflictive punishment in the next world for children who die with nothing but original sin on their souls, but only the privation of the sight of God [Denz., n. 1526 (1389)].[9]

Two Asides Concerning the Encyclopedia Excerpt

First aside: the last sentence of the encyclopedia article is notably problematic. It says, *"The doctrine of the Church supposes no sensible or afflictive punishment in the next world for children who die with nothing but original sin on their souls, but only the privation of the sight of God"* (emphasis added). I find the use of the phrase *"but only the privation of the sight of God"* to refer to the fate of unbaptized children who die to be troubling. If the *"sight of God*," more commonly referred to as the beatific vision (awareness of, and intimacy with, God in Heaven), is indeed, as Christians claim, the *summum bonum* (greatest good) for humans, then eternally depriving hundreds of billions of babies who die without being baptized of said highest good of the beatific vision, due to something completely beyond their control, would be extremely unfair—something unworthy of a being who is said to be maximally good and loving. The unbaptized babies did nothing to justify their eternal deprivation of that highest good of the beatific vision in heaven and also did nothing to justify their being eternally separated from their parents, siblings, and other family members who, given Christian theology, may well be in heaven. Furthermore, being aware of such a fate for the baby would likely bring severe consternation to the baby's parents and other loved ones while they are here on earth or in heaven

---

9. Harent, "Original Sin," para. 19. Brackets in the original.

ORIGINAL SIN: CAN'T LIVE WITH IT; CAN'T LIVE WITHOUT IT

as well. Yet, on the other hand, if such unbaptized infants *were* given the beatific vision, then that would be unfair to the many people who were not so privileged to get such an automatic admission into paradise. In sum, multiple serious problems arise if the claim in *The Catholic Encyclopedia* about the postmortem fate of unbaptized babies were true.

Important Relevant Data about Prenatal Mortality

One might be surprised about the figure of "hundreds of billions of babies who die without being baptized" that I cited in the previous paragraph. That figure has been confirmed by recent research in reproductive human science. According to Kathryn Kavanagh, associate professor of biology at the University of Massachusetts, Dartmouth,

> in people, the most common outcome of reproduction by far is embryo loss due to random genetic errors. An estimated 70% to 75% of human conceptions fail to survive to birth. That number includes both embryos that are reabsorbed into the parent's body before anyone knows an egg has been fertilized and miscarriages that happen later in the pregnancy.[10]

The article from which the above excerpt is taken is a trove of excellent data about prenatal mortality. What I have done in the following calculations is to use an intermediate figure of 72 percent of conceptions that fail to survive birth. If 72 percent is a reasonable estimate, then, of course 28 percent *do* survive to be born alive. Demographers estimate that about 117 billion human beings have lived in the three hundred thousand year history of our species.[11] If so, then simple math tells us that there have been about 418 billion conceptions (117 billion divided by .28 = 418 billion). Therefore, there have been some 301 billion human persons who were never born (418 − 117 = 301).[12] I bring this to your attention here because it will be used in a number places throughout the rest of the book.

Second aside, recall that *The Catholic Encyclopedia* states the following.

---

10. Kavanagh, "Most Human Embryos," para. 7. See also Benagiano, "Fate of Fertilized Human Oocytes," 732–43; Berger, *Developing Person*, 94; Ord, "Scourge," 12–19; Vaquero, "Diagnostic Evaluation," 79–84; Zinaman, "Estimates of Human Fertility," 503–9.

11. Routley, "How Many Humans," para. 10.

12. For the sake of argument here I'm accepting the Christian claim that human personhood begins at conception.

> It is not, however, intelligible that the prince, on account of a fault committed by a father, should order the hands and feet of all the descendants of the guilty man to be cut off immediately after their birth. This comparison represents the doctrine of Luther which we in no way defend.[13]

As I understand it, the encyclopedia is claiming that Luther's theology in the area of the legacy punishment for original sin is flawed because it's too harsh. That is, in the prince analogy, Luther's view would be similar to the Prince ordering "the hands and feet of all the descendants of the guilty man to be cut off immediately after their birth." The encyclopedia excerpt implicitly affirms that such an action by the prince would be self-evidently unjust. But a critic of humans' punishment due to original sin could persuasively note that it would be considerably harsher and, therefore, even more unjust, if the prince were to sentence all the descendants of the guilty man to death accompanied by much suffering beforehand, which is in essentially the penalty for original sin that the encyclopedia is defending.

Responses to the Preternatural Gifts Retort

First response is that *God's punishing humans for original sin and the prince's punishing his minions for infidelity are, at best, only weakly analogous* for the following reasons.

Under certain circumstances when the revocation of a gift would bring about great harm, it's morally impermissible to revoke it. For example, morally speaking, I can't demand my donated kidney back even if the recipient were disobedient to me. For a second example, if someone underwrites the expenses for economically poor breastfeeding mothers in order to get them to forego using their own breast milk and instead to feed their babies with formula sold to them at a good profit by the underwriters, then it's not morally permissible for the underwriter to rescind that gift since doing so would likely have serious life-threatening repercussions for the babies. In the case of God's original sin punishment, it's obvious that revoking his gifts would be catastrophic not only for the life, limb, and well-being of Adam and Eve, but also for hundreds of billions of their descendants (see chapter 1 section entitled "Important Relevant Data about Prenatal Mortality") and for uncountable numbers of sentient animals as well. On the other hand, the prince's revocation of the title he granted would not result in the

---

13. Harent, "Original Sin," para. 19.

ORIGINAL SIN: CAN'T LIVE WITH IT; CAN'T LIVE WITHOUT IT

kind of universal catastrophic harm that followed God's punishment for original sin and so should not be thought to be sufficiently analogous to the passed-on punishment for original sin.

Furthermore, there is not only much greater harm that results from God's rescinding his gifts to Adam and Eve compared to the prince's revocation of the hereditary title, but the infraction for which God revoked those gifts was much less serious than the infraction that caused the prince to revoke the hereditary title. The prince is likely operating within a system that requires loyalty from those so benefited with a hereditary title, such that the prince's well-being and that of his principality could be put into significant jeopardy by such breeches of loyalty. In the case of Adam and Eve there is no harm attached to their infraction. No one, especially not God, is harmed by their eating the fruit.

Christians cite that the prince only removed certain gifts from the family members of his disloyal minion that were not standard issue to them and to which they had no right, but otherwise still left the family's standing with the prince intact. Christians claim that God did something similar with the family (Adam and Eve's descendants) of his disloyal minions (Adam and Eve). He only removed certain gifts (preternatural elements of their natures) from the family members that were not standard issue to the descendants and to which they had no right, but otherwise still left the family's standing with God intact. Just as there was nothing immoral in the prince's doing what he did to the family of his disloyal minion, there was nothing immoral in what God did to the family of his disloyal minions either.

But it would seem that there *was* something unjustified about what God did compared to what the prince did. Christians hold that the non-preternaturally embellished "standard" human natures of Adam and Eve's descendants were all corrupted by the fall. Moreover, that corruption would not have been a part of their original "standard" non-preternaturally embellished human natures. It was something they suffered after the fall. This means that, unrelated to anything they ever actually did, all Adam and Eve's descendants were created estranged from God, their Father. It's not just that all humans come into the world having to deal with an *indifferent* creator/parent. That might be bad and unfair enough. Rather, they come into the world with what amounts to a *hostile* creator/parent who arranged, before they ever had a chance to freely choose anything with respect to him, that their default fate would be eternal perdition. That's punishment, not just removal of some preternatural gifts. There is nothing comparable to that in the situation concerning the prince.

Second response to the Christian preternatural gifts retort is that *the distinction between preternatural and natural properties is ad hoc and nowhere articulated in the garden of Eden story*, and with good reason. Ask yourself, why would God make Adam and Eve's natures with X-number of "standard" properties and an additional Y-number of "preternatural" properties? Such a move would make no sense from a divine point of view. After all, from the Christian perspective, *all* God-given properties, whether called "natural" or "preternatural," are sheer gifts to which humans would have no right. Thus, I contend that the natural/preternatural property division put forth by Christian apologists is an ad hoc distinction without a difference. Its main purpose seems to be to try to justify God's post original sin treatment of Adam and Eve and their descendants.

Third response to the preternatural gifts retort is that *God would have known with absolute certainty that stripping humans' natures post-fall of their so-called preternatural properties would lead to innumerable numbers of humans causing unimaginable amounts of pain, suffering, and death to be experienced by innumerable numbers of innocent humans and animals.* English philosopher Jonathan M. S. Pearce has developed this objection in a number of his YouTube presentations. He notes that if some scientist were to construct robots that the scientist knew with certainty would produce enormous amounts of pain, suffering, and death for innocent beings, along with some amount of good outcomes by some of the robots, no morally sensitive person would doubt for a moment that that scientist would be guilty of the horrendous atrocities committed by his robots. If so, then Pearce claims that God would have to be considered to be morally responsible for the incalculable amounts of post-fall horrendous harms caused by humans on whom God foisted corrupted natures that God would infallibly have known would incline them to produce serious harms. The fact that God knew that the humans with the defective natures that he gave them would commit those atrocities and did nothing to prevent them implicates God as the morally culpable party for the occurrence of those atrocities. And all this because a primal pair of humans ate a piece of fruit? Really?

Christians usually answer the foregoing challenges by pointing out that God took pity on humans and sent his Son to offer us a way that we could be reconciled with him.

The critic could answer that, even if this were true (which the critic disputes), God set things up so that his offer of reconciliation with humans didn't happen until thousands or hundreds of thousands of years after the fall, depending on how one dates things. Why such a long wait? For a more developed criticism concerning this delay, see chapter 16.

From the critic's perspective, the Christian's response that God sent his Son to redeem us is flawed because it would be like someone, S, intentionally breaking your leg because one of your relatives in the distant past ate one of S's apples without permission, but then solicitously offering to drive you to the hospital. Better that S never broke your leg in the first place. Similarly, it would have been better that God didn't so harshly punish post-fall humans in the first place than that he did and then had his Son suffer and die in a brutal, bloody sacrifice so that *maybe* we would thence get to the "hospital" of redemption.

Representation Retort against the Claim That the Doctrine of Original Sin Has a Moral Problem

Defenders of the doctrine of original sin might contend that God's treatment of Adam and Eve's descendants was not unjust because Adam and Eve were our representatives in the garden of Eden testing scenario. As such, if they passed the test, then we all passed the test; and if they failed the test, we all failed with them.[14] Hence, no divine injustice can be associated with God's treatment of Adam and Eve's descendants.

Responses to the Representation Retort against the Claim That the Doctrine of Original Sin has a Moral Problem

First, if Adam and Eve did indeed "represent" their descendants in the garden of Eden test, then one meaning of "represent" here could be that if any of their descendants were to have been put in their place in the garden of Eden scenario, they would have chosen the way Adam and Eve chose. That, in turn, would mean that all of Adam and Eve's descendants would have also failed the test, as Adam and Eve did.

The problem with that interpretation of "represent" is that it would strongly suggest a serious design flaw in God's creation of humans, a flaw

---

14. Thomas, "Why Did Adam's Sin," para. 1.

which, by the way, his foreknowledge would have made him well aware of from all eternity. (See this chapter's section entitled "Doctrine of Original Sin's Knowledge Problem.")

Second, a critic might claim that in the garden of Eden test, Adam and Eve should not be considered representatives of their descendants because the latter never explicitly gave their consent to be represented by Adam and Eve on such an important matter. Right now, would you or I consent to have two people about whom we have no knowledge whatsoever make a life and death decision on our behalf? I wouldn't think so. If so, then it would not be morally proper for God to have had Adam and Eve represent all of the hundreds of billions of their descendants without the descendants' consent and to punish the descendants of Adam and Eve for the latter's original sin.

Creator Retort against the Claim That the Doctrine of Original Sin Has a Moral Problem

This defense holds that, as their creator, God had the moral right to give his creatures any nature or properties he wanted and also to change any nature or revoke any property at any time for any reason without being guilty of violating any moral norm.

Response to the Creator Retort

A creator divinity who is maximally good would not be morally permitted to give his creatures just any nature or property that the creator chose. There are natures or properties which involve so much gratuitous pain, suffering, deprivation, harm, and hardship for innocent sentient creatures that a morally perfect creator would never give them to any creatures, especially if there would be benign alternatives. And, for God, there would be such benign alternatives. (See chapter 18.) It would be immoral to procreate when it's known that the nature, properties, or circumstances pertaining to resulting children would likely involve serious pain, suffering, deprivation, hardship, harm, or premature death for the offspring. Consider, for example, how most people judge human incestual breeding to be highly, and even grotesquely, immoral. The reason is that such inbreeding would put offspring in danger of being harmed by genetic abnormalities stemming from the inbreeding. As it turns out, the likelihood of there being such harm in any single case of inbreeding is fairly low, as is the seriousness of any resulting harm. Nevertheless, such inbreeding is almost universally morally condemned. If so, then, *a fortiori* (even more so), one could persuasively argue that an omnibenevolent God would never cause all human beings to come into existence and be the recipients of far more pain, suffering, and death than any human brought into existence by inbreeding, given above in the section entitled "Third Response to the Preternatural Gifts Retort" about how immoral it would be for a scientist to create robots that she knew would cause significant harm to the innocent.

Thus, a maximally morally good divine being would have no moral license to bring about a creation marred by such universal and unwarranted harm to the innocent resulting from the original sin, especially if God could have instead created a world that would maximize moral and human flourishing outcomes. For more on the feasibility of God's creating such a world, see chapter 18 of this volume.

Doctrine of Original Sin's Knowledge Problem

If God is all-knowing, then he would have known beforehand that Adam and Eve would fail his garden of Eden test. A good and loving deity would not let a lengthy human drama involving the pain, suffering, death, punishment, and estrangement of untold numbers of humans and animals play out over hundreds of thousands of years (or more in the case of animals) when there would be more benign alternatives. Again, see more about these alternatives in chapter 18.

Being all-knowing, God knows everything that has happened and everything that will happen. Many prominent Christian philosophers[15] claim that an all-knowing deity would also have knowledge of events involving human choices that neither have happened nor will ever happen, but would happen in some logically possible world or worlds.[16] This kind of knowledge is called "middle knowledge," for reasons we don't have to get into here. For example, if God has middle knowledge, then he knows what Abraham Lincoln would have eaten for breakfast on his eighty-fifth birthday in any possible world in which Lincoln would have eaten breakfast on his eighty-fifth birthday.

---

15. William Lane Craig, Alvin Plantinga, Terrance Tiessen, and Thomas Flint are examples.

16. A possible world is a complete and consistent way the world is or could have been. The actual world we live in is one of the countless possible worlds.

With respect to the doctrine of original sin, instead of creating Adam and Eve in a world in which God knew they would invariably freely fail his test, God could have used his middle knowledge and created them instead in a world in which he knew they would have freely passed his test. He could have thereby eliminated all the pain, suffering, and death that hundreds of billions of humans and uncountable numbers of animals have experienced over the last half of a billion years.

A Christian might respond that it's possible that God knows that Adam and Eve would have failed his test in every possible world in which he could create them. To that I would respond that then God could have created a different primal pair instead of Adam and Eve whom God would know *would* pass the test.

To the retort that perhaps there is no possible primal pair who would pass God's test, I would respond that that would suggest that the test was too difficult or that there was a design flaw in the creation of humans in the first place. An omnibenevolent God should then have altered his test, or created human beings with "better" natures, or should have simply foregone any test and just have given all humans a heavenly pass. Once again, see more about this in chapter 18.

I conclude, therefore, that Christianity "can't live with" such a flawed doctrine of original sin. Note that some Christians thinkers[17] accept that the doctrine of original sin is problematic enough to cause them to reformulate Christian theology on a foundation that does not depend on the doctrine of original sin. However, such a view is a decidedly minority one. The vast number of Christians and Christian denominations firmly accept the doctrine of original sin. In the section that follows we will see why.

CAN'T LIVE WITHOUT THE DOCTRINE OF ORIGINAL SIN

Unfortunately, for Christianity, it also can't live *without* the doctrine of original sin either. It can't simply evict this embarrassing crazy old aunt of a doctrine from the attic of the Christian mansion because the old girl holds title to the property, as it were, as I shall explain below.

The website Catholic Answers fielded the following relevant question concerning the facticity of Adam and Eve. Keep in mind that Roman

---

17. See, for example, Spencer, "Evolution, Middle Knowledge, and Theodicy," 215–33; and Swinburne, "Does St. Paul Believe," 291–313.

ORIGINAL SIN: CAN'T LIVE WITH IT; CAN'T LIVE WITHOUT IT

Catholics comprise about one billion of the approximately two billion Christians in the world today.

Question: What is the Catholic Church's teaching on the belief that Adam and Eve were merely symbols and not literally our first parents?

Answer: Pope Pius XII addressed this question in his 1950 encyclical Humani Generis. He identifies this belief as a "conjectural opinion" and denies the children of the Church the liberty to hold such an opinion. His reason is it's apparent inconsistency with the transmission of original sin:

> It is in no way apparent how such an opinion can be reconciled with that which the sources of revealed truth and the documents of the teaching authority of the Church propose with regard to original sin, which proceeds from a sin actually committed by an individual Adam and which, through generation, is passed on to all and is in everyone as his own (sec. 37).

It is true that Pius XII's rejection of "polygenism" (the belief that we descended from multiple sets of first parents) is not infallible. Nevertheless, it is a teaching that carries with it a high degree of magisterial authority. Even the Catechism of the Catholic Church (CCC) seems to affirm the belief that Adam and Eve were not mere symbols but literally our first parents.

It teaches that Eve in some manner was created from Adam (CCC 371).

It contrasts the first Adam with Christ (CCC 359).

It refers to Adam and Eve as our "first parents" created in an original state of justice and holiness (CCC 375), which they lost when they sinned (CCC 399-400).

It identifies Adam as the source of sin in contrast to Christ as the source of grace (CCC 388).

It affirms St. Paul's teaching in Romans 5:18 that by one man's sin all of humanity is affected (CCC 402).

It teaches that all men are Adam's descendants and are implicated in his sin (CCC 404).

It teaches that Adam and Eve transmitted to their descendants human nature wounded by their own first sin (CCC 417).

> There is no indication in these passages, or in the many other passages where the Catechism references Adam and Eve, that the Church believes the biblical Adam and Eve represent a number of our first parents.[18]

The above views do not represent only the Roman Catholic Christian position on the historical reality of Adam and Eve and original sin. Most Protestant denominations, especially those characterized as Fundamentalist or Evangelical, also hold very similar views. The reason that a large majority of Christian denominations holds to the factual, historical reality of the existence of Adam and Eve and their original sin is that if Adam and Eve were not real persons and their original sin not a factual occurrence punished by God as described in Genesis, then the truth of the following Christian signature claims would be jeopardized:

- *All* humans are guilty of serious sin.
- *All* humans suffer from a debilitating corruption of their natures which renders them inclined to sin further.
- *All* humans' natures, corrupted by the fall of Adam and Eve via original sin, prevent them from rehabilitating or redeeming themselves by their own efforts from the bondage to sin and the harsh punishment that accompanies it.

The above signature claims are important in the Christian scheme of things because they provide the main rationale for Jesus's incarnation, passion, death, and resurrection. Paul speaks to this in Rom 5:18–19 (KJV):

> Therefore, as by the offense [original sin] of one [Adam] judgment came upon all men to condemnation; even so by the righteousness of one [Jesus] the free gift [of salvation] came upon all men unto justification of life. For as by one man's disobedience many were made sinners, so by the obedience of one shall many be made righteous.[19]

---

18. Broussard, "Adam and Eve."

19. Note that in this passage Paul implicitly affirms the historicity of Adam and Eve, the garden of Eden story, and original sin. If Christianity were to jettison the doctrine of original sin, it would have to admit that one of its most influential theologians, if not *the* most influential, was in error in his belief about the reality of the original sin. If so, this could raise reasonable concerns about where else he might have erred in his influential theology.

Summary of the Christian Rationale for the Historical Truth of the Doctrine of Original Sin

Most Christians, such as the apostle Paul, have held that the original sin caused the broken world we experience, comprising conditions of universal, excessive, debilitating, and irremediable sinfulness and suffering. They also believe that God sent his son to repair this broken world. Therefore, if there is such a broken world we experience, then Christians must be committed to the belief that Adam and Eve must have broken it by their committing an historically actual original sin. This is why most Christians can't live without the historical truth of original sin.

Two Mistakes Involving the Christian Rationale for the Truth of the Doctrine of Original Sin

First Mistake Involving the Rationale for the Truth of the Doctrine of Original Sin

It's not the case that there are, in fact, such dire conditions of universal, excessive, debilitating, and irremediable sinfulness in the world, as Christians claim there are. Let me explain.

NOT ALL PEOPLE ARE SINNERS

For starters, people who die before reaching the age of moral accountability[20] are, by definition, not sinners.[21] If one accepts the Christian view that from the moment of conception a person exists, then induced or natural abortions involve intrauterine persons who were not sinners during their short lifetimes. This last fact is significant. As cited earlier in this chapter in the section entitled "Important Relevant Data about Prenatal Mortality," recent research in the science of human reproduction has shown that less than 28 percent of fertilized human eggs are born. That means that, absent the truth of the doctrine of original sin, more than 72 percent of all humans who have ever lived could not have been sinners.

---

20. Usually thought to be no earlier than age seven or eight for most people

21. Incidentally, according to UNICEF, some five million children under age five die every year around the world. See "Child Mortality."

In addition, people who have severe mental handicaps which prevent them from ever becoming morally accountable are not sinners.

Furthermore, experience suggests that there have been some people, not included in the groups just mentioned, who also never sinned. These include those who lived exceptionally saintly lives or who arrived at the age of moral accountability and then died shortly thereafter without ever having sinned.

All of this means that, without relying on the doctrine of original sin, at most, less than 30 percent of all the people who have ever lived have possibly been sinners.[22] But, with the doctrine of original sin, Christianity can say that the other 70 percent are also sinners.

Christian Claims about the Excessiveness of Human Sinfulness Are Exaggerated

Without the truth of the doctrine of original sin, it would be difficult to establish the excessiveness and irremediableness of human sinfulness that is baked into the Christian assessment of the world. However, experience suggests that the degree of moral transgression of most people is modest. To be sure, there have been despicable evildoers such as Hitler, Stalin, Pol Pot, Jack the Ripper, etc.; but there have also been untold numbers of people (not all of whom were Christian) who sacrificed life, limb, and property to stop evildoers, as well as large numbers who have labored tirelessly and selflessly to reduce the amount of pain, suffering, and premature death in the world. Thus, instead of the bleak pessimistic view of humankind's moral failings preached by Christianity, the evidence rather indicates that some form of bell curve more properly represents the distribution of people's moral behavior. At one end of the curve there are a relatively few people who are guilty of the most heinous immoral acts, while at the other end of the curve there are a relatively few people who commit very few or no immoral acts. In between, the vast majority of people lives with some modest moral failures but for the most part with a greater degree of moral decency. Notably, atheists and agnostics have been well represented among the ranks of those who have lived decent-to-exemplary moral lives.[23]

---

22. Note also that zero percent of animals are sinners and, yet, are still made by God to suffer and die, often horrendously.

23. For an excellent bibliography on the issue of atheism and morality see "On Average, Are Atheists as Moral as Theists?"; Narvaez and Lapsley, *Personality, Identity, and*

ORIGINAL SIN: CAN'T LIVE WITH IT; CAN'T LIVE WITHOUT IT

Christian Claims about the Irremediableness of Human Sinfulness Are Exaggerated

Not only has the level of moral transgression for most people been modest but, contrary again to the deficiency claimed by many Christians, evidence shows that people are far from impotent in affecting both personal and social moral improvement without supernatural involvement.

Secular Personal Improvement

One set of examples of secular personal improvement can be found in an article published by Steven Mohr in which he showed that the religiously tinged Alcoholics Anonymous (AA) had a rather dismal record of success and that alcoholics were able to do better on their own without AA.[24] Mohr reports,

> In 1995, the Harvard Medical School reported evidence that a significant number of problem drinkers recover on their own. Researchers wrote in the Harvard Mental Health Letter of October, 1995: "One recent study found that 80 percent of all alcoholics who recover for a year or more do so on their own, some after being unsuccessfully treated."[25]

There are innumerable other examples of secular personal self-improvement that could be cited.

Secular Social Improvement

There have been many instances of human beings improving societies in terms of morality and human flourishing without overt deference to any supernatural agency. Steven Pinker, acclaimed Harvard cognitive psychologist, psycholinguist, popular science author, and public intellectual, has recently published two well received books, *The Better Angels Of Our Natures*[26] and *Enlightenment Now*[27] in which he makes a compelling case that, by means

---

Character; Walter Sinnott-Armstrong, *Moral Psychology*.
   24. Mohr, "Exposing the Myth."
   25. Mohr, "Exposing the Myth," 44.
   26. Cliff Notes, "Plot Summary, 'The Better Angels.'"
   27. Find Qualia, "Enlightenment Now."

of virtually any meaningful measure, the world is actually getting better, not worse, in terms of human well-being.[28] For example, he substantiates that violence has been plunging worldwide for centuries, so that a smaller percentage of people today are victims of violent crimes or die in wars than in the past. In addition, a smaller percentage of people die of disease and starvation and a smaller percentage are illiterate. He reminds us of the significant scientific, technological, and sociological progress around the world in recent times that has led to impressive increases in human flourishing. I would add that all this progress has been achieved by the increasing use of reason, not by the increasing turn to religious faith. Thus, the Christian contention that original sin has rendered humans incapable of, one might say, "saving" themselves is inaccurate.[29] To conclude the discussion on the theme of increasing worldwide human well-being, I would mention that, although the causes for criminal activity are many, most sociologists are in broad agreement that environmental factors such as poverty, ignorance, fear, deprivation, bad fortune, insecurity, physical and psychological pathology[30] are significant contributors to crime or other immoral or, if you will, sinful, behavior.[31] In recent years human beings, especially in the more developed secular countries, have produced societies with first rate levels of prosperity, progress, safety, and justice by providing decent levels of education, health care, jobs, welfare, security, opportunity, and justice without any necessary genuflection to supernatural doctrine.[32]

---

28. Pinker, *Better Angels of Our Nature*; Pinker, *Enlightenment Now*.

29. For more on this, see PBS NewsHour, "How the World."

30. Add, also, curable false beliefs. Consider how many an ideology has caused immorality that ceased when the supporting ideology is abandoned for being discovered false; for example, Aztec human sacrifices.

31. See: Raine, "High Rates of Violence, Crime," 544–49; Kennedy, "Social Capital, Income Inequality," 7–17.

32. Paul, "Big Religion Questions Finally Solved," 24–36. See especially Figs. 6, 7, and 8. For a somewhat different take than Paul's, see Delamontagne, "High Religiosity and Societal Dysfunction," 617–57. Finally, two additional good works showing that secularization improves, rather than degrades, the morality of societies are: Zuckerman et al., *Nonreligious: Understanding Secular People*, and Zuckerman, *Society without God*.

Second Mistake Involving the Rationale for the Truth of the Doctrine of Original Sin

Even if one accepts the Christian claim that the punishing legacy of original sin has produced grim conditions of a broken world, there are good reasons to think that a loving God could have, and would have, alleviated those conditions in a way that would have significantly limited this world's brokenness. After all, as just described, in many instances humans have improved themselves and societies in terms of morality and human flourishing, without overt deference to any supernatural agency. If humans have been capable of substantially improving the moral and human flourishing aspects of the world by secular means, then surely an omnipotent God could have accomplished even more. If, as John 16:3 proclaims, God so loved human beings and wanted to save them from sin and its harmful effects, then there would clearly have been ways he could have done that that would not have violated human free will, if such there is, or required the brutal, bloody murder of his son. Instead, God could have simply offered forgiveness to truly repentant and restituting sinners. In addition, he could have improved the world by reducing negative environmental factors, such as those listed earlier in this chapter that foster sinful behavior. More positively, God could have produced a morally better creation suffused with more human flourishing than seen in this world by improving the genetic qualities of humans. That is, God could have made humans more resistant to false beliefs and illogical reasoning, and more instinctually prone to empathy and honesty, for everyone, but especially for those most broken by the legacy of the punishments associated with original sin. He could have prevented the creation or promulgation of any of the genes or gene combinations causing the existence of sociopaths, as well as preventing abusive parents, whom he knows would raise a criminally minded child, from ever raising such a child.

Thus, I conclude from this section that Christianity "can't live without" the doctrine of original sin because the Christian rationale for the incarnation, passion, death, and resurrection of Jesus would limp without that doctrine.

CONCLUSION

I've argued that Christianity has a problem. It can neither defend the historical and conceptual plausibility of the doctrine of original sin nor delete it from the list of its requisite beliefs without doing significant damage to Christianity's cogency and plausibility.

Chapter 2: **Petitionary and Thanksgiving Prayer: Innocuous but Pointless**

Preview

I argue that petitionary and thanksgiving prayer are not cogent practices.

INTRODUCTION

Petitionary prayer (PP) is prayer that asks God for some favor. It can be positive, asking that some desired thing or event be had or happen, or it can be negative, asking that some undesired thing or event not be had or happen. *Thanksgiving prayer* (TP) is prayer expressing gratitude toward God for some benefit he has bestowed. Both PP and TP are widely practiced in Christianity. I will refer to praying persons as orants, from the Latin word *orare*, meaning to pray.

I'll argue that proper analysis shows that PP and TP are not cogent practices, that is, that they don't make the kind of sense that Christians believe they do. Let me be clear. I'm not arguing that there is anything gauche, illegal, or immoral about engaging in PP or TP. All other things being equal, people in a free society should have the right to such expressions and I would certainly defend that right.

I will first examine PP and then TP.

PART I: CRITIQUES OF SELECT ASPECTS OF CHRISTIAN BELIEFS

REASONS WHY PETITIONARY PRAYER (PP) IS NOT A COGENT PRACTICE

PP Lacks Adequate Evidence Supporting Its Efficacy

There's no reputable empirical evidence showing that PP actually produces any positive results, even after being carefully and rigorously tested.[1] In fact, the largest and best controlled study of the efficacy of PP was done with post operative cardiac patients from the 2006 STEP project. It found no significant differences in patients recovering from heart surgery whether the patients were prayed for or not.[2]

Christians Never Hold God Responsible for Not Answering PP

PP orants judge unevenly by crediting God whenever what is requested by a particular PP occurs, but not faulting him when what is requested does not occur. It's heads God wins, tails he doesn't lose. Accountability, it seems, is expected in every serious public endeavor except PP. The absence of accountability in PP encourages fallacies of confirmation bias and motivated reasoning,[3] thereby tainting the Christian assessment of PP.

Christian Defenses of PP Are Weak.

Let-God-Know Defense of PP

A defender of PP might claim that PP is cogent because it lets God know what outcome the orant wants.

Response to the Let-God-Know Defense of PP

An all-knowing God would already know what our preferences are. He wouldn't need to be reminded or informed about anything.

---

1. Andersson, "Chronic Pain and Praying"; Finney and Malony, "Empirical Studies."
2. Benson et al., "Study of the Therapeutic Effects."
3. *Confirmation bias* is a tendency to interpret information in ways that confirm what we already believe—or want to believe. *Motivated reasoning* occurs when someone actively looks for reasons why they're right, doesn't look for reasons why they might be wrong, and rejects facts and research that don't fit their beliefs.

Just-Ask Defense of PP

This defense is rooted in the belief that God is the most perfect being possible. As such, he possesses maximal power, knowledge, and goodness. Such powers give him the means, method, and motivation to respond to PP. Thus, according to the just-ask defense, it's perfectly reasonable to petition such a credentialed deity on behalf of self or others. Furthermore, Christians believe that God, through the Bible, has made it clear that if orants ask, God will positively respond (Matt 7:7–8).

Responses to the Just-Ask Defense of PP

First, most PP orants seem to harbor the misconception that God is some kind of superhero who, say, like Superman, can be petitioned to fight against pain, suffering, and evil which run rampant in the world independently of him. However, this is a misconstrual because God, as the most perfect being possible, is responsible for everything that exists or happens, including suffering, such as that associated with, for example, an orant's stage four cancer or a horrendous earthquake and tsunami that took some 230,000 lives in the Indian Ocean area in 2004.[4] If so, then it would be highly unreasonable for an orant to beseech God, the very person responsible for the pain and suffering of those being prayed for, to now suddenly reverse course and remove the pain and suffering that he just caused or permitted. It would be like pleading with a bank robber to contribute to a fund to reimburse those whose money he just robbed from the bank.

Second, God is mandated by his maximally good nature to always bring about the morally best possible future. Consider a situation in which an orant prays for mitigation of her stage four cancer, or for mitigation of the effects of something like the aforementioned Indian Ocean disaster, or prays to be selected for some honor. The outcome prayed for in each of those kinds of cases is either a part of the morally best possible future or it's not. God, being omniscient, would know which. If the prayed-for outcome were, in fact, part of the morally best possible future, then God, being omnibenevolent, *must* bring it about. On the other hand, if the prayed-for outcome is not a part of the morally best possible future, then God *must not* bring it about.

---

4. Ironically, perhaps, such tragedies are often called "acts of God."

Thus, the just-ask defense is not cogent because, if what the PP orant is praying for were necessary for satisfying God's obligation to bring about the morally best possible future, then the PP would necessarily be superfluous, that is, God would already be obliged to bring about what is being prayed for anyway, even if it weren't being prayed for. On the other hand, if satisfying the orant's PP would not be in accord with God's bringing about the morally best possible future, then the PP would necessarily be ineffective. For example, imagine that the mother of Judas Iscariot prays to God and asks that her son be selected to be a member of the inner circle of disciples of the new prophet, Jesus of Nazareth. When that transpired, one might say that her prayers were answered. But, in fact, that would not be accurate because Judas's becoming such a close disciple of Jesus was always a part of God's divine plan. If so, then her PP was superfluous. Next, imagine that Judas's mother prays that Judas not betray Jesus. Suppose that Judas had confided in her that he planned to do so. As things turned out, one might say that her PP was denied by God. But the truth would be that her PP was ineffective, not because God deemed it in some way deficient and, therefore, unworthy of being granted. Rather, it was ineffective since what it petitioned for was not in accord with God's divine plan. Thus, since any instance of PP is either necessarily superfluous or necessarily ineffective, it would indeed be incoherent to engage in it.

Ironically enough, many orants seem to tacitly accept the reasoning just explained about PP being superfluous or ineffective. Their tacit acceptance may manifest when what they are praying for doesn't materialize. At that point, if they are challenged about the failure of their PP, they may dismiss the challenge by simply responding something along the lines of "well, God knows best what should happen." They don't seem to realize that if their response is correct, then their engaging in PP in the first place makes little sense. As detailed above, God must bring about the morally best future regardless of any PP or not.

If a Christian were nevertheless to insist that PP (properly done) can somehow be efficacious, then that would beget a serious problem about the fairness of PP. That is, efficacious PP would be unfair to all those in need who, through no fault of their own, have no one (including themselves) praying for them. To reiterate, if PP were efficacious, then these individuals would have no chance of receiving help from PP, compared to someone who had PP working for them. That would seem to be seriously unfair.

Speaking of unfairness associated with PP, one might ask whether someone who is earnestly prayed for by ten people would have twice the likelihood of receiving assistance than if only five people earnestly prayed for them? Christians seem to think it would be, considering how often we hear appeals for *everyone* to pray for a person, P. Christians might respond that an omnibenevolent God would take pity on the un- or under-prayed-for, and give them help, even without any PP being involved. But, if that were true, then, once again, PP would be unnecessary and, therefore, an uncogent practice.

To sum up, PP is either efficacious or it's not. If it's efficacious, then it would be inherently unfair for the un- or under-prayed-for. If it's not unfair to the un- or under-prayed-for, presumably because God helps all persons equally whether they're prayed for or not, then PP would be unnecessary. If PP is not efficacious, then it would be a useless practice. Or would it? Let's turn now to the character-enhancement defense of PP.

Character-Enhancement Defense of PP

The third main line of Christian defense of the cogency of PP, in addition to the let-God-know and just-ask defenses, I term the character-enhancement defense. It holds that PP is cogent because it leads to important enhancements of the orant's character, such as the development of compassion, humility, hope, or kindness that the orant would not otherwise have attained, or at least would not have attained as readily without PP. For example, Catholic priest and apologist Philip Dion put it this way.

> St. Augustine said, "There would be no martyrs if there were no tyrannical persecutions." Hence, it is by the wickedness He permits in some men, that God stimulates others to goodness and virtue and sanctity.[5]

I can only assume that part of the "goodness and virtue and sanctity" that Fr. Dion thinks suffering "stimulates" is engaging in PP.

Responses to the Character-Enhancement Defense of PP

First, given that people's characters are the complex products of genetics and years of social, economic, environmental, educational, and psychological

---

5. Dion, "Does God Will It," 19.

influences, there's little reason to think that engaging in occasional PP actually produces much significant character enhancement. In fact, I would say that, with respect to PP on behalf of others, it's more likely that already existing positive character traits of an orant cause the orant's PP, rather than that the orant's PP causes positive character traits in the orant.

Second, sometimes PP may not produce character enhancement, but, rather, character degradation. For example, it may be that an orant's PP is unfruitful in that those being prayed for continue to experience considerable pain, suffering, or losses. As a result, orants may experience disappointment, discouragement, disillusionment, and ultimately, at times, even lose their faith as a result of their engaging in unanswered PP.

Third, if a benevolent God wanted people to work toward character enhancement, he wouldn't have to use pain, suffering, and loss to accomplish it. There would be other morally preferable means available. For instance, God could encourage people to engage in supererogatory actions (actions that are above and beyond what is morally required) toward humans or animals, or to work at perfecting their athletic, intellectual, aesthetic, arts and crafts, or other talents to advance their character enhancement.

Fourth, the character-enhancement defense entails the morally questionable practice of God causing or permitting some person, P1, to suffer as *means* to enhance the character of another person, P2, through P2's engaging in PP. This is morally questionable since the gold standard in morality has usually been to respect a person's dignity by treating them as an end in themselves and not merely as a means to some other end.

Fifth, the character-enhancement defense also entails the morally counterintuitive and problematic conclusion that pain, suffering, and loss are good things, in part because they encourage PP which, in turn, enhances the orant's character. For example, the much esteemed and literally sainted Mother Teresa echoed such a view when she said, "The suffering of the poor is something very beautiful and the world is being much helped by the nobility of this example of misery and suffering."[6]

I take it that she (and probably Fr. Dion as well) would agree that the prompting of PP because of suffering is one of the ways "the world is being much helped . . . by misery and suffering." Now I don't think I'm going too far out on a limb here to say that most of those actually *doing* the suffering, as opposed to those just *opinionating* about it, would rather have their suffering ended, even if the cessation would eliminate an orant's PP

---

6. Hitchens, *Missionary Position*, 41.

from being a source of the orant's character enhancement. In this regard columnist Valerie Tarico relates that,

> By her own report, Mother Teresa once told a woman to imagine that her suffering was kisses from Jesus. Mother Teresa said: "Suffering, pain, sorrow, humiliation, feelings of loneliness, are nothing but the kiss of Jesus, a sign that you have come so close that he can kiss you." "Tell Jesus to stop," the woman responded."[7]

I think most of us can understand why the woman responded as she did. I sometimes told my students, "I've suffered and I've not suffered. Not suffering is better," elimination of character enhancement of orants through PP notwithstanding.

PP ASSESSMENT CONCLUSION

Even if it were conceded that PP is logically incoherent, one could still ask whether there is any real harm in engaging in it anyway or encouraging the practice in children. I think there is for at least two reasons.

First, engaging in PP on behalf of others is too often a poor substitute for providing substantive responses to tragedies. It's all too often an excuse to do nothing. For example, critics have charged that the US Congress's response to the appalling procession of mass shootings by only intoning PP (thoughts and prayers) has been grossly inadequate.

Second, normalizing PP helps to legitimize a religious worldview that too often denigrates reason and subordinates it to religious faith. In some jurisdictions this has resulted in ineffective or harmful public policies in such areas as reproductive rights, euthanasia, faith healing, LGBTQ+ rights, and stem cell research. My aim in showing the incoherence of PP has been to reinforce a beneficial commitment to reason with respect to evaluating PP, which, in turn, by my lights, makes a small, but worthwhile, contribution to shaping a safer and more just world for all.[8]

---

7. Tarico, "Why Right-Wing Christian," paras. 3, 4.
8. For additional lines of critique of PP see Davison, "Petitionary Prayer," 286–305 and Davison, "Petitionary Prayer."

PART I: CRITIQUES OF SELECT ASPECTS OF CHRISTIAN BELIEFS

REASONS WHY THANKSGIVING PRAYER (TP) IS NOT A COGENT PRACTICE

TP Is Incoherent

Consider the following TP scenario. A baseball player hits a home run that wins the game for his team. As he heads toward home plate to officially score the winning run, he engages in an overt act of TP, namely, he points skyward with one or both index fingers while reverentially raising his gaze to heaven. This TP practice has been becoming more and more a "thing" in many sports recently. Again, there's nothing immoral, illegal, or gauche about such a practice. However, as with PP, there is something rationally incoherent about it. Let me explain.

TP is problematic because a necessary condition for a sensible thanksgiving is missing in TP, namely, that the benefactor, in this case, God, *could have done otherwise*. Consider that it would make no sense for one to thank a programmed robot for successfully performing a life-saving surgery because the robot "benefactor" is required by its program to do exactly what it did. It literally could not have done otherwise. It's all about computer codes, not about the making of any free, intentional, gracious, and compassionate choice by the robot. In a similar vein, as we saw with PP, God is required by his most perfect nature to produce the morally best possible future. Since the home run happened, Christians must infer that its happening must have been part of the morally best possible future. If so, then God *had to* enable it. He could not have done otherwise. It was an essential part of his divine nature/plan to have facilitated the home run. It was all about metaphysical necessity. Had circumstances been different, God would have had to facilitate, say, the batter striking out. "Sorry batter. Nothing personal old boy. Most perfect being possible here, best of all possible futures and all that. You understand, right?" Thus, giving thanks to God in the homerun case would be as incoherent as it would be in the surgery case.

Well, it might be asked, wouldn't it at least make sense for the batter to thank God for having a nature that required him to actualize the morally best possible future which happened to include the homerun? Answer: no, not really, because God isn't responsible for his nature. He didn't choose it or work toward developing it or himself to be God. He was just always that way. He's due no particular thanks for that.

CONCLUSION

Whatever level of respectability and plausibility PP and TP have in the thinking of Christians comes from the fact that most Christians view the two forms of praying uncritically through the prism of a flawed theology. To them God is like some powerful superhuman autocrat to whom people can present their petitions for him to hopefully act on. In return, if their petition is granted, they're encouraged to lavish extensive thanks and praise upon God while acknowledging his peerless glory. That the most perfect being possible would actually want and even require praise and glory remains a mystery to me. (For more on God and glory, see material starting in chapter 8, part 3, "What's Up With God and Glory Anyway?") That such a TP and PP theology is flawed should be clear, given the critical discussion of them in this chapter.

Chapter 3: **Religious Faith: A Peek Behind the Curtain**

Preview

This chapter focuses on the fact that faith, that is, belief that some proposition is true without adequate evidence for its truth, is the ultimate Christian go-to "justification" for many of its doctrinal, moral, and social/political pronouncements. I think that faith has not received the critical attention it deserves, commensurate with its influence on personal belief and policy formulation. To address this shortcoming, this chapter examines the nature of faith and argues that there are serious problems with the claim that it can legitimately justify beliefs or behavior.

INTRODUCTION

The influence of religion on beliefs and behavior throughout the world is considerable. In the US, religion, principally Christianity, vigorously presses its positions in the public square on a multitude of moral and social issues such as those concerning abortion, birth control, sexual morality, gender issues, stem cell research, euthanasia, LBGTQ+ issues, education, environmentalism, and others. Religious views on these issues carry great weight with many people because they take religion to be the most appropriate source of correct moral and social beliefs. In other words, in their worldview religious faith provides the ultimate justification for social and moral beliefs.

RELIGIOUS FAITH: A PEEK BEHIND THE CURTAIN

In what follows, I critique the practice of defending any beliefs or practices by reliance on a faith-based method of justification.

FAITH

I define "faith" in the present context as "belief that something is true without having adequate evidence that it is" (See Heb 11:1–3). For Christianity, faith is a necessary condition for admission to heaven. According to Christianity, having faith in Jesus as Savior and the truth of the doctrines of Christianity manifests one's love and loyalty to God and their willingness to accept God's gift of eternal salvation. The importance of faith is stressed time and again in biblical stories involving such notables as Abraham, Noah, Job, the Israelites, as well as certain New Testament figures such as the apostle Thomas. John 20:19–29 records that after his resurrection Jesus appeared to the remaining apostles during Thomas's absence. When the others told Thomas that Jesus had appeared to them, Thomas was skeptical. Presumably, he felt that he didn't have sufficient evidence for believing such a remarkable claim. Sometime later, Jesus appeared to the apostles again when Thomas was present, at which point, with sufficient evidence now in hand (literally!), Thomas believed. Jesus went on to rebuke Thomas for his lack of faith, and, in contrast, praised the many who believe on faith alone, that is, without having to have adequate evidence to support their beliefs. The moral of the story is clear: in religious matters belief based on faith is more important, necessary, accurate, and worthy in the eyes of God than belief based on evidence and reasoning.

The primacy of faith in generating and defending important true beliefs is a standard theme in Christian doctrinal history. Paul of Tarsus, the organizing genius of early Christianity, makes this point early on.

> Jews demand signs and Greeks look for wisdom, but we preach Christ crucified: a stumbling block to Jews and foolishness to Gentiles, but to those whom God has called, both Jews and Greeks, Christ the power of God and the wisdom of God. For the foolishness of God is wiser than human wisdom, and the weakness of God is stronger than human strength. (1 Cor 1:22–25 NIV)

A century and a half later Tertullian of Antioch, an early church leader (c. 160–230), reaffirmed the anti-rationalist tenor of the priority of faith when, concerning the death and resurrection of Jesus, he said, "I believe because it is absurd; it is certain because it is impossible!"[1] The same glorification of faith and suspicion of reason were echoed 1,300 years later by the influential Protestant reformer, Martin Luther, when he asserted the following:

> If all the smart alecks on earth were to pool their wits, they could not devise a ladder on which to ascend to heaven. . . . He who would deal with the doctrines of the Christian faith (should) not pry, speculate, and ask how they may agree with reason, but, instead, merely determine whether Christ said it. If Christ did say it, then he should cling to it, whether it harmonizes with reason or not, and no matter how it may sound.[2]

The situation remains essentially unchanged for most Christians today. Faith continues to be Christians' ultimate go-to justification for many important religiously related convictions. In conservative Christian circles (echoing Luther) this point is pugnaciously made on bumper stickers such as those which declare that, "Christ said it, I believe it, and that settles it!"

Admittedly, sometimes Christians do engage in the public arena in support for some of their views using non-faith-based argumentation (see chapter 7), but even here faith drives reason. For Christian apologists, reason can, at best, give only supplementary support for the truths that faith has already made manifest. For example, William Lane Craig, one of the foremost Christian apologists (defenders of the faith) in the world today, has stated that "should a conflict arise between the witness of the Holy Spirit to the fundamental truth of the Christian faith and beliefs based on argument and evidence, then it is the former which must take precedence over the latter."[3] To see recent examples of Christians' use of faith to justify beliefs, we may ask why so many Christians continue to believe that homosexual activity is morally wrong even after all of the nonreligious objections to it have long since been discredited. Answer: the Bible, held to be inerrant *on the basis of faith*, considers it to be immoral. For another example, it may be asked why many Catholics disregard the sound arguments establishing the reasonableness and compassion of certain forms of euthanasia. Answer: the Pope, believed by Catholics *on the basis of faith* to be the vicar of Christ on earth, has affirmed God's disapproval of such procedures. Faith is a powerful epistemological (relating to the theory of

---

1. Miller, *God*, 119.
2. Luther, "Tenth Sermon," 80.
3. Craig, *Reasonable Faith*, 36.

knowledge) trump card played frequently and with apparent impunity in personal and public domains by religious advocates.

REASON

Reason can be defined as the activity which requires one to hold all and only those beliefs for which there is adequate support. The phrase *adequate support*, of course, requires specification. Logic, a branch of philosophy, has developed rules and procedures for ascertaining what are the proper criteria for such support. Although there may be instances where reasonable people can reasonably disagree on whether there is adequate support for some proposition, fortunately those instances are relatively infrequent and are often satisfactorily resolved with a later addition of probative (affording proof) evidence. Thus, the crucial phrase "adequate support" in the definition of reason is not hopelessly vague or subjective. Logic has, for the most part, given reason a clear and useful understanding.

The importance of reason in human affairs needs little elaboration. It largely accounts for the survival and progress of our otherwise physically undistinguished species. Moreover, reason underwrites the civilizing activities of morality, science, education, language, and government. In short, reason is indispensable for human survival and prosperity in a way that faith is not.

Problems Associated With Faith

Faith Contradicts Reason

The eighteenth-century French thinker Denis Diderot summed up this problem for faith when he said, "If reason was bestowed on us by Heaven and the same can be said of faith, then Heaven has presented us with two incompatible and contradictory gifts."[4] The contradictory directives of faith and reason are rooted in their contradictory definitions. Reason requires that one ought *always* to hold all and only those beliefs which have adequate evidential support; while faith says one ought *not always* do that, but rather one must hold some, namely certain religious beliefs, in the absence of adequate evidential support. Clearly, one cannot satisfy both directives. As I pointed out earlier in the chapter, the inconsistency between

---

4. Diderot, *Oeuvres Complètes*.

the two directives creates some serious tensions for religious adherents. For example, orthodox Roman Catholics must accept the condemnation of barrier methods of birth control on faith, even though reason informs them that such methods harm no one, can greatly enhance the physical and emotional well-being of women and men, can aid the formation of caring, nurturing, functional families, and can be very helpful in a world of finite and shrinking material resources. In the same vein, Christian fundamentalists are required to accept on faith that the earth has had a relatively short history (say, thousands instead of billions of years), that no significant biological evolution has taken place, and that a worldwide flood occurred in historical times which covered the entire planet, including the highest mountains. Yet, at least the educated fundamentalist can hardly be unaware of the veritable blizzard of scientific evidence which shows such beliefs to be rationally unsupported. Sometimes the inconsistency can literally be a matter of life or death as when some Christian parents reject standard medical treatment or preventive therapy (vaccines) for their children in favor of faith-based alternatives.

At this point, in order to make room for faith, a believer might challenge: Why must one always be "reasonable"? That is, why is it problematic to consider faith to be an alternative source of knowledge? The resolution of this dispute rests on whether faith can be justified as an alternative to reason for generating knowledge. Thus, it is to the examination of this question that I now turn.

Faith Is Not a Path to Knowledge

Many Christians, such as the medieval philosopher Thomas Aquinas, deny any serious conflict between faith and reason because they hold what has been called "the dual approach" to truth. That is, they claim that reason and faith both originate in some sense from God. As such, the two are different but not inconsistent with one another and are equally valid paths to understanding.

The most obvious problem with the Christian's dual-approach defense of faith is that there's no evidence that faith is a path to any knowledge whatsoever. To say that we can know that X is true through faith is to say, in effect, that despite having insufficient evidence for the truth of X, we can nevertheless know that X is true anyway. This claim that beliefs can be justified solely on the basis of faith runs counter to our personal and our species' experience of how knowledge about the world has been gained. One way to see this more clearly is to replace the word "faith" in sentences with its proper definition, "belief without adequate evidence." If this is done, then a claim such as "my *faith* gives me adequate knowledge that God has a morally sufficient reason for causing/permitting fourteen thousand children to die every day around the world,"[5] would be recast as "my *belief without adequate evidence* gives me knowledge that God has a morally sufficient purpose for causing/permitting fourteen thousand children to die every day around the world." The latter formulation would more clearly portray the emperor's nakedness, that is, the deficiency of appealing to faith as a knowledge-generator or guarantor.

One might try either a faith-based or a non-faith-based justification of the claim that faith is a legitimate alternative to reason as a path to knowledge. However, neither justification can succeed.

First, if one were able to demonstrate logically or empirically[6] that faith-based claims were true, then one would have thereby acknowledged the priority of reason over faith. This would, in effect, entail the redundancy and dispensability of faith. We cannot believe on the basis of faith what we can prove by reason. So, to the extent that Christian apologists could prove the truth of traditional faith-based claims such as the doctrine of the Trinity, the resurrection of Jesus, or the inerrancy of the Bible, to that same extent the apologists would eliminate the need for, and, therefore, the importance of, faith within Christianity. See more about this in chapter 7. This point has been noted by many Christians themselves, especially those in the fideist (faith-based) camp going back to Paul of Tarsus. It receives perhaps its most passionate and eloquent expression in the writings of the nineteenth century Christian thinker, Soren Kierkegaard, as in the following passage.

> Without risk there is no faith. Faith is precisely the contradiction between the infinite passion of the individual's inwardness and the objective uncertainty. If I am capable of grasping God objectively, I do not believe [have faith], but precisely because I cannot do this I must believe [have faith]. If I wish to preserve myself in faith I must constantly be intent upon holding fast to the objective uncertainty, so as to remain out upon the deep, over seventy thousand fathoms of water, still preserving my faith.[7]

5. Suzuki and Kashiwase, "New UN Estimates."

6. Based on, concerned with, or verifiable by observation or experience rather than theory or pure logic.

7. Kierkegaard, *Concluding Unscientific Postscript*, 182.

Second, a faith-based justification of faith as knowledge-generating also will not work. One cannot use faith as the legitimate justification for accepting faith as a path to knowledge, as this would be patently question begging. In response, the fideist might counter that it is the rationalist who is in fact begging the question by requiring reasons to prove faith. For this assumes the primacy of reason over faith—one of the points in contention between the fideist and the rationalist. The rationalist, however, can respond by pointing out that the preference for using reason and not faith as a justification for beliefs is not *assumed* but rather *justified* by facts which even religious people cannot deny, namely, the significant advances in human well-being, progress, and happiness made possible by the use of reason, especially over the last four hundred years or so, and unmatched by faith.

Third, there have been numerous instances where faith-based beliefs were shown to be false by the use of reason, but there have been no instances where reason-based beliefs have been shown to be false by the use of faith.

Fourth, it should be noted that all false religions are based on faith, which means faith is not just ineffective, it is maximally unreliable.[8]

In sum, we cannot justify faith as an alternative path to knowledge by rational means, as this would make faith redundant; nor can we justify faith as a knowledge-generator by appealing to faith itself, as this would be question begging. I conclude, therefore, that faith cannot be shown to be a path to knowledge.

Faith Cannot Objectively Judge Competing Faith-Based Claims

For example, Christians cannot objectively show that Muslims or Jews err when the latter deny on the basis of *their* faith that which Christians hold by *their* faith; for example, that God is a trinity. This inability of faith to objectively judge competing fideist (faith) claims, together with the fact that there are so many such important competing claims, is a serious flaw for an activity that claims to be knowledge-generating. On the other hand, if there is a disagreement about, say, which of two pieces of chalk weighs more, reason provides an objective method for settling the dispute, for instance, by putting both pieces on a balance; or, if reason cannot at a certain point decide which view is correct because of lack of conclusive evidence, then

---

8. See Loftus, *Outsider Test for Faith*, 66–77.

reason would require withholding judgement until conclusive evidence is had. Disputants with conflicting faith claims, however, simply deny the opposing view and remain intransigent in their own, regardless of the lack of evidence. This dogmatism is not a recipe for progress. In fact, it can produce dangerous tensions which often erupt in violence.

Since faith cannot adjudicate competing faith-based claims, it unintentionally becomes the great equalizer of all knowledge claims asserted in its name. This is ironic in light of faith's claim to be channeling absolute truth. But knowledge is surely not advanced by equalizing competing belief claims. It is advanced by rigorously investigating the matter in question, and then carefully evaluating the answers obtained therefrom. One of the rules of reasoning is that if an answer does not have adequate support, it must not be accepted. If it does have adequate support, then it may provisionally become part of our understanding of reality, at least until supplanted, if ever, by a better supported view. The knowledge engine generating great human advancement, especially over the past four hundred years, has not been faith, but reason. This is why worldviews substantially rooted in faith-based claims are so frequently irreconcilable, faulty, and harmful.

Faith Cannot Be Justified by Strength of Conviction

Some Christians maintain that faith-based claims get adequate support from the intensity of the believer's internal conviction. For example, a Christian may claim to know that Jesus is Lord on the basis of the internal subjective feeling of certainty she has about the lordship of Jesus when praying, reading Scripture, or witnessing to others, etc. The certainty associated with faith-based claims is similar to the certainty one gets about, say, being in love or being hungry by being directly aware of one's internal feelings on the matter.

In response, *first* of all, it is a faulty analogy to compare knowing by introspection that you're in love or hungry and knowing by introspection that a faith-based claim is true. To consult your internal feelings to determine something about one's own romantic feelings or hunger feelings is quite appropriate. In fact, that's precisely where reason would have one look for adequate evidence about something such as whether you are in love or hungry, for example. However, it's inappropriate to consult internal feelings or reactions to get adequate evidence for the truth of things *outside* ourselves, such as whether God exists or whether using barrier methods of birth control will send an unrepentant person to eternal damnation.

Second, there's no evidence whatsoever that strength of conviction has any plausible connection to the truth of what is believed. Simply believing something about the world strongly or even passionately is no indication that what is believed is true. Many patients in mental care facilities unfortunately bear not so mute testimony to this fact. Nature has certain objective characteristics which reason, not faith, has the better track record of revealing to us. To the extent that we ignore this we detach ourselves from reality, sometimes dangerously so.

Faith Is Not Found in Everyone

Christians sometimes charge that critiques of faith falter when they neglect the fact that virtually everyone has faith in *something*, whether it be the veracity of their spouse, the punctuality of the 5:53 evening train, or their own self-worth. Christians also claim that faith-critiques falter when they fail to acknowledge that even scientists believe in many things they haven't or can't see, such as electricity or the fact that meteors caused the bulk of the craters on the moon. Thus, Christians charge that it is unfair to single out religious faith-based claims for special criticism.

There are two major ambiguities in this attempted defense of faith. The first concerns the word "faith" itself. Besides its use in a religious context as belief in the absence of adequate evidence, "faith" is also often used to indicate a sense of trust, but trust *based on adequate support*. One might say, "I have faith that the 5:53 train will be right on time." But here we are actually talking about a belief which, unlike religious faith-based claims, *is* supported by past experience, in this case by the past record of the punctuality of this particular train. We can refer to this as "supported faith," as opposed to the "unsupported faith" characteristic of religious claims. Anyone can reasonably have supported faith in all sorts of things. The fact that virtually everyone accepts supported faith does not establish that everyone really accepts, or should accept, the legitimacy of unsupported faith as a knowledge-generator.

The second ambiguity resides in the word "see" or some similar external sensing term. Some Christians fail to recognize that words like "see" are not always meant in their literal sense. To say that scientists can never *see* electricity, and that therefore their belief in it is faith-based, is to miss the point. Scientists do, in fact, have rich and abundant empirical (having to do with the five external senses: sight, hearing, smell, taste, and touch) evidence supporting the existence of, say, electricity, partly in the form of many successful predictions, involving precise, directly observed instrument readings, which would otherwise be unpredictable and unexplainable. These accurate, explainable predictions make belief in "unseen" scientific posits, like electricity, a matter of reason and not faith.

CHAPTER SUMMARY

I've argued that faith has the following serious deficiencies: (1) it contradicts reason; (2) it's not a proven path to knowledge; (3) it cannot objectively judge its conflicting claims; (4) it cannot be justified on the basis of strength of internal conviction; and (5) it is not found in all people. Given the aforementioned deficiencies, it is surprising that faith continues to enjoy a revered status as a source of justified beliefs for many people. I conclude with the caution that serious personal and public policy is too important to be anchored on unsupported faith-based beliefs, no matter how sincerely they may be held and offered.

Chapter 4: **Does God Send People to Hell?**

Preview

I take issue with the conservative Christian claim that God does not send people to hell; rather, people who are there want to be there.

INTRODUCTION

It's difficult to write a chapter critiquing *the* Christian conception of hell because it's difficult to determine exactly what that is. All agree that hell comprises the most undesirable type of existence in a state of separation from God. Most hold that existence in hell includes some form of pain or suffering and is relentless and eternal. This conception of hell has critics, some even from within Christianity itself. The critics have registered some serious and pointed criticisms about hell's severity, permanency, and eternality vis-à-vis the nature of the transgressions and the conditions that led to the transgression that bring a person to hell.[1] I think those criticisms are telling. However, I won't dwell on them here. Rather, what I'm concerned to do is critique a common conservative Christian claim used to defend against the criticisms of hell just referred to. That defensive claim is that God doesn't send people to hell. Those in hell are there because they want

---

1. See Parsons, "Hell: Christianity's," 233–54.

to be there. Noted Christian apologist and writer C. S. Lewis put it this way: "The doors of hell are locked on the inside."[2]

I read a transcript of a debate on Jesus's resurrection in which the conservative Christian debater, Michael Horner, echoing Lewis, said the following.

> God doesn't send anyone to hell. . . . We each have the number one choice to make in our life, and that is, do we want to commence a relationship with the Creator and submit to Him as a creature to a Creator, or do we say, "No thanks. I don't want that relationship." Now if we say, "No, thanks" to God, what can God do? Apart from, if you'll excuse the expression, spiritually raping us, he just has to give us our free choice to be apart, separate from Him.[3]

Clearly, for Christians, the defensive value of the claim that God doesn't send anyone to hell because they want to be there is that if it were true, then most criticisms of hell would be blunted. In response, I'll argue that there are compelling reasons to hold that no sane person would want to be in hell and if Christians insist that there are people in hell, then it could only be because God does indeed send and keep them there. Let's look now at my reasons for holding this.

DEBUNKING THE CLAIM THAT GOD DOES NOT SEND PEOPLE TO HELL

First, there are a goodly number of scriptural proof texts supporting the claim that God does send people to hell. Not only do the textual references indicate that God sends people to hell, they indicate that God sends *a lot of people* to hell (Matt 7:13–14; Luke 13:23–24). Matt Slick, in an article from June 6, 2014, entitled "Do People Send Themselves to Hell or Does God Send Them There?," says the following.

> It is biblically true that God sends people to hell. There are too many verses that show God's active involvement in executing judgment upon people. Let's take a look.

---

2. Lewis, *Problem of Pain*, 130.
3. Barker and Horner, "Did Jesus Really Rise," Questions from the Audience, para. 104.

PART I: CRITIQUES OF SELECT ASPECTS OF CHRISTIAN BELIEFS

> "Then He will also say to those on His left, 'Depart from Me, accursed ones, into the eternal fire which has been prepared for the devil and his angels,'" (Matthew 25: 41).

> "For if God did not spare angels when they sinned, but cast them into hell and committed them to pits of darkness, reserved for judgment . . ." (2 Peter 2:4).

> "he also will drink of the wine of the wrath of God, which is mixed in full strength in the cup of His anger; and he will be tormented with fire and brimstone in the presence of the holy angels and in the presence of the Lamb. 11 And the smoke of their torment goes up forever and ever; they have no rest day and night, those who worship the beast and his image, and whoever receives the mark of his name" (Rev 14:10–11)."[4]

These verses give rise to two problems for the views of Christian debater, Michael Horner, cited above. First, scripture does not support the idea of a hell bereft of human denizens. Second, only a very small proportion of Christians has ever believed that hell is empty of humans.[5] In fact, according to the most common forms of Christianity, there are many people in hell.

Second, Horner's comments claim that the only reason people are in hell is that they want to be there. If so, then either there isn't, and never has been, anyone in hell or anyone in hell is insane. No fully informed sane persons would ever opt to be there. Implicit biblical support for this is found in Luke 16:19–31, the story of Lazarus and the rich man in hell. The passage makes it clear that the rich man in hell does not want to be there because he is fully experiencing the horror, pain, and suffering of being there.

Third, if Christians nevertheless still insist that there that there are people who want to be there, then that raises a problem with respect to divine justice. Perhaps the most important reason Christians give to justify the existence of hell is that divine justice requires that the people in hell be punished for their transgressions. But a reasonable and necessary condition for something to be a punishment is that it be the imposition of an unpleasant or undesirable outcome on the one being punished.[6] If so, then if the

---

4. Slick, "Do People Send Themselves," para. 4. See also Matt 5:22, 29–30; 7:21–23.

5. For more on this see the section in chapter 15 entitled "Third Christian Retort to the Claim of Divine Invidious Discrimination against the Unables Vis-à-Vis the Ables: The Salvific Universalism Defense."

6. According to the *Merriam-Webster Dictionary*, "punishment" is defined as (1)

people in hell want to be there, then they really aren't being punished, and God is not instantiating justice with regard to hell.

Fourth, God, as the most perfect being possible, would have the means, method, and motivation to convince, without forcing, any sane human that opting for hell would be a very bad idea. For example, if, postmortem, someone were so foolish as to initially opt to be there, a good and loving Father God could give them a brief "taste" of what hell is like (as well as some inkling of what heaven would be like). That brief experience would "scare them straight," as it were, by enabling them to realize how foolish their opting for existence in hell would be for them. My point here is that even with such a brief taste of hell, any individual would still be able to opt to be in hell, though I find it hard to imagine anyone exercising such an option. Analogously, imagine, for a moment, that you had a fourteen-year-old daughter who told you that she didn't want a relationship with you. Instead, she wanted to commit suicide. Would you think to yourself, à la what Horner claims God would do, "Oh well I guess that's it. My hands are tied. I shouldn't stop her because doing so would be 'raping' her free-will-wise. I just have to respect her free choice to be apart from me—and dead." The answer you're looking for here is a big "hell no!" (Pun intended). A maximally perfect and loving God would facilitate a suitable alternative to the spiritual suicide of hell, just as you, as a loving parent, would facilitate a suitable alternative to physical suicide. Furthermore, if, according to Horner, God must honor a person's free will choice to be in hell, then presumably God would also have to honor a person's free will choice not to remain there. If so, then anyone foolish enough to initially opt to be in hell would, sure as hell (oops, there I go again), not opt to remain there. So, yes, I believe that if there were a hell and people could choose whether to be there or not, then no one would so choose.

Fifth, the conservative Christian view that God doesn't send people to hell, they just choose to be there, suggests that *all* human beings in hell were explicitly offered a clear alternative to hell, namely, salvation through accepting God's invitation to experience the *summum bonum* (highest good) of being with him forever in heaven. But, as it turns out, many human hell-denizens obstinately and arrogantly rejected God's invitation, thereby,

---

"suffering, pain, or loss that serves as retribution"; (2) "a penalty inflicted on an offender through judicial procedure"; (3) "severe, rough, or disastrous treatment." See "Punishment."

PART I: CRITIQUES OF SELECT ASPECTS OF CHRISTIAN BELIEFS

ensuring that they will spend eternity in hell instead. However, such an explanation is questionable for a number of reasons.

1. Some people didn't reject the invitation to join God in heaven because they died before it was ever sent out, that is, before Jesus inaugurated Christianity in the first century.

2. Others, such as preborns, infants, and young children who died as such, or those who lived with significant mental impairment, also didn't reject the invite because they never developed sufficient cognitive faculties to be able to understand it. As we saw from the section in chapter 1 entitled "Important Relevant Data about Prenatal Mortality," this group would number more than 300 billion since relatively recent studies have shown that less than 30 percent of all human fertilized eggs are born alive. Demographers have estimated that about 117 billion humans have been born in the approximate three-hundred-thousand-year history of our species. That means that, given the results of the research just cited, more than 300 billion human persons have died as preborns, infants, and young children. Unless Christianity discovers some long lost doctrine of karma that shows that preborns, infants, and young children who died as such, or those who lived with significant mental impairment, deserved their bad fortunes, these folks too should skate on the charge that they *rejected* God's invitation.

3. Others who lived in parts of the world where delivery of the invitations was pretty spotty or nonexistent cannot reasonably be said to have rejected God's invitation. For instance, there were no Christian missionaries in seventh-century America or Australia. Here, as with (1) above, ignorance of the law *is* a defense.

4. Still other denizens in hell may have found their mailboxes stuffed with tempting postmortem fate invitations from all sorts of religions, including multiple versions of Christianity. Many of these people didn't accept God's invitation because they couldn't figure out what was junk mail and what was the real deal. Even today, this sort of frustration may be at least partially responsible for fueling the increase in the number of people who describe themselves in such terms as "I'm not religious, but I *am* spiritual." Nevertheless, for conservative Christians the rules are clear: no shirt, no shoes, no

acceptance of the divine invitation—then no hell-canceling service. OK, maybe not the first two.

5. After rational deliberation during their lifetimes some individuals concluded that the invitation was bogus because there was insufficient evidence to show that any supernatural Inviter exists, or that there really had been any such invitations issued at all. Note: even if these people were mistaken about there being inadequate evidence for the correct invitation, that would at worst constitute only an error in reasoning, not an instance of dissing or rejecting God, punishable by eternal torment in hell.

6. Even if people somehow genuinely were to choose to reject God, then, according to Christianity, God creates and sustains hell as the only option for them, but that is akin to your spouse saying they want to leave you, and you offering them as the only alternative to be chained up and tortured in a pit in the basement. That's actually criminal coercion, a violation of free will, not a respecting of it. Someone who respected free will would have to allow the person who wants to leave them to build their own home and life, independently. Since it is logically possible for God to allow people who don't like him to live in nicer places than hell (since he can create and sustain any place for them that he wants), God is actually morally obligated to do so, by the Christian's own moral standards (respect for free will requires it, per the principle of noncoercion; compassion and love require it, per the Golden Rule; justice and fairness require it, per the principle of proportionality. All three moral standards would be violated by the doctrine of hell.

In sum, according to the conservative Christian doctrine of hell, people in scenarios 1–6 would end up in hell because they *rejected* God's invitation to join him in heaven. But, as I just argued, most of the humans that Conservative Christianity would say are in hell would never have explicitly rejected God's invitation to not spend eternity in hellish torment. Therefore, they must be there because God put them there.

Chapter 5: **How to Assure Christian Salvation through Murder!**

Preview

This chapter explains how, if Christianity were true, its doctrine of salvation would be fatally flawed because it would entail the morally deficient fact that person A could assure that person B would receive the *summum bonum* (highest good) of eternal salvation by murdering B!

INTRODUCTION

In Italy there is a particular form of revenge known as *la gran vendetta* designed to inflict maximum punishment on a person by bringing about his death and eternal damnation. The tactic is to wait for the victim to commit, or to lure him into committing, a mortal sin,[1] and then to assassinate him immediately thereafter before he repents. Later, the avenger can repent of his murderous act and still achieve eternal reward, thus completing the scheme of ultimate retribution. If one accepts the most commonly promulgated Christian soteriology (doctrine of salvation) with respect to divine judgement and eternal damnation for an unrepentant mortal sinner, then the logic of *la gran vendetta* is unassailable.

This chapter deals with the converse strategy of ensuring the eternal *happiness* of an individual by selected homicide. I'll argue that if standard

---

1. In the Catholic tradition a mortal (deadly) sin is one which if not forgiven by a proper confession would send the sinner to eternal damnation.

Christian soteriology is true, then a logically compelling case can be made for the rationality of abortion, infanticide, and young-child homicide. If so, then that would undermine the plausibility of Christian soteriology and, ultimately, therefore, of Christianity itself. Note that this chapter develops a form of *reductio ad absurdum* argument[2] against the cogency of the Christian theory of salvation. That is, if the Christian theory of salvation is held to be true, then abortion, infanticide, and young child homicide, all considered immoral on the basis of Christian moral principles, must be accepted as a sure-fire means of obtaining salvation for the aforementioned decedents. In short, it's salvation through homicide!

GENERAL CHRISTIAN SOTERIOLOGY

General Christian soteriology holds that our life is in part a trial whose verdict, rendered by God, irrevocably determines our postmortem eternal fate. If our lives satisfy certain standards, then we receive from God a gift of eternal heavenly bliss. If our lives fail to satisfy those standards, then we forfeit heaven, and, according to most Christian interpretations, we receive the eternal damnation of hell. Clearly the salvific (pertaining to salvation) stakes involved in living properly are high for Christians.

CHRISTIAN ASSURED-SALVATION STRATEGY

All good parents want their children to attain goals which are in the children's best interests. The most important goal for Christians, their *summum bonum* (greatest good), is to be reconciled with God and to thereby receive God's gift of eternal salvation and, at the same time, to avoid eternal damnation. The Gospels of Mark and Matthew make this point emphatically. "For what shall it profit a man, if he shall gain the whole world, and lose his own soul?" (Mark 8:36; Matt 16:26 KJV). Thus, good Christian parents should, above all else, want their children to attain eternal salvation and avoid eternal damnation. Moreover, the Bible makes it clear that not all will be saved. In fact, it says that most humans will *not* be saved (Luke 13:23–24; Matt 7:13–14).

---

2. A method of proving the falsity of a view by showing that the logical consequence of the view is absurd or contradictory.

Among the most commonly claimed Christian requirements for salvation are the performance of good deeds, and/or the acknowledgement and faith that Jesus is one's Savior, and/or repentance for one's sins. But clearly these can only be requirements for those who have attained the age of moral and rational accountability, which is no earlier than seven years of age. The requirements can't be satisfied by those who are non-accountable, such as preborns (zygotes [human fertilized eggs], embryos, and fetuses), infants, and young children. It seems fair and reasonable that a perfectly good God would waive the salvific requirements for nonaccountables. As a result, all preborns, infants, and young children who die at that stage of their development should be guaranteed eternal salvation from a maximally benevolent God. To deny them the *summum bonum* of salvation because of an accident of birth would be cruel and unfair. For more on this theme see chapter 15.

In today's world many preborns, infants, and young children do not die as such. Parents, however, could bring it about that they do by practicing abortion or infanticide on them. Think about it for a moment. For parents to do that would guarantee eternal salvation for their offspring which, as we already pointed out, is the paramount Christian parental goal. At the same time it would guarantee that their children would avoid the worse fate of humans, being damned to eternal torment in hell. Therefore, if Christian soteriology is really true, good, loving Christian parents *should* practice abortion or infanticide.[3] I'll call the strategy leading to this radical, some might even say absurd, conclusion the *Christian assured-salvation strategy*.

Noted atheist philosopher Bertrand Russell wrote,

> The Spaniards in Mexico and Peru used to baptize Indian infants and then immediately dash their brains out: by this means they secured that these infants went to Heaven. No orthodox Christian can find any logical reason for condemning their action, although all nowadays do so.[4]

If challenged about the moral and religious propriety of their murderous actions, the Spaniards could have cited something like what I have called the Christian assured-salvation strategy.

---

3. For example, on June 20, 2001, in Houston, Andrea Yates drowned each of her five children, aged six months to seven years, in her bathtub because she thought that would prevent them going to hell. See Broussard, "Adam and Eve."

4. Russell, *Why I Am Not*, 35.

OBJECTIONS TO THE CHRISTIAN ASSURED-SALVATION STRATEGY AND MY RESPONSES

FIRST OBJECTION:

God would find the cost-benefit approach entailed by the Christian assured-salvation strategy to be odious and would never reward such a base calculation.

Response

The carrot of eternal reward and the stick of eternal punishment have long been staples of Christian missionaries. Christians have never been shy about attracting adherents by preaching that the highest benefit of being a Christian (eternal salvation) far exceeds the costs, nor have they held that conversions based on anticipated eternal salvation are unacceptable to God. In fact, Christian apologists have explicitly affirmed its acceptability in what has become known as Pascal's Wager, named after the seventeenth-century French thinker Blaise Pascal. The essence of the wager is that we should believe in God because from a cost-benefit perspective it is more profitable to do so than not, because if God does exist, belief would gain us eternal salvation, while if he doesn't exist, belief would cost us hardly anything. Thus, it would be inconsistent to accept the calculation aspect of Pascal's Wager and yet reject the calculation aspect of the Christian assured-salvation strategy.

Second Objection:

Abortion and infanticide would violate God's will by taking innocent lives.

Responses

First, these transgressions couldn't harm God since, as the most perfect being possible, he is quite beyond being harmed. Moreover, abortion and infanticide contribute to the realization of an end that God desires, namely, that all people be saved. "For this is good and acceptable in the sight of God our Savior; Who will have all men to be saved, and to come unto the knowledge of the truth" (1 Tim 2:3–4 KJV).

Second, if standard Christian salvation doctrine is true, then abortion, infanticide, and young child homicide would not ultimately harm its targets either. Indeed, it would guarantee their eternal happiness. In fact, if Christianity is true, then it's likely that Adolph Hitler is in eternal hell—presumably ruing the fact that his parents didn't exercise the Christian assured-salvation strategy on/for him.

Third Objection:

Practicing abortion or infanticide would harm the parents by bringing about their eternal damnation.

Responses

First, the offspring would still receive their salvation even if this objection were sustained.

Second, in the Christian tradition the only unforgivable sin is blasphemy of the Spirit, which is deliberate resistance to the Holy Spirit (Matt 12:31). Since the parents' sin is not blasphemy of the Spirit, they could, like the avengers practicing *la gran vendetta*, repent later and seek God's forgiveness. Furthermore, there is at least some reason to think they could receive that forgiveness. After all, Christian scripture says, "Greater love hath no man than this, that a man lay down his life for his friends" (John 15:13 KJV). If parents would be willing to trade not only their own lives but also possibly even their own chances of salvation for the eternal happiness of their children, this should strengthen the case for their forgiveness from a loving and compassionate God who could not fail to see the selfless quality of such willingness.

Fourth Objection:

True repentance necessary for God's forgiveness requires that sinners totally reject their sinful actions. But parents could not plausibly claim total rejection of their sinful actions in this matter since they committed them with the intention of subsequently renouncing them. God would realize such renunciations were programmed and would therefore withhold his forgiveness. Thus, parents would indeed lose salvation and suffer damnation.

HOW TO ASSURE CHRISTIAN SALVATION THROUGH MURDER!

Response

Don't many sinners reason that they will sin now and repent later? The New Testament nowhere holds this attitude to be an insurmountable impediment to divine forgiveness. No less a Christian luminary than St. Augustine prayed, "[God] Give me chastity and continency; only not yet," suggesting his intention not to repent until his passions sufficiently subsided.[5] Christians believe that he eventually received forgiveness as indicated by his elevation to sainthood and by his status as one of the most universally revered church fathers. Therefore, performing sinful actions with the intention of repenting later does not appear to preclude obtaining forgiveness from God.

Fifth Objection:

All humans are biologically conceived participating in the original sin of Adam and Eve. Consequently, abortion or infanticide would, in fact, doom preborns, infants, and young children not baptized to eternal damnation.

Responses

Putting aside, for the sake of argument, the implausibility of inheriting moral culpability (see more about this in chapter 1), two responses are in order here.

First, this objection would, at most, only be a problem for preborns, given that infants and young children could be baptized first, thereby, according to most widely practiced Christian traditions,[6] freeing them from the taint of original sin.

Second, it would seem that an omnibenevolent God would not condemn the unbaptized for something for which they are not responsible. The synoptic Gospels certainly emphasize Jesus' concern for infants and young children.

> And they brought unto him also infants, that he would touch them: but when his disciples saw it, they rebuked them. But Jesus called them unto him, and said, "Suffer little children to come

---

5. Augustine, *Confessions of St. Augustine*, 125.
6. Principally, Roman Catholicism and some Protestant denominations. The former alone comprises more than half of all Christians (some one billion adherents).

unto me, and forbid them not: for of such is the kingdom of God." (Luke 18:15–16 KJV)

There is no reason to think God would have any less concern for those who were aborted. Thus, one could reasonably conclude that those aborted would not be denied salvation because of original sin.

Sixth Objection:

All, or most, Christians will be saved anyway and, therefore, abortion and infanticide need not be used for achieving salvation.

Response

It's not clear that all or most Christians will be saved. (For more on this, see material in chapter 15, the section entitled "Rebuttal to the Salvific Universalism Defense.") Jesus in fact suggested that many will not be saved.

> Said one unto him, "'Lord, are there few that be saved?' And he said unto them, 'Strive to enter in at the strait gate: for many, I say unto you, will seek to enter in, and shall not be able.'"(Luke 13:23–24 KJV; see also Matt 7:13–14)

Moreover, it would be irrational to eschew a course of action that would *guarantee* an outcome of infinite value (eternal reward), even if the chances were decent, though not certain, that the outcome could be achieved without the action.

Seventh Objection:

If everyone were to commit abortion or infanticide, the human race would soon die out.

Responses

First, the "what if everyone . . ." line of reasoning is notoriously weak in that, if it proves anything, it proves too much. This line of reasoning, for example, could equally well "prove" the unreasonable claim that being a

Catholic priest or nun is immoral since they commit to celibacy which, if everyone were celibate, would result in the end of the human race.

Second, it would be extremely unlikely that everyone would carry out the conclusion of the Christian assured-salvation strategy. Certainly, non-Christians, who still constitute about two-thirds of the human race two millennia after the founding of Christianity, would undoubtedly reject the Christian assured-salvation strategy.

CONCLUSIONS

There are three important conclusions I draw from the preceding analysis: one logical, one moral, and one psychological.

The logical conclusion: my defense of the soundness of the Christian assured-salvation strategy is meant as a *reductio ad absurdum* argument against the plausibility of standard Christian soteriology and, by extension, against standard Christianity itself. That is, if the Christian assured-salvation strategy unavoidably leads to the horrific conclusion that it is rationally justified and desirable for all parents to abort all pregnancies or commit infanticide on all children under the age of accountability, then standard Christian theory of salvation is implausible, as well as inconsistent with other doctrines of Christianity. But since this theory of salvation is an indispensable part of standard Christianity, then standard Christianity itself is seriously crippled.

The moral conclusion: in recent battles over induced abortion Christians have led the opposition to its moral and legal acceptance. However, if the essence of immorality is causing unwarranted harm to another, then the Christian assured-salvation strategy shows that it is inconsistent for Christians to judge abortion to be immoral. For, given Christian soteriology, abortion causes no harm. On the contrary, it guarantees the eternal salvation of those aborted, enhances the good of Christian parents by satisfying their most important parental goal of securing salvation for their offspring, and pleases God insofar as he wants all to be saved. Thus, the Christian claim that abortion is immoral is undermined.

The psychological conclusion: it seems safe (I hope!) to say that under virtually no circumstances would the vast majority of Christian parents ever embark on the Christian assured-salvation strategy. If one's true degree of conviction about something is most accurately reflected in high stakes decisions concerning it (for example, [supposedly] no atheists in foxholes), then the reticence of Christian parents to follow the Christian assured-salvation strategy *may* be an indication of their lack of conviction about the truth of Christianity's soteriological claims. Just sayin'.

SUMMARY

What the argument in this chapter shows is that God himself does not make moral sense within standard Christian theology. A moral God would be a universalist, working all his wits and means (from the very design of persons to how they are educated) to ensure that everyone, eventually, is saved. In that system, the Christian assured-salvation strategy would be defeated, since killing kids would then be unnecessary. It would do nothing for them that they couldn't get elsehow. The Christian assured-salvation strategy only arises when you introduce hell as a soteriological doctrine. The Christian assured-salvation strategy refutes the moral and logical coherence of hell as a doctrine. Christians, therefore, to be morally coherent and head off the Christian assured-salvation strategy, should abandon any doctrine of hell and be universalists (everyone ends up in heaven eventually).[7] Yet the resistance to this moral and logical conclusion demonstrates that persons' commitment to Christianity is dogmatic rather than rational, which is actually evidence that Christianity is false; people aren't believing it on sound reasons.

---

7. For more on the problems that salvific universalism poses for Christianity see in chapter 15 the section entitled "Rebuttal to the Salvific Universalism Defense."

Chapter 6: **Christianity And The Meaning Of Life**

> *Tomorrow, and tomorrow, and tomorrow,*
> *Creeps in this petty pace from day to day,*
> *To the last syllable of recorded time;*
> *And all our yesterdays have lighted fools*
> *The way to dusty death. Out, out, brief candle!*
> *Life's but a walking shadow, a poor player*
> *That struts and frets his hour upon the stage,*
> *And then is heard no more; it is a tale*
> *Told by an idiot, full of sound and fury,*
> *Signifying nothing.* —Macbeth 5.5.19–28

Preview

This chapter looks at the question "What is the meaning of life?" from the perspective of Christianity and secularism, that is, a worldview devoid of deities and other supernatural entities. The two perspectives on the question are laid out and evaluated.

INTRODUCTION

Shakespeare is duly celebrated not only for his unrivaled genius with the language, but also for his insight into basic issues of human concern. The subject of the meaning of life is one of the most significant of these. In the passage cited, Macbeth expresses the view, shared by many, that human life, alas, has no real significance. Yet eloquent, as well, have been the voices that have proclaimed that every human life has profound meaning. Clearly, this is a subject of great importance, dealing so intimately as it does with the very nature of our existence. It's with precisely such topics as the meaning of life—momentous, controversial, nonscientific—that philosophy can make its most important contributions to the understanding of ourselves and the world around us. In this chapter I'll analyze the question of the meaning of life from a Christian and a secular perspective. I'll henceforth refer to this question as "Q."

Q = *What is the meaning of life?*

CLARIFICATION OF "MEANING OF"

The first thing we must do is to clarify what, from a Christian or secular perspective, Q could be interpreted as asking. This requires that we determine what the phrase "meaning of" at the heart of Q means. One way to do this is to list the different ways the phrase "meaning of" is used in ordinary language. Consider the following sentences.

1. What is the *meaning of* "bachelor"?
2. What is the *meaning of* the play's last scene?
3. What is the *meaning of* the hastily caused press conference?
4. What is the *meaning of* this year's sparse rainfall for Texas farmers this season?
5. What is the *meaning of* this mess, young man?

Sentences 1–5 represent different, although sometimes overlapping, connotations of "meaning of." In (1) the phrase has a purely linguistic function. It's simply asking for a word or words in English that could be substituted for the word "bachelor" so that any resulting sentence would always have the same truth value (true or false) as the original sentence had with the word "bachelor" in it.

Sentence (2) is asking for meaning in terms of *significance*. The sense of sentence (2) would be "What importance has the playwright attached to the play's last scene?"

Sentence (3) seems to be stressing "meaning of" in terms of *purpose of*. The reading would be "Why did they call a press conference on such short notice?"

Sentence (4) would appear to be a call for ascertaining the *effect*(s) of the circumstances described. That is, it's asking what's the likely result of the sparse rainfall this year to farmers in this area.

Finally, sentence (5) suggests a desire for an explanation in terms of *cause*, that is, who or what is the cause of something or event.

These five uses of "meaning of" can be usefully grouped into two broad categories and a number of sub-categories. "Meaning of" can be used in (I) a linguistic or (II) a descriptive sense. (II) comprises requests for nonlinguistic information about something, either in terms of significance, purpose, effect, or cause, or, in fact, any combination of these. Table 6.1 summarizes the scheme of distinctions described so far.

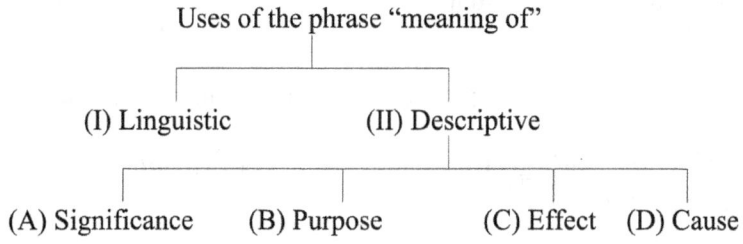

Table 6.1

As seen in table 6.1, there are five categories: I, IIA, IIB, IIC, IID. Sentences 1–5 above are examples, respectively, of those five categories. Now let's connect the scheme in table 6.1 with Q. First of all, clearly no one who poses Q is using the phrase "meaning of" in the sense of category I (linguistic sense). Q is clearly not a request for a definition of the word "life." But Q has at times been used in ways which stress one or more of the remaining categories. Some people have understood Q to be a request concerning the *significance* of life (IIA), the *purpose* of life (IIB), an inquiry into the *effect* of any person's having lived (IIC), or, finally, the *cause* of life (IID). Table 6.2 presents four plausible reformulations of Q (R1–R4) which correspond to the four categories (IIA, IIB, IIC, IID) sketched in table 6.1.

Category	Emphasis	Reformulation Of Q
IIA	meaning-in-significance	R1: What gives my life significance?
IIB	meaning-in-purpose	R2: What is the purpose of my life?
IIC	meaning-in-effect	R3: Does it really matter that I live and will die?
IID	meaning-in-cause	R4: Why am I living?

Table 6.2

Remember, as we begin to look more closely at R1–R4, we are not attempting to judge which is the correct reformulation of Q. That's not the issue; and anyway, there's no correct reformulation. I'm simply pointing out that these are possible reformulations of Q which reflect the different ways to interpret and use the phrase "meaning of." Let's take a closer look at each of the proposed reformulations.

EXAMINATION OF REFORMULATIONS OF Q (R1–R4)

R1: Meaning-in-Significance; What Gives My Life Significance?

One might argue that any life has significance to the extent that it leaves an observable or measurable impact on the world such as, for example, in a positive vein by substantially adding to the world's stock of truth, beauty, goodness, or other positive values. This might be brought about directly through one's actions or indirectly by a descendant.

There are, however, a number of drawbacks to this interpretation of meaning as significance.

First, many human lives thought meaningful to those who led them would have to be judged unmeaningful since they left no discernibly noteworthy or lasting marks on the world.

Second, in many cases a judgement about whether a particular life has meaning or not would have to be deferred for quite some time, perhaps even long after the death of the individual involved. It seems a bit strange that, according to R1, a person may not be able to determine whether her life has meaning while she is living it.

Third, there is the unsettling fact that significance must also be associated not only with acts of great good but also of great evil, since, alas, the latter could be very impactful.

Fourth, there must be the realization that the significance which any life may have will never be permanent. Whatever changes in the world we may have wrought by our lives will eventually be forgotten, indiscernible, or forever lost. Nothing in the physical world (the world of matter and energy) can have permanently lasting significance. The reason this is the case has to do with the most well-attested and accepted cosmological (the study of the origin and development of the physical universe) view of the origin of the universe called the Big Bang Theory. It holds that the universe that we know today developed from an event which occurred about 13.8 billion years ago. Since then the universe has grown to its present enormous dimensions by expansion. Most cosmologists believe that the expansion of the universe will continue without ever ceasing. If so, then the final fate of our never ending expanding physical universe after trillions of years will be that all organization of matter and energy within the universe will be forever dismantled or dissipated, and with that, the possibility of anything which exists in time and space (like human lives) having lasting significance will have vanished. There is also a competing theory, sometimes called the Pulsating Universe Theory, in which the expansion of the universe slows, stops, and is followed by a gradual contraction, resulting eventually in a reconstitution of the original primal mass of matter and energy, which will then repeat the cycle—endlessly. Even in the Pulsating Universe Theory all organization of matter and energy is periodically totally obliterated, leaving no traces from the previous forty-or-so-billion-year cycle (twenty-billion-year expansion—twenty-billion-year contraction). Here again, obviously, the possibility of any spatio-temporal life having lasting significance is nil. So, regardless of which of the two current major cosmological theories is true, material lasting significance is not to be had.[1]

Christian Interpretation of the Meaning of Life

There is, however, yet another approach to try to establish that human life has lasting significance, and that is to associate it in some way with a nonphysical

---

1. Actually, there are a number of other less prominent cosmologies on offer besides the two main ones just sketched out. However, all have the same concluding point: nothing can last "forever" in them.

transcendent (outside of time and space) reality. A common interpretation of the transcendent reality is that it is the personal God of Christianity who is held to be, among other things, the divine designer, creator, and sustainer of the universe. In the Christian tradition an answer to R1 (*What gives my life significance?*) is extracted from a divine worldview as specifically interpreted by Christian scripture and doctrine. This divine worldview describes the world, its origin and history, as a grand, purposeful drama "produced, written, directed, and, at times, starred in" by God. Each individual lives in conformance with the role that has been divinely ordained for him as part of God's overall scheme for this world.

This interpretation, if true, would satisfy the idea of lasting significance with respect to R1 in at least two ways. First, God's cosmic plan and our place in it would be a part of God's divine *eternal* ideas. Second, the Christian tradition, like a number of other religious traditions, claims that each individual has a unique, nonmaterial component, referred to as a soul. Being nonmaterial and of divine origin, it is held to be impervious to the destructive fate of matter and energy sketched out in the Big Bang and Pulsating Universe theories. The most common Christian view is that an eternal life of either reward or punishment awaits each person according to how she lives her life. Such a view is said to produce lasting significance to a human life.

Many philosophers have rejected the foregoing Christian attempt to demonstrate that human life has lasting significance because they hold that there is simply insufficient credible evidence to prove either: (I) the existence of God, or (II) the existence of any nonmaterial, enduring aspect of each person (a soul).

With regard to (I), there are many strong arguments which support the contention that no God exists. I refer the reader to part III, chapters 14–18 for five novel ones.

With regard to (II), there have been many philosophical and scientific attempts to prove the existence of a nonmaterial human aspect (soul) since at least the fifth century BCE. Despite many ingenious arguments and experiments, there simply have been no successes. Of course, we should keep an open mind on the subject and remain alert for any evidence that may prove the existence and nature of a soul. However, absent such evidence, reason requires that we consider its existence unproven and that our personhood ceases at death. This is not exactly a welcomed conclusion for many people, but we should not reject truth simply because we take it to entail unpleasantness.

To recap this section, then, we sought an answer to Q, reformulated as R1: What gives my life significance? I suggested that an answer could be given in terms of public, noteworthy changes in the world associated with one's life. In this interpretation, some, but not all people, have meaningful lives, although sometimes in a destructive sense. However, if significance comes only with the permanence of the changes wrought, then no human life has meaning, for, as I argued, no change wrought by human beings will be permanent. The ultimate destiny of matter and energy in the universe, and the lack of evidence supporting the existence of a nonmaterial source of permanent significance (soul or God), preclude any meaning of life having permanent significance.[2]

R2: Meaning-in-Purpose; What Is the Purpose of My Life?

Assuming that we have satisfactorily ruled out a role given to us by a cosmic Divine Being, the only role or function that could even remotely be associated with an answer to Q as R2 is that of a purely biological or sociobiological nature. It may be said that each individual has a kind of biological mandate or purpose to see to its own and, collaterally, the species' survival. There are various physical, and perhaps psychological, pleasure/pain incentives associated with eating, drinking, resting, procreating, eliminating, etc., to insure that we do the actions necessary for biological or sociobiological advancement purposes.

The major drawback to this reformulation of Q as R2 is that the goals associated with this reformulation seem too trivial to serve as a meaningful meaning of a human life in any significant or interesting sense. These kinds of biological drives, goals, or functions operate "blindly" for all living systems. They involve more instinct-related, rather than reason/will-related, actions. If we agree that humans have a uniqueness rooted in highly developed capacities, such as reason and self-reflection, which are suited to achieve more than just biological mandates, then it would seem that the R2 Q reformulation in terms of biologically or sociobiologically set goals is philosophically uninteresting.

---

2. The lyrics to the incongruously upbeat song "History of Modern (Part I)" (by Orchestral Manoeuvres in the Dark) are spot on. See Orchestral Manoeuvres in the Dark, "History of Modern (Part I)."

R3: Meaning-in-Effect; Does It Really Matter That I Live and Will Die?

R3 contains the crucial but vague phrase "really matter." One must ask "matter to whom or what?" and "'matter' in what sense." If you count the fact of being mourned or remembered after your death as sufficient for making your life "really matter," then for many, although not all, the answer to the R3 formulation of Q is yes. The answer is also yes if we accept a purely physical interpretation of what it is to matter. It can easily be shown that, had any individual not been born, the makeup of the universe would have been different in at least some small physical ways involving the position and status of the universe's matter and energy. After all, any physical body, including, of course, a human body, affects, and is affected by, every other material body in the universe to some very small degree, at least, for example, by gravitational attraction.

Again, however, I suspect that such interpretations are unlikely to satisfy most people's understanding of what it means to "really matter." It certainly doesn't satisfy mine. The trouble is, if we discount a role for a transcendent Divine Being, then I don't see any other plausible answers for this R3 reformulation.

R4: Meaning-in-Cause; Why Am I Living?

Ignoring the philosophically uninteresting explanation of R4 in terms of the successful mating action of one's parents, and having already ruled out the role of any divine transcendent planner, we seem to be left with precious little at this point. There isn't any evidence of any conscious "hand" of fate or destiny operating in human doings or comings and goings, although we sometimes flatter ourselves thusly. True, we can, as a matter of historical exercise, go back and trace certain patterns of causes, effects, and coincidences in individual lives or in history in general. Some people have, after the fact, claimed to see the working of agency in these patterns. However, this cannot be considered satisfactory evidence for the existence of a guided plan, since patterns can always be discerned with or without a pattern-maker responsible for them. Numerous patterns can be identified in ink blots or clouds, for example. This should not count as evidence for the claim that either were intentionally fashioned.

There remains nothing, therefore, but the bare biological facts of mammalian reproduction to provide an answer for the R4 reformulation of Q, "Why am I living?" However, this is hardly the stuff which will provide satisfactory meanings-of-life for most people. R4 seems to fall far short of how most people think of Q.

Let's summarize the entire endeavor so far. We have seen that question Q, "What is the meaning of life?," has a number of different interpretations. We proposed and examined four possible interpretations of Q (table 6.2) based on four identified uses of the expression "meaning of" (table 6.1): (R1) significance, (R2) purpose, (R3) effect, and (R4) cause. The analyses of these four reformulations yielded three basic answers:

i. permanent meaning could be associated with a transcendent Being (God);
ii. there is no meaning of life; or
iii. the meaning of life is transitory, and often of a frankly trivial nature.

I rejected (i) on the basis of the fact that there is insufficient evidence to support it. In the next section I'll try to show that there are good reasons for rejecting (ii), and that meaning, although unavoidably transitory, can be reasonably and *non-trivially* ascribed to human life. To show this, I will introduce a fifth usage of the phrase "meaning of" which I'll argue is sensible, and then, based on this usage, I'll offer a fifth reformulation, (R5), and answer for Q.

MY PROPOSED INTERPRETATION AND ANSWER TO Q

I now propose a third broad usage category for the phrase "meaning of." In addition to the (I) linguistic and (II) descriptive uses, I propose a (III) prescriptive use category for the phrase. In this usage, to ask for the meaning of something is to ask for a set of action-guiding principles related to a proper functioning of the item under consideration. The following are some examples of what I have in mind with this kind of usage.

- What is the meaning of the cross?
- What is the meaning of charity?
- What is the meaning of being a marine?

In each of these cases the answer has something to do with setting out prescriptions based on the nature of the thing which is being inquired into. One might say that the meaning of the cross is *to emulate* the life of Jesus; that the meaning of charity is *to treat* others lovingly as brothers and sisters; that the meaning of being a marine is *to be* brave, courageous, strong, and, of course, *semper fi*. Table 6.3 is table 6.1 with the additional prescriptive use category added.

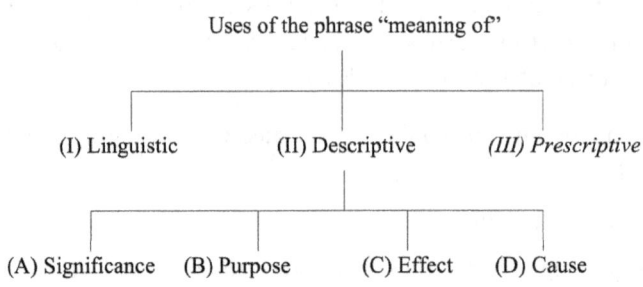

Table 6.3

R5: Meaning-in-Prescription; What Procedures, Standards, Virtues Should Guide Human Life to Satisfaction?

On the basis of the prescriptive use (III), we can generate a fifth reformulation, R5, of Q. Since life is at the heart of what Q is inquiring into, it seems only reasonable that something about life should hold the key to a suitable answer to Q. I think Q is best understood as asking about the *value* of life, that which makes it worth living. It should be evident that simply existing, although an obviously necessary condition for life having meaning as value, is equally obviously not sufficient. There are, regrettably, instances of human existence where death may in fact be preferable and more reasonable. I have in mind, for example, cases of irremediable severe pain, depression, or incapacitation. If life has value, it exceeds the simple fact of existing.

I maintain that reflection and experience reveal that the value of life lies in the likely possibility or actual realization of personal satisfaction. By "satisfaction," I mean "either a feeling of contentment, or a feeling of making acceptable advancement toward contentment in our lives." This notion of satisfaction would seem to be related to the popular psychological notion of "feeling good about ourselves." Experience confirms that such a feeling is not only good in itself, but is also a most effective inducement to additional achievements. It is this concept of a satisfied life which I feel holds the key to unlocking a suitable answer to the question about the meaning of life. Table 6.4 is table 6.2 with the R5 reformulation added.

Category	Emphasis	Reformulation Of Q
IIA	meaning-in-significance	R1: What gives my life significance?
IIB	meaning-in-purpose	R2: What is the purpose of my life?
IIC	meaning-in-effect	R3: Does it really matter that I live and will die?
IID	meaning-in-cause	R4: Why am I living?
IIIE	meaning-in-prescription	R5: What procedures, standards, virtues should be followed to guide human life to satisfaction?

Table 6.4

In searching for the proper R5 prescriptions for living a satisfying life, we are led to the notions of a fulfilling life (for more on this, see the section of chapter 13 entitled "Starting Point: A Fulfilling Life"), which incorporates each individual's conception of his or her understanding of intrinsic goods, namely, those experiences we hold to have highest value, that is, value in and of themselves apart from anything else they may lead to. Examples of intrinsic goods would be physical pleasure, relationships of intimacy, aesthetic enjoyment, personal achievement and creativity, and possession of certain kinds of knowledge. Each person and her circumstances are unique, and her version of a fulfilling life to realize her unique desires and goals will likewise be unique. In this sense one cannot suitably propose a meaning of life that prescribes detailed behavior for all individuals. We can, however, illuminate the evident, namely, point out that meaning is to be found in each individual's freedom to have a plausible opportunity to weave the threads of her own interpretation of what are intrinsically good experiences for her into the fabric of her life. However, reason dictates that the quest to achieve one's fulfilling life cannot be most efficiently carried out in an environment of *unregulated* competition with other fulfilling life achievement seekers. The most effective way of achieving one's fulfilling life is to recognize and follow fair rules of engagement for the lifelong effort to achieve one's fulfilling life. This is the role I propose for the moral code I call Ethical Rationalism, which is thoroughly explained and defended in chapter 13.

MEANING OF LIFE—PROPOSED

> The meaning of life is to be found in the value of formulating, striving to achieve, and, if fortunate, achieving our own freely chosen version of a fulfilling life, consistent with a rational moral code (see chapter 13) designed to regulate and assist all individuals in these activities. More specifically, *my life has meaning in my seeking truth, doing good, enjoying beauty, having fun, and loving.*

In summary, I hold that every human life can have meaning grounded in the unique desires, goals, interests, and talents of each human being. To be sure, as I admitted earlier, this sense of meaning is transitory with respect to each person. The evidence indicates that once we die, all meaning ceases for us because there is no more "us." But this interpretation of a meaningful life is one which is life-affirming and exhorts us to take full advantage of the time we have to pursue life's fulfillments in love, pleasure, beauty, creativity, and truth in peaceful and productive cooperation with other beings.

To conclude: let me leave you with the thoughts of the American writer Bessie Stanley on what a life well-lived could be.

> To laugh often and love much; to win the respect of intelligent persons and the affection of children; to earn the approbation of honest citizens and endure the betrayal of false friends; to appreciate beauty; to find the best in others; to give of one's self; to leave the world a bit better, whether by a healthy child, a garden patch or a redeemed social condition; to have played and laughed with enthusiasm and sung with exultation; to know even one life has breathed easier because you have lived—this is to have succeeded.[3]

Hear, hear!

---

3. Stanley, "Success." Bessie A. Stanley was responding to a contest held in 1906 by the *Emporia* (Kansas) *Gazette*, which put its readers to the task of defining success. People loved it and recycled it, and by 1951 Stanley's winning paragraph was being misattributed to Ralph Waldo Emerson in a syndicated newspaper column by midwestern journalist Albert Edward Wiggam. From here it was off to the races.

Chapter 7: **Christian Apologists: Why Do They Even Bother?**

Preview

When the topic of Christian apologetics (hereafter simply "apologetics") arises, the usual focus is on whether it accomplishes its goal of rationally establishing the truth of Christianity. In this chapter I examine whether the general apologetical enterprise itself is coherent, rather than whether any version of it achieves its goals. I argue that, from the perspective of the apologists' own Christian tradition, their efforts are not coherent because they are, ironically, unchristian and spiritually dangerous.

CHRISTIAN APOLOGETICS IS UNCHRISTIAN!

Almost all Christian denominations deny the possibility of rationally demonstrating the truth of Christianity. Roman Catholicism, Christianity's largest branch, explicitly declares in its canon law that,

> If anyone say that in Divine Revelation there are contained no mysteries properly so called, but that through reason rightly developed all the dogmas of faith can be understood and demonstrated from natural principles, let him be cursed.[1]

Hilarion Alfeyev, Russian Orthodox bishop of Austria and representative of the Orthodox Church to the European Union, sums up the Eastern

---

1. Arieti and Wilson, *Scientific and the Divine*, 309.

PART I: CRITIQUES OF SELECT ASPECTS OF CHRISTIAN BELIEFS

Orthodox Christian view of the possibility of rational demonstration of the Christian faith as follows.

> "Unless I see I will not believe." This is how people who demand from us logical, tangible proof of the Christian faith often answer us, the faithful. But there are not and cannot be such proof, for the Christian faith is beyond the grasp of rational thought, being super-rational. Nothing in the Christian faith, be it the existence of God, the resurrection of Christ or other truths, can be proven logically: one can only accept them or reject them on the basis of faith.[2]

Much of Protestant Christianity has also always insisted that the truth of Christianity cannot be rationally demonstrated. For example, the apostle Paul, the most important figure in early Christianity, many of whose views align with Protestantism, declared,

> Jews demand signs and Greeks look for wisdom, but we preach Christ crucified: a stumbling block to Jews and foolishness to Gentiles, but to those whom God has called, both Jews and Greeks, Christ the power of God and the wisdom of God. For the foolishness of God is wiser than human wisdom, and the weakness of God is stronger than human strength. (1 Cor 1:22–25 NIV)

As cited in chapter 3, the emblematic Protestant reformer, Martin Luther, echoed this same theme when he asserted the following.

> If all the smart alecks on earth were to pool their wits, they could not devise a ladder on which to ascend to heaven. . . . He who would deal with the doctrines of the Christian faith (should) not pry, speculate, and ask how they may agree with reason, but, instead, merely determine whether Christ said it. If Christ did say it, then he should cling to it, whether it harmonizes with reason or not, and no matter how it may sound.[3]

John Calvin, who along with Luther is one of the most influential founding figures of Protestantism, maintained that the natural human intellect is so blinded and distorted by the effects of Adam and Eve's original sin that it cannot make an adequate approach to divine truth. As the Internet Encyclopedia of Philosophy article on Calvin comments,

> Sin has corrupted not only the will, but also the intellect. After the introduction of sin into the world, human possibility (natural

2. Alfeyev, "Blessed Are Those," para. 2.
3. Luther, "Tenth Sermon," 80.

knowledge) is radically limited, and no un-aided intellect, not even the sharpest, will be able to penetrate into the mysteries of God's truth and God's current will for humanity.[4]

In sum, apologetics creates for itself a kind of liar's paradox (A liar says: "I am lying." Is she?). If the apologist is successful, then he succeeds in rationally showing that Christianity is true. But one of the truths of Christianity is that Christianity cannot be rationally shown to *be* true!

Besides being unchristian, Christian apologetics is dangerous.

CHRISTIAN APOLOGETICS IS DANGEROUS

As I pointed out in chapter 3, having religious faith can be described as believing that religious claims are true in the absence of adequate evidence that they are. If apologists could actually demonstrate the truth of Christianity, there would be no psychological space, as it were, within which religious faith could operate, or any role for it to play in one's religious life. Rational demonstration would render faith redundant. One cannot believe as a matter of faith that for which one has adequate evidence. For example, I cannot believe *by faith* that you have a watch on your left wrist if I am presently staring at that watch on your wrist. The observational evidence is simply too dominant. One might say that the floodlight of evidence prevents one from seeing anything using the candle of faith. However, if you put your arms behind your back, then I could believe as a matter of faith that you have a watch on your left wrist. The floodlight of evidence is turned off and the candle of faith can now shed light on the situation, so to speak. As I pointed out in chapter 3, Soren Kierkegaard, the notable nineteenth-century Danish Christian philosopher noted that if Christianity were rationally provable, then there would be no risk in believing it. He explained his view thusly.

> Without risk there is no faith. Faith is precisely the contradiction between the infinite passion of the individual's inwardness and the objective uncertainty. If I am capable of grasping God objectively, I do not believe, but precisely because I cannot do this I must believe. If I wish to preserve myself in faith I must constantly be intent upon holding fast the objective uncertainty, so as to remain

---

4. Holder, "John Calvin," para. 16.

out upon the deep, over seventy thousand fathoms of water, still preserving my faith.[5]

But, if there be no role for religious faith to play or room for it to operate, then salvation would be jeopardized since virtually all Christian denominations claim that faith is indispensable for salvation. In this regard, Christian scholar Charles Hodge wrote, "There is no faith, therefore, where the Gospel is not heard; and where there is no faith, there is no salvation."[6] Recall, also, how Jesus rebuked the apostle Thomas for his lack of faith: "Because you have seen me, you have believed; blessed are those who have not seen and yet have believed" (John 21:29 ESV).

Christian apologists commonly argue that the reason that God doesn't give us indisputable evidence of his existence or his gospel's truth is because that would violate our free will. But if that were the case, then it would follow that Christian apologetics would violate our free will, precisely by attempting to give us adequate evidence. Thus, I contend that from a Christian perspective apologetics is dangerous for Christians because its success would preclude faith, and thereby imperil salvation.

SO, WHY DO CHRISTIAN APOLOGISTS EVEN BOTHER THEN?

It's difficult to imagine that any informed Christian apologists would be unaware of the points just mentioned. So why do they persist nevertheless? Let me suggest some reasons.

Fame And Fortune

In the emerging cottage industry of Christian apologetics, there is certainly the potential for considerable fame and fortune for the most visible practitioners. I imagine that apologists William Lane Craig and Frank Turek, for instance, are well compensated for their many writings and appearances. "Not that there's anything wrong with that"—as TV comedian Jerry Seinfeld would say.[7] Atheists, too, have their fame and fortune rewards (see works of the "new atheists," including Richard Dawkins, Sam Harris, Daniel

---

5. Kierkegaard, *Concluding Unscientific Postscript*, 182.
6. Hodge, *Systematic Theology*, 648.
7. Cherones, "Outing."

Dennett et al.). However, unlike their theist counterparts, the new atheists aren't irrationally laboring to achieve a goal whose ultimate success is precluded from the start by the very view they are defending.

Half a Loaf Is Better Than None

Some apologists may accept that Christianity may not be fully rationally justifiable, but still feel that effective apologetics may at least justify *some* aspects of Christianity, thus making apologetics meaningful. Setting aside whether apologists *can* rationally justify even some aspects of Christianity, this "half a loaf" justification is weak.

First, the professed aim of most apologists is to provide a rational justification for the *entire* Christian corpus. Josh McDowell, for example, in his popular *Evidence That Demands a Verdict*, explicitly says that the goal of apologetics is to "give valid, convincing, historical, documented reasons for faith in Jesus Christ," not to rationally justify, say, 57 percent of Christian faith.[8]

Second, of what use would a partial justification of Christianity be anyway? Why bother to struggle through apologetic contortions to justify only some aspects of Christianity, only to ultimately cede the field to faith anyway? By the way, I don't understand what McDowell means by saying that the goal of apologetics is to give "documented reasons for faith." If one believes something is true on the basis of faith, then why would they want or need a rational justification for it? In sum, apologetic success would seem to be, like the proverbial pregnancy, an all or nothing affair.

It's the Faith, Stupid!

Finally, apologists might see themselves in the role of buttressing the faith of Christians who suffer from what might be called (with apologies to Freud) "reason envy." Such Christians feel threatened by what they fear (correctly) are formidable rational challenges to their faith. For example, the late Catholic Supreme Court justice Antonin Scalia said in an address some years back that "the modern world dismisses Christians as fools for holding to their traditional beliefs. . . . Surely those who adhere to all or most of these traditional Christian beliefs are to be regarded as

---

8. McDowell, *Evidence That Demands a Verdict*, iii.

simpleminded."[9] Apologetics might then be justified by its providing assurance to these Christians that they are not "fools for holding to their traditional beliefs." After all, apologists are no dummies—right? Thus, apologetic support could still be claimed to be effective even if, as seems likely, most of the assurance-needing Christians are largely unfamiliar with, or uninterested in, the details of the apologetics themselves.

However, this justification of apologetic practice falls short on two accounts.

First, the claims of the success of Christian apologetics have been vigorously, and I would say, successfully, challenged by atheists, agnostics, and other non-Christians.

Second, as pointed out earlier in the chapter, major Christian figures have made it very clear that the ultimate success of apologetics is precluded by the Christian affirmation of the preeminence and indispensability of faith-based justifications.

CONCLUSION

I've striven to show that, despite its current celebrity in Christian religious circles, Christian apologetics is incoherent in that it incurs Christian historical and doctrinal disapproval and is such that, were it to achieve its goals, the Christian *summum bonum* of eternal salvation could very well be jeopardized.

---

9. Biskupic, "Scalia Blasts."

Chapter 8: Critiques of Three Miscellaneous Christian Topics

Preview

This chapter responds to two common Christian complaints about atheists. It also examines God's peculiar predilection for glory. More specifically the items covered are the following.

1. Why do atheists always blame God for suffering in the world?
2. Why do atheists always seem so angry at religion, especially at Christianity?
3. What's up with God and glory anyway?

WHY DO ATHEISTS ALWAYS BLAME GOD FOR THE SUFFERING IN THE WORLD?

Although some atheists may give that impression, it's actually inaccurate for the very simple reason that, by definition, atheists don't believe there is a God. So, it would make no sense for them to blame anything on a being that they don't believe exists. For the same reason, Christians don't blame Zeus for any destructive lightning strikes.

What atheists are actually saying is that there are things we observe in the world that we wouldn't expect to observe if God existed, such as massive quantities of unjustified pain, suffering, and harm to innocent beings (see chapter 17), God's hiddenness (see chapter 16), unfairness with regard human well-being (see chapter 14) and salvation opportunities (see chapter 15), and the existence of the world we inhabit rather than a world akin to what Christians call heaven (see chapter 18). For atheists to point these things out is not to complain about God. It's to show that the existence of God is very unlikely.

WHY DO ATHEISTS ALWAYS SEEM SO ANGRY AT RELIGION, ESPECIALLY CHRISTIANITY?

I can't, of course, speak for all "angry" atheists, but my sense is that at the heart of whatever "anger" they might have is their belief that religious folk too often seek to impose their religious beliefs, most often by law, on all other members of a society. Moreover, atheists feel that the justification offered for imposed religious beliefs in most cases is faith-based, not reason-based. Atheists see this as not only wrongheaded but also detrimental to many innocent persons who are harmed by such faith-based Christian claims. For one salient example among many, think of how many LBGTQ+ people in the past, and even today, have been harassed, discriminated against, and persecuted on the basis of faith-based religious claims condemning LBGTQ+ behavior.[1] Many atheists see these sorts of religious efforts to be an affront to proper morality and rationality which coarsens society and weakens its ability to function as a prosperous commonwealth benefitting all its inhabitants; hence, the atheists' "anger."

Finally, I'd be remiss if I didn't point out that there are plenty of Christians who harbor explicit or implicit anger toward atheists. For example, polls show that Americans hold atheists in lower esteem than they do members of any other major social group.[2] In addition, in most US states it's practically impossible for an avowed atheist to win election to any public office.[3]

---

1. For more examples of what might irk atheists about Christianity and religion in general, see chapter 12. Also, see Christina, *Why Are You Atheists?*

2. See "Atheists Remain Most Disliked."

3. For more info on this point see the Wikipedia article entitled "Discrimination against Atheists."

CRITIQUES OF THREE MISCELLANEOUS CHRISTIAN TOPICS

WHAT'S UP WITH GOD AND GLORY ANYWAY?

Glory Defined

glo·ry: noun[4]

1. "high renown or honor won by notable achievements"
2. "magnificence or great beauty"

God Likes Glory

In reading or listening to Christian commentators expound on the nature of God, it's hard to miss the fact that, according to them, God really likes glory—a lot, and a lot *of* it. For example, as a student at a Catholic Jesuit high school, I was told to write the initials AMDG at the top of my test sheets or graded papers. AMDG is the motto of the Society of Jesus (Jesuits). It is a Latin acronym for *Ad majorem Dei gloriam* (For the greater glory of God). As *Catholic Answers* says, "the [Catholic] Church teaches that God freely chose to create the world for his glory."[5] In the Protestant tradition, too, God's glory is prominently affirmed. Just to give you a sample of how much God values his glory, consider the following Biblical citations collected by noted Protestant author, commentator, and pastor John Piper.[6]

John Piper's Comments on God and His Glory (Following in Italics)

> Probably no text in the Bible reveals the passion of God for his own glory more clearly and bluntly as Isaiah 48:9-11 where God says [emphasis added],
>
> For my name's sake I defer my anger, for the sake of my praise I restrain it for you, that I may not cut you off. Behold, I have refined you, but not as silver; I have tried you in the furnace of affliction.

4. "Glory."

5. See Maggiolini, "World Was Created," sec. 293-94, and Horn, "Why Did God Create."

6. John Piper is founder and teacher of desiringgod.org and chancellor of Bethlehem College and Seminary. For thirty-three years, he served as pastor of Bethlehem Baptist Church, Minneapolis, Minnesota. He is author of more than fifty books, including *Desiring God: Meditations of a Christian Hedonist* and most recently *What Is Saving Faith?*

> *For my own sake, for my own sake, I do it, for how should my name be profaned? My glory I will not give to another [emphasis in Piper's original].*

Piper continues.

> *What this text hammers home to us is the centrality of God in his own affections. The most passionate heart for the glorification of God is God's heart. God's ultimate goal is to uphold and display the glory of his name [emphasis added].*

Piper goes on.

> *God chose his people for his glory. . . .*
> *(Ephesians 1:4–6, cf. vv.12, 14, NASB). . . .*
>
> *God created us for his glory. . . . (Isaiah 43:6–7)*
>
> *God called Israel for his glory. . . . (Isaiah 49:3); (Jeremiah 13:11)*
>
> *God rescued Israel from Egypt for his glory. . . . (Psalm 106:7–8)*
>
> *God raised Pharaoh up to show his power and glorify his name. . . . (Romans 9:17)*
>
> *God defeated Pharaoh at the Red Sea to show his glory. . . . (Exodus 14:4, 18; v. 17)*
>
> *God spared Israel in the wilderness for the glory of his name. . . . (Ezekiel 20:14)*
>
> *God gave Israel victory in Canaan for the glory of his name. . . . (2 Samuel 7:23)*
>
> *God did not cast away his people for the glory of his name. . . . (1 Samuel 12:20, 22)*
>
> *God saved Jerusalem from attack for the glory of his name. . . . (2 Kings 19:34; 20:6)*
>
> *God restored Israel from exile for the glory of his name. . . . (Ezekiel 36:22–23; v. 32)*
>
> *Jesus sought the glory of his Father in all he did. . . . (John 7:18)*
>
> *Jesus told us to do good works so that God gets glory. . . . (Matthew 5:16; 1 Peter 2:12)*
>
> *Jesus warned that not seeking God's glory makes faith impossible. . . . (John 5:44)*

CRITIQUES OF THREE MISCELLANEOUS CHRISTIAN TOPICS

Jesus said that he answers prayer that God would be glorified. . . . (John 14:13)

Jesus endured his final hours of suffering for God's glory. . . . (John 12:27-28). . . . (John 17:1)

God gave his Son to vindicate the glory of his righteousness. . . . (Romans 3:25-26)

Jesus receives us into his fellowship for the glory of God. . . . (Romans 15:7)

The ministry of the Holy Spirit is to glorify the Son of God. . . . (John 16:14)

God instructs us to do everything for his glory. . . . (l Corinthians 10:31; cf. 6:20).

God tells us to serve in a way that will glorify him. . . . (l Peter 4:11)

Jesus will fill us with fruits of righteousness for God's glory. . . . (Philippians 1:9, 11)

All are under judgment for dishonoring God's glory. . . . (Romans 1:22,23); (Romans 3:23)

Herod is struck dead because he did not give glory to God. . . . (Acts 12:23)

Jesus is coming again for the glory of God. . . . (2 Thessalonians 1:9-10)

Jesus' ultimate aim for us is that we see and enjoy his glory. . . . (John 17:24)

Even in wrath God's aim is to make known the wealth of his glory. . . . (Romans 9:22--23)

God's plan is to fill the earth with the knowledge of his glory. . . . (Habakkuk 2:14)

Everything that happens will redound to God's glory. . . . (Romans 11:36)

In the New Jerusalem the glory of God replaces the sun. . . . (Revelation 21:23) [emphasis added].[7]

That ends Piper's comments.

---

7. Piper, John. "Biblical Texts."

My Comments

As those many citations attest, it appears that God loves his glory. The question is, why? Why would the most perfect being possible care a wit about amassing and flaunting his glory, that is, his renown and magnificence, to any of his creations, let alone to his sin-stained, natures-corrupted, infinitely inferior human creations?[8] The situation of God, glory, and humans reminds me of the Seinfeld episode where Kramer is taking a martial arts class with children at a Dojo and is asked by Jerry why he's doing that. Kramer responds triumphantly "Jerry, I'm dominating!"[9]

Popular cultural allusions aside, God's attraction to glory is a bit of a head-scratcher. A plausible non-pious explanation is that the Judeo-Christian-Islamic tradition arose in circumstances wherein humans projected the characteristics, highly enhanced, of the most powerful human beings they could actually encounter or possibly imagine, namely kings, emperors, pharaohs, etc., onto preternatural or supernatural beings.[10] Among those enhanced characteristics were manly lust for power and glory. However, for obvious reasons, that explanation is not suitable to the pious. So, my question persists to them: why would God be so insistent on flaunting his glory to such inferior beings like us, or anyone, for that matter?

I suppose a Christian could reply that the phrase "magnificence and great beauty" from the definition of "glory" quite appropriately applies to the Christian God. However, the critic could challenge applying the phrase "high renown or honor won by notable achievements" to God. A glory-worthy "notable achievement" would have to be some endeavor of high value that was accomplished only with great effort, often accompanied by great personal risk, against considerable odds and opposition. Such endeavors would be the kinds of actions attributed to the heroes of epic literature. If so, then the above criteria for a glory-worthy achievement would not be satisfied by any of God's works. For if God is indeed the most perfect being possible, then all the great things Christians say he has done and accomplished were done without such glory-making criteria as great effort, great personal risk, against considerable odds and opposition. In fact, my swooshing a mosquito away from the face of a sleeping baby

---

8. By the way, I have a similar question about God and worship—but that's a topic for another day.

9. Ackerman, "Foundation."

10. See Tarico, "God's Emotions," 155–77.

would involve more glory-making criteria, though nowhere near enough to be described as a glory-making act, than any divine actions cited in Piper's list—at least in terms of personal effort, risk, against considerable odds and opposition. This would be the case, because if you are the most perfect being possible, you can do anything logically possible with virtually no effort, risk, or opposition at all.

There's one other criterion that I think is necessary for glory-making, namely, the glory attainer must somehow be responsible for the development of their glory-making characteristics or nature. This criterion could not be had by God because God could not be responsible for the development of his glory-making maximally perfect nature. God was always the most perfect being possible. He didn't start "small" and by dint of great effort develop into the most perfect being possible.

Finally, for what it's worth, the Christian God comes across to me as a kind of insecure autocrat who needs to be bolstered by the constant glory-adulation, praise, and worship of his subjects. The fact is that the most perfect being possible would not need or care about being glorified, adulated, or worshipped and would not be offended by not being so. So, God's relentless pursuit and demand for praise and glory comes across (to me, at least) as pathological, not commendable, an indication of insecurity, an ungodly flaw that has the greasy fingerprints of human contrivance all over it. If you think I exaggerate, I suggest you reread John Piper's remarks and citations about God, glory, and humans laid out earlier. By the way, I don't see any problem in God's wishing or accepting being loved by his human creations. Although I do see something amiss in God's *commanding* that humans love him. Love can only be given voluntarily.

Part Two: **Christianity and Ethics**

Chapter 9: By Their Fruits Ye Shall Know Them

Chapter 10: Jesus Christ: Ethical Sage?

Chapter 11: Two Inconsistencies in the Christian Antiabortion Stance

Chapter 12: American Christianity and Political Conservatism

Chapter 13: A Novel Defense of Objective Ethics Without Christianity or Any Religion

Chapter 9: By Their Fruits Ye Shall Know Them

Preview

In this chapter I respond to what I call Christians' Atheist Atrocities Argument, which concludes that atheism is immoral because it has spawned mega-fatalities of the innocent in the recent past.

ATHEIST ATROCITIES ARGUMENT

In his article, "The Atheist Atrocities Fallacy—Hitler, Stalin and Pol Pot," Michael A. Sherlock describes what he calls "the atheist atrocities fallacy" committed by some Christians. He writes,

> Religious apologists, particularly those of the Christian variety, are big fans of what I have dubbed, the atheist atrocities fallacy. Christians commonly employ this fallacy to shield their egos from the harsh reality of the brutality of their own religion, by utilizing a most absurd form of the *tu quoque* ("you too") fallacy, mingled with numerous other logical fallacies and historical inaccuracies. . . . Should an atheist present a believer with the crimes committed by the Holy See of the Inquisition(s), the Crusaders and other faith-wielding misanthropes, they will often hear the reply; "Well, what about Stalin, Pol Pot and Hitler? They were atheists, and they killed millions!"[1]

---

1. Sherlock, "Atheist Atrocities Fallacy," para. 1.

Christians also often add former Chinese leader Mao Zedong to their list of atheistic mega-killers.

Sherlock begins his response to what I have called the Atheist Atrocities Argument by pointing out that Hitler, Stalin, and the Cambodian, Pol Pot, were actually influenced to some extent by their religious backgrounds. In the cases of Hitler and Stalin it was Christianity, and for Pol Pot it was Theravada Buddhism. Mao seems not to have been religiously influenced. Actually, I'm not interested here in evaluating Sherlock's contentions about possible religious influences on Stalin, Hitler, and Pol Pot. Those interested can read his article and decide for themselves how sound his points are. Rather, I'll give my response to the Christian criticism of atheism that states, "Well, what about Stalin, Pol Pot and Hitler [and Mao] [or SPHM for short]? They were atheists, and they killed millions!"

For starters, I don't contest the claim that SPHM were morally responsible for the deaths of millions. Determining the exact numbers is difficult, but reasonable estimates have been made. In particular, I refer to a 2018 article[2] by Ian Johnson, a Pulitzer Prize-winning writer, researcher, and Senior Fellow for China Studies at the Council on Foreign Relations. His best researched estimates are that Mao was responsible for 42 million, Hitler 11 to 12 million, Stalin 6 to 9 million, and Pol Pot 1.7 million[3] fatalities. The total is 62.7 million fatalities.

RESPONSE TO THE ATHEIST ATROCITIES ARGUMENT

First, and importantly, SPHM didn't murder in order to explicitly support, bolster, or further the interests of atheism per se. In fact, as Sherlock annotated in his article, there is evidence that Hitler and Pol Pot may not themselves have even been atheists. But even if they were, as were Stalin and Mao, the SPHM-caused fatalities served these individuals' military, social, political, and economic purposes, not the purpose of supporting or advancing atheism. In contrast, the fatalities committed by Christians, shown below in table 8.1, *were* done for the explicit purpose of upholding, expanding, or protecting the Christian faith.[4]

Second, as you will see below in tables 8.1 and 8.2, the mega-numbers of fatalities brought about to explicitly uphold or advance Christianity,

2. Johnson, "Who Killed More."
3. "Cambodia."
4. Elaboration of this point can be found in Avalos, *Fighting Words*.

when adjusted for populations at the time, dwarf the number of fatalities attributed to SPHM.

Fatalities From the Old Testament Era

Noachian Flood: some Christian fundamentalists say that the population of the earth at the time of the flood was some eight to nine billion,[5] out of which only eight humans survived.[6]

Biblical genocides and other Old Testament killings: various genocides (see, for example, Deut 7:1–2) are estimated to have had some twenty-five million victims, if the Old Testament is to be believed.[7] For instance, Exod 12:37 (involving the conquest of Canaan in the thirteenth century BCE) tells us that the Hebrews utterly destroyed seven tribes, each with more than two million people. Also, we should note and count people executed according to Jewish law (gay people, rape victims who didn't cry out, apostates, unbelievers, people who pick up sticks on the Sabbath, etc.) over what Christian and Jewish believers must accept to be more than a thousand years of Jewish society. That must have constituted a significant number of their own people who were murdered on a weekly and yearly basis for centuries upon centuries.

Fatalities from the New Testament Era

Fatalities Caused by Christian Ideology

These fatalities, listed in table 8.1 below, involved Christian-on-Christian, Christian-on-Muslim, and Christian-on-Jew fatalities. The first column of the table names the fatality event. The second column gives the date or dates of the event. The third column gives the best estimate of the number of fatalities for the event. The fourth column gives the population of the region during the time when the event took place, as well as the population of the region in 1944, roughly the time when Hitler's and Stalin's fatalities were being brought about. Mao's and Pol Pot's fatalities occurred a number of decades later. Finally, column five shows what the number of fatalities would have been if the region in which the original fatalities occurred

5. See, for example, Dolphin, "World Population Since Creation."
6. Noah, his wife, and their three sons and their wives
7. See, for example, Wells, "How Many Has God Killed?"

PART TWO: CHRISTIANITY AND ETHICS

had had the population it had in 1944. The purpose of the last column is to make it easier to more properly compare the numbers of Christianity-caused fatalities with the numbers of SPHM-caused fatalities.

Name	Dates	Number of fatalities in 1200	Population of Europe + West Asia in 1200/ Population of Europe + West Asia in 1944	What the number of fatalities in 1200 would have been in 1944
Crusades to the East	1095–1291	4 million[8]	88 million /758 million	34 million

Name	Dates	Number of fatalities in 1300	Population of France in 1300/Population of France in 1944	What the number of fatalities in 1300 would have been in 1944
Albigensian Crusade	1209–29	1 million[9]	20 million /41 million	2 million

Name	Dates	Number of fatalities in 1500	Population of France in 1500/Population of France in 1944	What the number of fatalities in 1500 would have been in 1944
French Wars of Religion	1562–98	3 million[10]	16 million /41 million	7.7 million

Name	Dates	Number of fatalities in 1600	Population of central Europe in 1600/ Population of central Europe in 1944	What the number of fatalities in 1600 would have been in 1944
Thirty Years War	1618–48	8 million[11]	68 million /200 million	23 million

8. Johnson, "Who Killed More."
9. "Albigensian Crusade."
10. McNeill, "How Many People."
11. Mark, "Thirty Years' War."

Name	Dates	Number of fatalities in 1650	World population of Jews in 1600/World population of Jews in 1933[12]	What the number of fatalities in 1650 would have been in 1944
Jews killed in Poland/Ukraine	1648–56	100,000[13]	1.2 million /17 million	1.4 million
Totals		16.1		68.1

Table 8.1

You can see from table 8.1 that the total number of Christianity-caused fatalities in targeted populations, adjusted for 1944 (roughly about the time of the SPHM-caused fatalities) was some 68.1 million compared to the estimated total 63 million SPHM-caused fatalities. Note that the 68.1 million count is just for five specific Christianity-caused fatality events. It doesn't include the large number of smaller Christianity-caused fatality events, such as ecclesiastical inquisitions and witch killings.

12. DellaPergola, "Some Fundamentals."
13. "Bogdan Chmielnicki."

PART TWO: CHRISTIANITY AND ETHICS

Fatalities Carried Out by Christians for Nonreligious Reasons

Name	Dates	Number of Fatalities
Belgium Congo atrocities	1885–1908	10 million[14]
Rwandan genocide	1994–2003	5 million[15]
Middle Passage Fatalities (African slave trade)	1501–1866	1.8 million[16]
British Raj in India	1880–1920	165 million[17]
Totals		181.8 million

Table 8.2

Although the fatalities listed in table 8.2 were not caused by Christianity, per se, they were certainly formulated and carried out by Christians and, very pertinently, were not disapproved of by most authoritative Christian leaders.

Tale of the Tape

If we add the totals of Christianity-caused fatalities from table 8.1 and 8.2, the final tally is an astounding 250 million (normed for 1944 populations) compared to 63 million SPHM-caused fatalities. The total of Christianity-caused fatalities, then, is 187 million more than those caused by SPHM, or about three times the SPHM total. Also, it's important to note that many of those who carried out or enabled the Hitler and Stalin-caused fatalities were themselves Christians. Germany, at that time, had an overwhelmingly Christian population, as did Nazi-assisting countries

14. Rannard and Webster, "Leopold II."
15. "Rwanda Genocide."
16. O'Neill, "Estimated Share."
17. Economic anthropologist Jason Hickel and his coauthor Dylan Sullivan gave this number in an article in the respected academic journal *World Development* titled "Capitalism and Extreme Poverty: A Global Analysis of Real Wages, Human Height, and Mortality Since the Long Sixteenth Century." In their analysis, they estimated that India suffered 165 million excess deaths due to British colonialism between 1880 and 1920. "This figure is larger than the combined number of deaths from both World Wars, including the Nazi holocaust," they noted (5). See the article's section 3.4 on South Asia.

of Eastern Europe such as Hungary and Romania. The Soviet Union had at least a plurality, and likely a majority, of Christians in its population. Finally, comparing the number of Christianity and SPHM-caused fatalities per se doesn't tell the full story.

While we're on the subject of caused fatalities, consider the following claim, GA.

CLAIM GA: GOD IS MORALLY RESPONSIBLE FOR CAUSING FOUR THOUSAND EIGHT HUNDRED TIMES MORE DEATHS THAN WERE CAUSED BY SPHM

Argument in Support of Claim GA

1. According to most Christian denominations, every fertilized human egg (zygote) is a human person. See chapter 11 in the section entitled "Violence against Abortion Providers.".

2. As we've seen a number of times earlier in this volume, recent research into the laws of human reproduction shows that more than 72 percent of zygotes die in the early stages of pregnancy because they never properly adhere to the walls of the uterus. See chapter 1 in the section entitled "Important Relevant Data about Prenatal Mortality."

3. In the history of our species demographers estimate that there have been about 117 billion human births.[18]

4. The recent research in reproductive science just cited above in (2) indicates that the 117 billion live births constitute less than 30 percent of the approximate 418 billion human conceptions there must have been. That means that there have been some 301 billion zygotes, embryos, and fetuses who died in utero because they didn't attach to the uterine walls or for other reasons.

5. God established the laws governing human reproduction and knew that those laws would result in the deaths of those 301 billion zygotes, embryos, and fetuses who died in utero.

6. Therefore, God is responsible for the deaths of those 301 billion zygotes, embryos, and fetuses who died in utero, which is about 4,800 times the number of human deaths for which SPHM were responsible.

18. See Routley, "How Many Humans."

PART TWO: CHRISTIANITY AND ETHICS

Christian Retorts to Claim GA and My Responses

Devil-Is-Responsible Retort to Claim GA

The devil, who is consummately evil, caused the deaths of the 301 billion zygotes, embryos, and fetuses who died in utero.

RESPONSE

The Devil, assuming he exists, could only be responsible for the deaths of the 301 billion zygotes, embryos, and fetuses who died in utero if God permitted him to be responsible. That is, God had the power to prevent the devil from doing anything that God did not want the devil to do. If so, then God, not the devil, would be the primary cause of those deaths. Moreover, as I shall point out below in the discussion of the *Summum Bonum* retort, the devil actually wouldn't want those zygotes et al. to die in utero since that would guarantee that all of them would end up in heaven (see chapter 5 in the section entitled "Christian Assured Salvation Strategy") and, therefore, be beyond the devil's reach to be corrupted.

Soul-Making Retort to Claim GA

This retort is associated with Christian philosopher John Hick's theory of soul-making as a plausible justification for at least some of the suffering in this world.[19] The claim is that suffering in the world makes possible the development of important and valuable character traits, such as courage, compassion, and heroism. Thus, according to this retort, God caused the death of the 301 billion zygotes, embryos, and fetuses who died in utero so as to make possible the development of such important and valuable character traits.

RESPONSE

Most of the deaths of the 301 billion zygotes, embryos, and fetuses who die in utero occur so early in a pregnancy that, for the most part, no one is even aware that such deaths happen. Consequently, those deaths could not

---

19. Hick, *Evil and the God*, 255.

be said to have "made" any souls, that is, to have built any positive character traits in anyone.

Summum Bonum Retort to Claim GA

God's causing the death of the 301 billion zygotes, embryos, and fetuses who died in utero would not be immoral because all the aborted souls would end up being gifted the *summum bonum* of spending eternity in heaven. To say otherwise would be to portray God as unfairly denying those 301 billion zygotes, embryos, and fetuses the opportunity to be saved for reasons completely out of their control—something an omnibenevolent God would never do.

Response

God would be acting unfairly in guaranteeing eternal salvation for the 301 billion zygotes, embryos, and fetuses who died in utero while not guaranteeing it for the 117 billion or so human persons who were born in the three hundred thousand year history of our species. That would be a case of immoral divine discrimination against the latter 117 billion persons, especially since the Bible says that many, or even most, (born) humans will not be saved. Furthermore, such a retort would exist in tension with the general Christin view that abortion is a grave moral wrong. How could guaranteeing the *summum bonum* to 301 billion aborted persons be judged to be a grave moral wrong? No harm; no foul, right? For more on this see chapter 5.

CONCLUSIONS

First, nothing in the above analysis should be construed as in any way excusing or downplaying the immorality and horror of the SPHM-killing sprees. They were certainly horrendous events.

Second, the above estimates for the Christianity-caused and SPHM-caused fatalities are the best reasonable estimates from accredited, nonpartisan sources that I could find. Your mileage may vary. However, it's hard to imagine that the perfectly accurate numbers, whatever they may be, would tell a significantly different story.

Third, I haven't been arguing that, because Christianity-caused fatalities were significantly greater than those caused by SPHM, that shows that Christianity is false and atheism true. What I have been arguing is that Christians seriously err if they argue that the extent of the SPHM-caused fatalities constitutes substantial or, for that matter, *any* evidence for the truth of Christianity and the falsity of atheism.

Chapter 10: **Jesus Christ: Ethical Sage?**

Preview

In this four-section chapter I argue that the moral wisdom of Jesus can be called into question by the implausibility of seven of his important signature moral imperatives. Section I assesses four moral prescriptions from the Sermon on the Mount. Section II assesses his endorsement of "the two greatest commandments." Section III critiques his imperative "do not judge, lest you also be judged." In Section IV I critique a frequently heard moral cliché that conservative Christians believe Jesus implicitly endorsed, namely "hate the sin; love the sinner."

SECTION I: ASSESSMENT OF FOUR MORAL PRESCRIPTIONS FROM THE SERMON ON THE MOUNT

In Matt 5:38–48 and Luke 6:27–36 Jesus propounded four important and distinctive Christian moral prescriptions which I abbreviate as JEP (for "Jesus's ethical prescriptions").

JEP: (1) Love, (2) Don't Resist, (3) Turn the Other Cheek To, (4) Do Good to Your Enemies.

It's been said that familiarity often dulls the critical faculty. This seems to be the case in Christians' stance toward JEP. They either don't see or don't acknowledge that complying with it would not only be psychologically and socially problematic but also, at times, even seriously unethical. My case that there are major shortcomings with JEP starts with a pertinent counterexample to it.

Counterexample to JEP

> A morally accountable predator kidnaps a young girl whom he tortures and rapes for several weeks, after which he slowly and brutally murders her. Furthermore, he is totally without remorse. In fact, he previously committed similar atrocities and intends to commit more.

According to JEP, it would have been immoral for, say, the victim's mother or anyone else to have resisted the predator. What's more, the mother would have acted immorally if she did not love and do good to the torturer/rapist/murderer. Worse yet, the mother would have acted immorally if she didn't hand over another of her daughters to the torturer/rapist/murderer in order to satisfy the turn-the-other-cheek imperative of JEP. Surely, something is amiss here.

The sting of the counterexample to JEP is rooted in the fact that, first of all, serious malicious predation is unfortunately not all that rare. Second, there is simply no rational justification for claiming that morality requires one to behave toward the child's torturer/rapist/murderer as JEP commands. On the contrary, moral propriety requires that innocents be protected. All other things being equal, anyone who could have stopped the predator should have, including by the use of force, if necessary. If someone were to have done so, then, contrary to JEP, she would have been a moral hero, not a moral reprobate. It's noteworthy that throughout history Christians have rebuked people over their violations of a wide assortment of Christian moral principles. Yet, aside from a few marginal incidences, few Christians or their authorities have ever castigated anyone for violating any JEP-imperative in counterexample-to-JEP-type situations, although, alas, as I mentioned, such situations have not been rare. This form of "jury nullification" is evidence that even Christians and their authorities have serious, albeit mostly unacknowledged, doubts about the moral cogency of JEP. The kinds of counterexamples to JEP, similar to the one described above, present a major challenge to JEP and, therefore, also to the moral wisdom of Jesus and the moral authority of Christianity.

CHRISTIAN DEFENSES OF JEP EVALUATED

Christians have offered a variety of defenses of JEP. Here follow a representative sample of them, together with my responses.

JEP Is Cogent Because It Prevents Resisters from Becoming Harm-doers

For example, Walter Wink, professor of biblical interpretation at Auburn Theological Seminary in New York City, states, "'Don't resist one who is evil' *probably* means something like, don't turn into the very thing you hate. Don't become what you oppose" (emphasis added).[1]

Response

Forcefully resisting murderers, rapists, terrorists, and others rarely turns resisters into evildoers. One may cite the overwhelming majority of honorable law enforcers, military personnel, battered women, rape victims, and the like who have forcefully resisted counterexample-to-JEP-type villains without thereby becoming morally tainted.

JEP Embodies a More Elevated Morality Than Previously Practiced.

For example, Ralph Wilson states,

> Now let's consider what his [Jesus's] words [JEP] *don't* mean. They don't mean that we as a society should let criminals run free to do violence on any citizen. It doesn't mean we shouldn't call the police when robbed. It doesn't mean that we should stand idly by when someone is assaulted. Jesus's words aren't about crime or pacifism in war. They are about loving enemies in a radical way. If we seek to make a new law that overrides the civil law in Exodus against violent crime [the *lex talionis*—an eye for an eye etc.] we miss the point. Then we're trying to make a new law where Jesus intended that we look underneath the law intended to restrain sinful people. Having now a glimpse of love, don't try to legislate it.[2]

1. Wink, "Third Way," para. 8.
2. Wilson, "Love Your Enemies," para. 49–50.

PART TWO: CHRISTIANITY AND ETHICS

Response

I take it that the gist of Wilson's defense of JEP is that we may resist evil persons, but we must also love them—a version of "hate the sin, love the sinner." (For more on this, see section entitled "Section IV: Assessment Of 'Hate the Sin; Love the Sinner'" in this chapter.) The main problem with Wilson's interpretation is that the context and content of Matt 5:38–41 neither explicitly nor implicitly supports it. For example, the "do not resist" command, like the other JEP imperatives, is given as holding unconditionally. It does not say we can resist if we also love the evil person. Presumably, if Jesus meant that, he could have easily said it. That he does not warrants concluding that Wilson's interpretation is not what Jesus meant. Furthermore, it's hard to see how Wilson's interpretation would be reasonable with regard to the other JEP imperatives: turn the other cheek, do good to your evildoer, or love your evildoer.

The remaining claims in Wilson's defense are veiled in obscurity. For example, it's unclear what he means by "if we seek to make a new law." To what "new law" about what is he referring? Also, how and why do we find love as opposed to, say, justice or nothing at all "underneath" the law (*lex talionis*)? In fact, to what sense of "underneath" is Wilson referring? Finally, his last sentence adds more puzzlement: "Having now a glimpse of love, don't try to legislate it." What is the "it" that we are not to try to legislate? Love? If so, then who would seek to legislate love anyway? If the "it" is not love, then what is it? One would think that if love is to be brought into the moral response to evil actions, then instead of JEP's requirement that it be given indiscriminately to terrorists, rapists, batterers of women, child abusers, torturers, and such, morality and victims would be much better served by people rejecting JEP and acting on the basis of love of justice and love of those suffering predation. The Sufi sage Saadi of Shiraz sums this up pithily: "Doing good to evildoers may be equivalent to doing evil to the good [victims]."[3] I would add that Saadi's remarks are even more pertinent when "the evildoers" are Counterexample-to-JEP-level perpetrators.

---

3. Shah, *Reflections*, 86.

JEP Is Cogent Because It's Actually Hyperbole Designed to Enhance the Clarity of Jesus's Message.

Dr. Wilson continues and posits the above interpretation of JEP in the following two excerpts:[4]

> Hyperbole has a respected place in teaching. Don't make the mistake of expecting every word Jesus says to be LITERALLY true. What he says *is* true, of course. But we must take it as it is meant. And we must take it very seriously. He probably uses hyperbole only to highlight a concept that his hearers are likely to miss without it. When Jesus speaks in hyperbole, we must be a thousand times more careful to listen. But we'd better discern when Jesus is speaking in hyperbole, or we'll make big mistakes in interpreting Scripture. [Emphasis in the original.]

The only notion of hyperbole with respect to defending JEP that makes any sense is that Jesus exaggerated when he implied that JEP was to apply to *all* enemies. One might say that he did not intend it to apply to counterexample-to-JEP-type predators. This interpretation seems to be what Wilson is getting at when he lists the kinds of enemies we face when adhering to JEP. He says the following.

> Who are your enemies? . . . Often they are the people close to us who have been hurt. A spouse or former spouse. A parent. A son or daughter. A co-worker at the job. An enemy of God who takes it out on you. Someone whose evil action you have exposed and is now out to get you. . . . Remember, the context is enemies, those who insult us and seek to embarrass us. . . . We need Jesus to do a heart change . . . toward our enemies . . . God haters, vulgar, foul-mouthed, unfaithful to spouses, lying, cheating, stealing, selfish [people].

Response

Noticeably absent from Wilson's list of enemies are counterexample-to-JEP-type most horrific evildoers, suggesting that he feels that Jesus's use of hyperbole involved using the universal claim, "resist not evil persons," when he really meant a more restrictive claim like "resist not lesser evil

---

4. Wilson, "Love Your Enemies," paras. 40, 19.

persons," such as those Wilson lists. There are a number of difficulties with this interpretation however.

First, there is no evidence that Jesus *was* speaking hyperbolically in giving JEP. In fact, the claim of hyperbole seems suspiciously ad hoc, put forth merely to inoculate JEP from charges of being unreasonable—especially when applied to counterexample-to-JEP-type immorality. If Jesus meant JEP to be applied only to lesser slights and harms, then, once again, he could have easily and clearly said as much without having to use hyperbole. In fact, hyperbole would likely have unnecessarily confused his largely uneducated and rhetorically unsophisticated audience. It is frankly implausible to think that Jesus, as God incarnate, would have given such new and momentous moral imperatives by solemnly intoning one thing but really meaning another, so that it would take human interpreters two thousand years to clarify what he *really* meant.

A *second* problem with Wilson's defense is that even in cases of lesser harm than that which the counterexample to JEP describes, there's no obvious reason why one should be morally required to not resist, but to love, bless, seek the good of, and turn the other cheek for a person acting immorally. Granted, there may be something to be said for forgiveness and mercy considered on a case by case basis, but this could be done without morally requiring people to adhere to JEP. It's interesting to compare Jesus's views with those of Confucius on these matters. In the *Analects* XIV, 36, it is written: "Someone inquired: 'What do you think of requiting injury with kindness?' Confucius said 'How then do you requite kindness? Requite injury with justice and kindness with kindness.'"[5]

JEP Is Cogent Because It Rules Out Only Retaliatory or Vengeful Resistance.

Patrick Rose gives voice to this defense as follows.

> When the Lord commands us "not to resist evil," He is, then, speaking of a universal law. His words might at first seem puzzling. On the surface they might seem to be advocating an extreme and impractical form of pacifism. "But I tell you not to resist evil. But whoever slaps you on your right cheek, turn the other to him also." In the light of the Writings, though, the true meaning of this becomes clear. The Lord is not forbidding people from defending

5. Confucius, "Lunyu XIV."

themselves and their rights. Rather He is talking about something quite different. He is talking about revenge. Indeed, He refers directly to what is sometimes called the *lex talionis* or law of retaliation or revenge in the Old Testament. "You have heard that it was said, 'An eye for an eye and a tooth for a tooth.' But I tell you not to resist evil . . ." The Lord is talking of the need to avoid a vengeful spirit if we are to come into charity.[6]

Response

Let's suppose that Jesus (like many before and after him) did oppose acting vengefully. It's still unlikely that his purpose in commanding JEP was only, or even primarily, to forbid vengeful resistance to evil persons. Once again, if that were his purpose, he could have very simply said something like: "You may resist evil persons, but only in a non-vengeful manner." But, of course, he did not. He forbade *any* resistance. To make this perfectly clear he described three brief scenarios (Matt 5:39–41) involving *absolute* non-resistance. They include turning the other cheek to one who has unjustly assaulted you, giving your cloak to one who has unjustly taken your tunic, and volunteering additional servitude to an unjust authority.

In giving these three scenarios Jesus is implicitly endorsing the position that one ought never resist evil persons in any fashion. If so, then we can rule out Rose's suggestion that in JEP Jesus was only ruling out vengeful resistance. If Rose's suggestion were really what Jesus meant, then Jesus would have had each of those subjects in the three scenarios I just described resist the evil doers since they could have been described as doing so without vengeance. In other words, Jesus could have used each as an example of resisting evil doers properly, that is, without vengeance. But, obviously, he didn't, thereby strongly indicating that he was advocating not only complete passivism, but, even more, offering themselves to further abuse by the evil doers. In effect, the behavior of the persons in the three examples was highlighted as being prime examples of what Jesus was radically and unconditionally requiring in JEP, namely, ruling out all, not just vengeful, resistance. Noted conservative biblical scholar R. T. France says as much in the following: "Jesus's position is shockingly radical: not only no retaliation, but even no resistance to one who is admittedly 'bad.'"[7] France continues,

6. Rose, "Resist Not Evil," para. 4.
7. France, *Gospel of Matthew*, 217.

> Jesus is often quoted as opposing retaliation, a stance for which there are several parallels in the Old Testament and other Jewish writings... and among pagan philosophers. But Jesus's words go further than that: even resistance is forbidden, and no distinction is made between active and passive resistance, violent and nonviolent, legal and illegal.[8]

If France is correct, then Rose is on shaky ground in claiming that JEP rules out only vengeful or retaliatory resistance.

JEP Is Cogent Because It Should Not Be Understood Literally

Christian preacher Doug Apple expresses this defense as follows.

> For example, First Timothy 5:8 says that I must provide for my family. So what if an evil person wants to take my provision for my family? Or what if someone simply asks for everything I own. Am I supposed to give it to them?... So should I just let them (harm me or my family), not resist them? That's not what Jesus did, so that must not be what He meant by, "Do not resist an evil person" and "Give to everyone who asks." So what *did* He mean? What did Jesus mean by *anything* He said? We find out by looking at the entirety of His teaching, not just by pulling one thing out here and there and treating it like a blanket statement. Yes, we do what Jesus said—within the context of all that He said.[9]

Response

As you might imagine, there are some problems with Apple's response.

First, Apple claims that we should try to discern what Jesus "really" meant by JEP in any particular case by looking at the entirety of what he taught and did. However, making such JEP-type decisions would become an exegetical (having to do with interpreting biblical passages) nightmare. One would have to be familiar with the entirety of everything Jesus taught and did as well as determining if and how Jesus's teaching and acting are to be understood and applied or not to that particular situation. Not easy. Moreover, in many cases what Jesus taught and did, such as JEP itself, is obscure—hence

---

8. France, *Gospel of Matthew*, 219–20.

9. Doug Apple, from radio station WAKU 94.1 FM, Tallahassee, Florida, Sep 18, 2009.

the reason for this chapter in the first place. For example, sometimes Jesus adheres to JEP and sometimes he doesn't. Sometimes, he resists malefactors (evildoers) as when he cleansed the temple or evaded Jewish authorities wanting to arrest him.[10] Yet, at other times, he turns the other cheek and does not resist malefactors as, for example, when he lets the temple police arrest him in the Garden of Gethsemane and lets Roman soldiers abuse and crucify him. Moreover, there doesn't appear to be any roadmap to guide us when to do what with regard to JEP. Therefore, Apple's "solution" to the problem of when we should adhere to JEP and when we should not by simply following the whole of Jesus's teachings comes up short.

Second, if Apple's explanation is correct, then why didn't Jesus, himself, explain it thusly? As God incarnate, he would certainly have been capable of doing so. In addition, his explicitly doing so would have very much helped his not very well educated and rhetorically unsophisticated audience to understand what he was getting at. It also would have made two thousand years of Christian speculation about what Jesus "really" meant unnecessary.

JEP Is Cogent Because It Should Be Understood More as Suggestions Applying to Private Individuals Rather Than Public Authorities

The following excerpt from the *New Catholic Encyclopedia* gives this defense.

> His [Jesus's] pronouncement on nonresistance to evil is taken as a counsel rather than as a precept, and for private individuals rather than for public authorities, since these latter would fail in an essential duty were they to offer no forceful resistance to violent aggressors from within or without.[11]

---

10. "Then took they up stones to cast at him: but Jesus hid himself, and went out of the temple, going through the midst of them, and so passed by" (John 8:59 KJV). See also John 10:39.

11. McReavy and Meehan, "Pacifism," 747.

PART TWO: CHRISTIANITY AND ETHICS

Response

One can reasonably surmise that McReavy and Meehan employ this explanation in the *New Catholic Encyclopedia* article in order to block the otherwise unavoidable unpalatable conclusion that JEP requires a controversial pacifism which would be exceedingly objectionable to the vast majority of Christians (among others).

The problem with the *New Catholic Encyclopedia* explanation, as we've seen time and again with defenses of JEP, is that there is no indication whatsoever that Jesus did, in fact, intend it to be merely "a counsel rather than a precept, and for private individuals rather than for public authorities." Yet, once again, if this were what Jesus meant, then why wouldn't he have just said so? There is no precedent for the counsel versus precept or private individuals vs. public authorities distinctions in any of Jesus's other Sermon on the Mount prescriptions. One would think that, as with any unqualified imperatives, unless there are clear indications to the contrary, Jesus's imperatives should be understood as applying to all moral agents, public and private, and as strictly binding rather than merely suggestive (if that is indeed what the *New Catholic Encyclopedia* means by a "counsel"). Note finally that the *New Catholic Encyclopedia* explanation still leaves unanswered all the difficulties exposed by the Counterexample to JEP that are associated with even a limited application of JEP only to private individuals.

JEP Is Cogent Because It Permits One to Resist Evil, But Only Nonviolently.

Walter Wink, for one, expresses this as follows:

> In the past, we have thought we had only two choices, either resist evil or don't resist evil. Jesus seemed to be saying, "Don't resist evil," and, therefore, non-resistance seemed to be the only alternative. Be supine, submit, surrender, flee, give up. It seems as if Jesus were asking us to be a doormat for God, to give up all concern for our own justice as well as the justice of others. Now we see in this passage interpreted in a new light, Jesus is not calling on people to be non-resistant. He is calling on them to be non-violent. He is calling on them to resist, yes, but to resist in a way that is not injurious or harmful to the other person.[12]

---

12. Wink, "Third Way," para. 19.

Response

I will first repeat the pertinent comments of biblical scholar R. T. France presented earlier.

> Jesus is often quoted as opposing retaliation, a stance for which there are several parallels in the Old Testament and other Jewish writings . . . and among pagan philosophers. *But Jesus's words go further than that: even resistance is forbidden, and no distinction is made between active and passive resistance, violent and nonviolent, legal and illegal* [emphasis added].[13]

Clearly, France does not endorse Wink's interpretation of how JEP should be implemented. Nevertheless, for the sake of argument assume, contrary to fact, that ruling out only violent resistance was what Jesus had in mind. That assumption would still not rescue JEP from charges of implausibility or worse. History records that in the vast majority of cases resisting counterexample-to-JEP-type malefactors nonviolently has proven to be ineffective in countering, stopping, or making up for the great evil that they do. For example, resisting Holocaust Nazis, the Khmer Rouge, or the murderer from the counterexample to JEP "in a way that is not injurious or harmful to the other person" would not only have been unavailing but in some instances would have been a substantial dereliction of moral duty. Add to this the other requirements of JEP to love, do good to, and "turn the other cheek to" Nazis, the Khmer Rouge, and counterexample-to-JEP murder-rapist-torturer types, and the unacceptability of JEP becomes even more manifest. It's very likely that if the nonviolent interpretation of JEP were normative and followed, no reasonably just society could survive for long. France put it this way.

> Those who have understood the true thrust of Jesus's teaching here [JEP] have often declared it to be not only extreme and unwelcome, but also practically unworkable in the real world. You cannot live like this. It would be to encourage the unscrupulous and the feckless and so to undermine the proper ordering of society.[14]

I agree. I wonder, then, how France *would* interpret JEP.

---

13. France, *Gospel of Matthew*, 219–20.
14. France, *Gospel of Matthew*, 217.

PART TWO: CHRISTIANITY AND ETHICS

JEP Is Cogent Because Its Prescriptions Were Meant as Divinely Sourced Moral Ideals

In support of this interpretation one might cite Matt 5:48: "Be ye therefore perfect, even as your Father which is in heaven is perfect" (KJV). Obviously, there is no way a human being can be perfect like God; but Christians could argue that JEP should be understood as a call to use the ideal of God's perfect moral character, partially embodied in JEP, to guide and encourage our best moral efforts.

Response

The problem with this defense, however, is not just that socially and psychologically JEP is nearly impossible to live up to, but that there is insufficient justification for claiming that it even *should be* lived up to. This was argued for all along in this chapter by defending the efficacy of the counterexample to JEP by showing the weaknesses of the various Christian defenses of JEP. In short, JEP is by no means an ideal standard that should be followed. In fact, its imperfection is manifest.

Conclusions about Section I

First, if the defenses of JEP examined above are the best that have been mustered (note: they were the best I could find) and if my critiques of them are sound, then the counterexample to JEP is not adequately answered. The result is that the credibility of Jesus as a moral sage, Christian morality, and even Christianity itself are significantly tarnished.

Second, given the emblematic status of JEP within Christian ethics, it's rather surprising that after nearly two millennia the best minds in Christendom still have not presented a conclusive coherent defense of JEP or even come to a consensus on what Jesus meant by it. It is quite unexpected to hear Christians talk about what Jesus "seems" to be saying, or what he "probably" meant by this or that JEP imperative. And they are the honest ones. Most of the others are really dispensing conjecture even though their language is categorical. This level of disagreement and uncertainty likely accounts for the relative reticence of Christians to comment much on JEP. The strategy, for the most part, seems to be to ignore the JEP tar baby as much as possible—out of sight, out of mind.

SECTION II: ASSESSMENT OF CHRISTIANITY'S TWO GREATEST COMMANDMENTS

When a Pharisee approached Jesus and asked him what the greatest commandment of the law is, Jesus responded by saying:

> "Love the Lord your God with all your heart and with all your soul and with all your mind." This is the first and greatest commandment. And the second is like it: "Love your neighbor as yourself." All the Law and the Prophets hang on these two commandments." (Matt 22:37–40 NIV)

The problem with Jesus's response is that, by any meaningful understanding of love,[15] it cannot be commanded. It must arise "internally," as it were. It must be elicited in some fashion by what is loved, and it must be given freely. Even if, contrary to fact, commanded love were to make sense, who'd want to be the recipient of it anyway, and who'd demand it? Given the passage above from Matthew and the reference below from *Beautiful in Jesus*, apparently God wants and demands it.

From Beautiful in Jesus,

> Next, we need to acknowledge that love is our primary command from God. A command is an order given by a superior authority that requires obedience. Walking in love is of first importance to God and, therefore, should be to us as well. It is not an option, suggestion, or request. To put it bluntly, if we are not walking in love, we are disobeying God.[16]

In contrast to Jesus's claim that loving God and one's neighbor constitute the two most important ethical prescriptions, I argue in chapter 13 that we have no moral obligation to love, or even like, anyone.[17] Our moral obligations to others are to not harm the innocent and to render them assistance when needed by them and feasible for us. If my contention in this chapter is correct that Jesus's two greatest commandments are incongruous with the concept of love, then his proclamation that "all the Law and the Prophets hang on these two commandments," would pose a serious challenge to the cogency of Christian ethics.

---

15. For example, from the Oxford Learner's Dictionary, "'love' is 'an intense feeling of deep affection.'"

16. Idahosa, "Love Is a Command," para. 6.

17. Notice, interestingly, that even the fifth commandment only requires that we *honor* our father and mother, not *love* them.

PART TWO: CHRISTIANITY AND ETHICS

SECTION III: ASSESSMENT OF "DO NOT JUDGE, LEST YOU ALSO BE JUDGED"

The above Christian aphorism, call it A1, is from Matt 7:1. I assume the judging involved is meant to be about the morality of certain human actions. My position is that when A1 is properly scrutinized, it turns out to be much less sensible than Matthew presumably thought it was. I'll analyze why I believe this is the case by examining several possible interpretations of what A1 might mean.

Face Value Interpretation of A1

I take this interpretation to mean exactly what it says, namely, "don't judge" (others) period, full stop, end of story. The face value interpretation receives support from the fact that A1 seems to be presented categorically in Matthew, that is, with no exceptions or conditions being specified. The face value interpretation would clearly strain the reasonableness of A1, since, if that interpretation were implemented, then, among other things, no legal systems could function. After all, if one is prohibited from judging others, courts of law would, ipso facto, violate A1. Moreover, people would be barred from making appropriate judgements about the horrendous actions of others, such as mass murderers, rapists, child abusers, and so on. Thus, the face value interpretation of A1 would clearly render it unacceptable.

Be-Not-Hypocritical Interpretation of A1

Perhaps A1 could be defended under what I call the be-not-hypocritical interpretation. According to this interpretation, we may judge (the morality of the actions of) others, however we shouldn't do it hypocritically. That is, we shouldn't morally criticize significantly immoral actions of others if we ourselves are guilty of committing our own significantly immoral actions. Many might say that this interpretation of A1 is perfectly sensible, since most persons believe that hypocrisy is a moral lapse. However, there are some problems with this interpretation.

First, one might ask why someone, P1, should be morally forbidden to criticize the significantly immoral behavior of another person, P2, if P1, himself, is guilty of significant moral transgression. There would seem to be nothing intrinsically immoral in such judging. For example, Hitler would not have done anything immoral per se if he had criticized Stalin's significant moral transgressions, even though Hitler himself was guilty of significant moral transgressions. What *would be* immoral is for the criticizer, say, Hitler, to continue to commit his own significant moral transgressions, whether criticizing Stalin's behavior or not. In other words, it's not P1's judging P2's behavior hypocritically that needs to cease. It's P1's own immoral behavior that needs to cease (and P2's also, of course). If so, then A1 would be a flawed prescription.

Second, under the be-not-hypocritical interpretation, if P1 judges others hypocritically while acting immorally himself, principle A1 warns that the penalty for that for P1 would be that others would in turn be motivated to judge P1's own immoral actions. However, that wouldn't necessarily be a penalty for P1. Consider that if P1 judges hypocritically, that is, while he himself is acting immorally, then he's not living a morally upright life, although not necessarily because of his hypocrisy, but rather because he's acting immorally apart from his acting hypocritically. If so, then A1's penalty for P1, namely, that others will judge P1's actions, would actually be a good thing for P1, not a penalty, because it may result in P1's discontinuing his immoral behavior, either voluntarily or through social or legal pressures. Note that, under the be-not-hypocritical interpretation of A1, if hypocrisy were the focal point of P1's immorality, then although his stopping his judging others' bad behavior would end his hypocrisy, it wouldn't end his immorality. Hence, the be-not-hypocritical interpretation of A1 is flawed.

SECTION IV: ASSESSMENT OF "HATE THE SIN; LOVE THE SINNER"

The above aphorism, call it A2, is heard from time to time from Christians, especially, it seems, when dealing with the morality of homosexual behavior that most versions of Christianity hold to be a sin. The idea that most Christians entertain with respect to A2 is something like, since God loves all human beings but hates all sin, we should do the same.

Responses

First, as I argued in assessing section II above, by its very definition and nature love cannot be ordered or morally required. Love can only be freely given. If so, then the "love the sinner" mandate of A2 is inappropriate.

Second, when one considers *serious* breaches of morality or, if you wish, serious sins, A2's plausibility is open to serious counterexample challenges. For instance, it would be inconsistent for person, P, to say that she hates the sin of genocide, but loves the concentration camp's enforcing personnel who knowingly, by their free choices, promulgate genocide in the camp. The enforcing personnel's actions are so horrendous that such actions should rule out any talk of P's "loving" the personnel or having any reaction toward them other than utmost condemnation. For more on this point see the earlier section in this chapter entitled "JEP: (1) Love, (2) Don't Resist, (3) Turn the Other Cheek to, (4) Do Good to Your Enemies."

In order to determine the proper response that P should have to any particular human behavior, P should determine whether the freely done behavior in question harms (or is intended to harm) any innocent party. If it does, then, P would be justified in "hating", that is to say, condemning, both the behavior and the doer for her "doings." If the behavior does not harm (nor is intended to harm) any innocent party, then P ought to refrain from hating/condemning the behavior and the doers.

Third, most Christians believe that God causes persons in hell to experience eternal conscious torment. If so, then it can be charged that God, himself, doesn't live up to the "hate the sin; love the sinner" admonition. This follows because, by any reasonable understanding of what loving someone means, causing them to experience conscious eternal tormenting is clearly not a part of that understanding.

CODA: WHAT JESUS SHOULD HAVE SAID

In this chapter I scrutinized seven of Jesus's ethical prescriptions, four from the Sermon on the Mount and three others summarizing important prescriptions of Christian ethics. I argued that all seven are flawed in one sense or another. At this point a question might be posed as to what Jesus, as the omnibenevolent, providential God incarnate, *should have prescribed* instead of those questionable seven prescriptions. Philosopher Richard Carrier has suggested some useful and relatively simple things that Jesus could have prescribed that his audience could have easily understood and put into practice.[18] Unlike the seven he prescribed, these alternatives, if implemented, could have saved or improved the lives of countless human beings.

18. Carrier, "Why Didn't Jesus Tell Us."

First, wash your hands a lot—preferably with hot water—

- before eating and after pooping and urinating,
- before handling, preparing, and eating food,
- before and after treating sickness and wounds,
- after contact with dead bodies.

Second, boil your "medical" tools/instruments in water before and after use.

Third, treat women with as much respect as you treat men.

Chapter 11: **Two Inconsistencies in the Christian Antiabortion Stance**

Preview

I argue that Christianity is inconsistent in claiming that abortion is immoral while at the same time affirming that (1) violence against abortion providers is immoral and (2) there is no moral obligation to implant unwanted frozen fertilized human eggs and bring them to term.

VIOLENCE AGAINST ABORTION PROVIDERS

According to a report from the respected Guttmacher Institute there were some 930,000 abortions performed in the U.S. in 2020.[1] More than 500,000 of those were in moderate or liberal so-called blue states such as California and New York where abortion still remains a legal option. That means that, despite the Supreme Court's overthrowing Roe v. Wade, there will likely still be upwards of half a million abortions performed every year in blue states for the foreseeable future.

Christians have been in the forefront of opposition to abortion. In particular, the Catholic Church and conservative Protestant-based groups have publicly admonished those seeking or providing abortions while also assiduously campaigning in legal and political arenas to outlaw the practice. At the heart of their objection to abortion is their endorsement of the following crucial claim.

1. See Diamant and Mohamed, "What the Data Says."

> *Ensoulment-at-Conception Claim*: at the moment of conception God provides an immortal soul to each fertilized human egg (zygote), thereby making it a human person endowed with full moral protection.

A large majority of Christians believes that the ensoulment-at-conception claim is true, and, therefore, that abortion is essentially the murder of babies. From their perspective, given the number of abortions each year in the US, we are truly in the midst of an immense holocaust of innocents. The point I wish to highlight here is that, despite their acceptance of the Ensoulment-at-Conception Claim, the vast majority of antiabortion Christians and their organizations nevertheless reject, and even condemn, violent action to stop abortions, including bombing clinics and executing abortion providers. What's wrong with this picture?

I contend that if antiabortion Christians condemn violence against abortion providers and clinics, they act against two ethical beliefs they presumably strongly endorse.

1. Abortion is murder, inferred from the ensoulment-at-conception claim.
2. It is morally permissible, and in some cases morally required, to protect the innocent with force proportionate to the threat, if there are no alternatives.

With respect to (1) and (2), there do not seem to be any nonviolent alternatives to prevent abortions in the blue states. If so, then violence, including fatal force, would appear to be the only option left to stop what antiabortion Christians consider to be a very grave violation of morality, namely, the mass murder of babies.

To see this more clearly, imagine that you come upon an intruder in your house who is about to stab your newborn baby. Few, if any, morally sensitive people would condemn you for killing the intruder, if that were the only way to prevent the likely fatal stabbing. Why, then, do antiabortion Christians consistently disavow the actions of people who have used violence to stop abortions being performed, such as John Salvi, who killed abortion providers?[2] It certainly won't do to reply that Salvi's actions were against the law. Christians have always held that a law may, and sometimes must, be disregarded if it permits God-condemned

---

2. John Salvi was an antiabortion extremist who carried out two fatal shootings at two abortion facilities in Brookline, Massachusetts, on December 30, 1994.

immorality, especially grave immorality like murdering babies. Furthermore, no major non-passivist Christian group of which I am aware has held that fatal force against those slaughtering innocents, say, during the Nazi era (1933–1945), was morally wrong.

If in our country today it were *really believed* that more than a half a million *babies* were being murdered each year, morally sensitive persons would not condemn violent resistance to such a slaughter, just like they didn't condemn the violent resistance to the Nazi slaughters. More likely, they would consider such violent resistance to be positively heroic. However, most antiabortion Christians do not think that. But why? If they accept that (1) abortion is the murder of babies and that (2) it is morally permissible to protect the innocent with force proportionate to the threat, then why wouldn't they consider someone like John Salvi to be a moral hero?

Make no mistake. I'm not arguing in support of antiabortion violence. In fact, I think it is morally unjustified. I have been arguing two points—one logical and one psychological.

First, the logical point: a serious and unavoidable logical consequence of the claim that abortion murders babies is that those who assist or perform abortions *should be* assassinated, if no other method will stop them.

Second, the psychological point: the fact that only relatively few antiabortion Christians support violence against abortion clinics and providers suggests that, in fact, "down deep" most antiabortion Christians don't really believe that abortion is actually the murder of babies.

In short, I conclude that Christian abortion opponents need to get right with logic and either endorse antiabortion violence straight out or repudiate their claims that abortion is the murder of babies.

ABORTION AND THE FATE OF FROZEN FERTILIZED HUMAN EGGS

The Centers for Disease Control and Prevention reports (2018) that of about four million births per year in the US, about 1 to 2 percent (forty to eighty thousand) of them are via in vitro fertilization (IVF).[3] In the most common IVF procedures eight or more eggs are harvested from the prospective mother with all being fertilized at one time in a petri dish. Then two to four of the fertilized eggs (zygotes) are put into the prospective mother's body, hoping that they will successfully implant in the womb

---

3. "IVF by the Numbers."

and eventually result in a live birth. The unused zygotes are frozen and stored in liquid nitrogen so that they can be thawed out for future use, if so desired. Most of the frozen zygotes are in a very early (4-64 cells) stage of undifferentiated development.[4] According to the US Health and Human Services Department, as of 2018 there were some 600,000 frozen zygotes in the US alone in which the creating parties have no further interest.[5] That number has very likely grown significantly at this time.

The ethical question which interests us here is what is the morally correct way to deal with unclaimed frozen zygotes? They cannot survive indefinitely in their frozen state. For antiabortion Christians who accept the Ensoulment-at-Conception Claim, that is, who accept that at the moment of conception God associates an immortal soul with the fertilized egg thereby creating a human person, the answer would seem to be clear. The frozen zygotes must be rescued, that is, be unfrozen and implanted in uteruses and set on a path to complete their natural development. To do nothing would be to accept the eventual deterioration and death of these innocent ensouled human persons.

If the frozen zygotes are ensouled human persons, their plight is similar to that of a human person who is a young child drowning in a shallow pond. In both the frozen zygote and pond situations rescue of the human person at risk would be a pressing moral necessity, not an optional gesture. Yet, while antiabortion Christians would undoubtedly acknowledge the moral necessity to rescue the young child in the pond, most of them apparently do not recognize the corresponding necessity to rescue frozen zygotes stored in IVF clinics. In fact, neither the Catholic Church nor any other religious antiabortion group has required or even asked that women rescue the zygotes by implanting them into their uteruses whenever feasible.

Evaluation of Two Christian Retorts to the Claim That Rescuing Unwanted Frozen Zygotes Is Morally Required

First Christian Retort

The analogy of the plight of the frozen zygote to that of the drowning child is weak because rescuing the drowning child requires only a few seconds

---

4. "Undifferentiated development" means that the cells of the zygote have not yet become specialized as being, say, skin cells, or brain cells, or liver cells, or blood cells, etc.

5. "After IVF," para. 3.

of effort, while rescuing the frozen zygotes may take up to nine months of discomfort and inconvenience. Moreover, there is usually no financial liability incurred in rescuing a drowning child, whereas there would be some financial burden involved in bringing a zygote to term.

EVALUATION

The discomfort, inconvenience, or financial difficulty of bearing a pregnancy, when offered by the pro-choice side as justifications for having an abortion, has always been rejected by antiabortion Christians as insufficient on the grounds that when the lives of innocent persons, such as zygotes, are at stake, mere inconvenience, discomfort, or economic difficulty are not acceptable excuses for having an abortion. If frozen zygotes truly are morally protected human persons in danger of being destroyed unless someone comes forward to rescue them, then it would seem that Christian female abortion opponents are morally obligated to use their available reproductive capacities to bring the unwanted zygotes to term.

Second Christian Retort

Judging that a woman would be morally wrong if she had an abortion is not analogous to judging that she would be morally wrong if she declined to rescue an abandoned frozen zygote by implanting it in her uterus. In the situations concerning abortion, the women involved would be personally responsible, often along with the fathers, for the plight that their preborns would be in because they would be responsible for the pregnancy itself; whereas, in the implantation scenarios the women called upon to rescue the frozen zygotes are not responsible for the situation the frozen zygotes are in because they are not responsible for producing them in the first place.

EVALUATION

First, lack of responsibility for producing a circumstance does not always excuse one from the responsibility of assisting the innocent who are in grave danger in that circumstance. Under pain of moral negligence I can't decline to wade into a pond to save a drowning child because I'm not responsible for the child's falling into the pond, or even because I warned the parents about their negligence with the child around the pond. My moral obligation to rescue is not lifted by such factors. Likewise, even though the women called upon to rescue the abandoned zygotes are not responsible for their production or plight, they may still be said to be morally responsible for doing their part to save an innocent person's (zygote's) life.

Second, in more than just a few instances women are *not* responsible for their pregnancies in any morally liable sense, for example, because of rape, non-culpable ignorance, or reasonably unexpected failures of normally reliable contraceptive procedures. Yet, the great majority of abortion opponents remains unmoved by such extenuations and holds that in such circumstances women are nevertheless morally obliged to bring their pregnancies to term since the life of the innocent unborn trumps the "not responsible" card. Thus, female abortion opponents are not on strong ground in refusing to implant the frozen zygotes into their uteruses on the basis of their not being responsible for the production of the zygotes.

CHAPTER SUMMARY

I've argued that Christianity has erred by inconsistently affirming the ensoulment-at-conception claim while also (1) condemning those who perpetrate violence against abortion providers, and (2) not mandating the implantation and bringing to term all available unclaimed frozen fertilized eggs.

Chapter 12: American Christianity and Political Conservatism

Preview

This chapter lays out and critiques some of the reasons why in the last five decades or so a large segment of American Christianity, namely, conservative Christianity, including traditional Roman Catholics, Evangelicals, Fundamentalists, Pentecostals, Mormons, and assorted nondenominationalists, has developed a close working relationship with political conservatism.

INTRODUCTION

In a recent article, "How Do Christians Become Conservative?,"[1] Mike Lux makes quite a compelling case that one would not expect Christianity and conservatism to have become as chummy as they have become.[2] What he doesn't do, however, is explain *why* they've become so closely associated, especially in the US. In order to better understand the current political and religious situations in the US I think it's important to try to answer this question.

I believe the answer starts with the recognition that, despite its claim to infallibly channel immutable truths from the divine, Christianity has, in fact, from time to time changed some of its nontrivial doctrines. For

---

1. Lux, "How Do Christians Become Conservative?"

2. Lux's point has been made even stronger with the ongoing alliance between the elements of conservative Christianity listed above and Trumpism.

example, by the fourth century it had jettisoned the pacifism of Jesus, and by the sixteenth it abandoned its fifteen-hundred-year prohibition on charging interest. The association of conservative Christianity and political conservatism is yet another such change. More specifically, conservative Christianity has distanced itself from Jesus's Social Gospel, that is, from his collectivist, anti-materialistic teachings and concern for the poor, and has moved to an un-Jesuine (not Jesus-like) de facto toleration of zealous individualism, material acquisitiveness, social Darwinism, jingoistic nationalism, xenophobia (fear of foreigners), environmental and climate change irresponsibility, and chastisement of the poor and disadvantaged, all coupled with a dismissive attitude toward criticism of excessive consumerism.[3] Once again, this prompts the question: why the change from Jesus's Social Gospel? Let me offer some explanations.

BIRDS OF A FEATHER

The alliance between conservative Christianity and political conservatism is facilitated by the fact that they share certain perspectives.

Those Were the Days My Friend . . .

Both esteem the past as a repository of truth and goodness. Conservative Christianity acknowledges the importance of the Old Testament and gives at least lip service to the claim that Jesus's pronouncements, as well as the actions and beliefs of the early church, are normative. Political conservatism, for its part, gives pride of place to tradition, historical precedent, and venerable documents as guides to proper contemporary beliefs, practices, and institutions. They don't call it *conserv*atism for no reason. It's no coincidence, for example, that American political conservatives evince an almost religious reverence for the US Constitution. They hold it to be the quintessential embodiment of legal and political rectitude, which, like fundamentalist Christian Scripture, should always be understood and implemented in the most literal fashion. The late Supreme Court Justice Antonin Scalia's fetish for "original intent" in interpreting the Constitution is illustrative.

Additionally, conservative Christianity and political conservatism, not surprisingly, both reject nontraditional secular humanist values such

---

3. For more on this see Carrier, "Dear Christian."

as tolerance of sexual preferences and identity, equitable gender treatment, environmental stewardship, autonomous reasoning, addressing climate change, and ameliorating social and economic inequalities by governmental means.

The Enemy of My Enemy Is My Friend

Besides a shared reverence for the past, conservative Christianity and political conservatism both also share a disdain for social democracies: political conservatives because they believe that the levels of taxation and regulation in such polities are obstacles to conservatives realizing their highest good, namely, the maximization of individual freedom, while conservative Christians are concerned that the prosperity, freedom, and fairness in social democracies reduce the need for church outreach services, which thereby reduces Christianity's influence and control within the society. Sociologist Gregory Paul has shown a strong correlation between, on the one hand, a state's success in delivering substantive social and economic benefits, and, on the other hand, a diminished religiosity within such a state.[4] The idea is that people tend to turn to religion when they feel there are serious problems that their state isn't redressing, and to dispense with it when conditions are good. For instance, church attendance in the US increased substantially in the immediate aftermath of 9/11 and then fell back to normal when conditions stabilized. Also, evangelical preachers stage most of their religious revivals in troubled countries such as Haiti or Guatemala rather than in successful humanist democracies like Denmark or New Zealand.

The successes of social democracies also undercut a number of core Christian religious doctrines, starting with the original sin of Adam and Eve in the garden of Eden. Many versions of Christianity maintain that one consequence of original sin is that all people's natures became corrupted. Moreover, people are unable to rectify that corruption or substantially improve the world at large without supernatural redemption, the foundation of which is putatively supplied by Jesus's passion, death, and resurrection. In effect, as far as Christianity is concerned, the human species has fallen and it can't get up. However, the achievements of largely secular polities adds to the evidence that shows that the doctrine of original sin is flawed. For problems

---

4. See the Paul footnote in the section entitled "Second Mistake Involving the Rationale for the Truth of the Doctrine of Original Sin" in chapter 1.

with the doctrine of original sin see material in the section entitled "Can't Live With the Doctrine of Original Sin" in chapter 1.

The successes of the largely secular countries also call into question other key Christian religious doctrines dependent on the truth of original sin, such as Jesus's incarnation and resurrection. Clearly, then, humanist-oriented liberal societies present a formidable challenge to the core philosophy of political conservatism as well as to the conservative Christian worldview.

YOU SCRATCH MY BACK AND . . .

Quid pro quos are also important in explaining conservative Christianity's unholy alliance with political conservatism.

Religion Bakes No Bread

Without significant donations religions would have a difficult time sustaining themselves. Those in the best position to provide the most support are the well-off, who are, in the main, politically conservative. Since their wealth and power is associated primarily with their business activities, conservative Christianity provides lush moral and theological validation for those activities in return for material support from the wealthy. Peter Montgomery at *People for the American Way* reports that conservative Christians are claiming to find biblical justification for such business friendly conservative policies as "opposition to progressive taxation, opposition to unions and collective bargaining, opposition to the minimum wage, opposition even to social welfare spending and Social Security."[5] This basically amounts to conservative Christianity muting the Social Gospel. Christians today are as likely to hear sermons about how difficult it is for rich people to get into heaven, as they are to hear about the sinfulness of working on the Sabbath—which is to say almost never. Many conservative Christians have sharply curtailed their commitment to social justice as an important part of their Christian ethos. Recently, Russell Moore, former top official for the Southern Baptist Convention who is now the editor-in-chief of *Christianity Today*, was critical of this turn away from the Social Gospel. He said during a recent interview aired on NPR's *All Things*

---

5. Hargerty, "Christians Debate," para. 10.

Considered that Christianity is in a "crisis" due to the current state of right-wing politics and warned that conservative Christians are now rejecting the social teachings of Jesus as "liberal talking points."[6]

In light of the great disparity between the politically conservative and Jesuine (of Jesus) ethoses, one might expect Christian liberals to go all "Old Testament prophet" on those Christians colluding with conservatism. But that expectation is not often realized. Oh sure, on some occasions there may be an "ahem" or two from some of the liberal-leaning mainline Protestant sources or the US Conference of Catholic Bishops about some particularly unsavory aspect of the Christian-conservative alliance; but those protestations are usually as mild as they are rare. Perhaps, Christian leaders who might have been expected to more forcefully advocate the Social Gospel have not because they're aware that the fastest growing Christian groups are those most ardently committed to making nice with political conservatism. To get along, conservative Christianity goes along. The payoff for accommodation is substantial.

Philosopher and historian Richard Carrier points out[7] that Christianity evolves on differential success just like species do. If your community comprises significant numbers of, say, homophobes, sexists, and members eager to support police violence, then your church simply won't grow or succeed if it opposes those positions. So churches get "naturally selected" into the mindset of the masses, which means that if the masses are cool or indifferent to matters of social justice, then Christianity's churches become so as well. Churches that run against the mindset of the masses shrivel and die out. In short, because churches have to tell people what they want to hear, they have to shift conservative if their members are largely conservative. If the population shifts liberal, then you get the opposite phenomenon (we see this happening to the Anglican Church in the UK for example, not without resistance, but the writing is on the wall). But then, people start to see no value in the church at all. They don't need churches in order to hold and advance their progressive ideas. On the other hand, conservatives feel beleaguered by what they see as a growing liberal/progressive/social democratic world. Thus, they need churches to bolster their mission. This involves, among other things, wealthy conservatives financially, and in other ways as well, supporting conservative Christian churches and their agendas.

6. Slisco, "Evangelicals," para. 1.
7. Richard Carrier, email message to author, March 8, 2023.

Onward Christian Soldiers!

For some time now, Christianity has felt threatened by secular humanism in a struggle that has become known as the Culture Wars. Some of the salient battles therein involve conservative Christianity trying to weaken church-state separation, promulgate the US as a Christian nation, protect or increase tax advantages for religious-based institutions, procure exemptions for parents to use faith healing rather than standard medical therapy to treat their minor children, and impose conservative Christian beliefs in areas such as sexual behavior, contraception, procreation, abortion, euthanasia, and gender/LBGTQ+ rights. In order to have any chance of winning these battles, conservative Christianity needs, in addition to generous resource donations, the political, legal, and media support from politically conservative organizations, pundits, politicians, media outlets, and think tanks. Political conservatism has been willing to provide that assistance to conservative Christianity—for a price, of course—namely, a legion of Christian foot soldiers supporting conservative political and economic causes. The reasoning is simple. It's all about the tale of the demographic tape. Absent its alliance with conservative Christianity, political conservatism would be unable to attract a sufficient following to achieve electoral success, given that its policies primarily favor big business and the well-off few at the expense of the rest. American political conservatism without Christian numbers would be, well, something more akin to libertarianism—an acquired niche political taste. But with Christian numbers political conservatism has become a formidable political force.

What happens is that conservative Christian leaders provide the peoplepower of their congregations to support conservative plutocratic (big money) interests electorally and otherwise. In return, those plutocratic interests extend to conservative Christianity the resources needed to fight the Culture Wars. Paging Dr. Faustus?

The obvious question at this point is how conservative Christianity gets its followers to support policies favorable to big business and the well-off, often even against the followers' own social and economic interests. The answer, in part, is that conservative Christianity convinces its followers that wealth and power reflect God's favor. St. Ayn Rand anyone? The late influential fundamentalist Christian leader, Jerry Falwell, was once asked whether his sumptuous lifestyle was consistent with the teachings of Jesus.

His response was "yes" because God favors those who put him first.[8] One would think that Falwell's view would be rejected by the non-wealthy people in the pews. One would think that they would keep in mind that the New Testament includes no hymns to wealth and conspicuous consumption, that the Gospel of Matthew has Jesus giving a "bleeding heart" *Sermon on the Mount*, not a "me first" *Investment-Strategy Seminar on the Countinghouse Floor*.[9] Alas, one would be mistaken. As the Christian-conservative alliance shows, religion is one of those institutions that can get people to voluntarily act against their own legitimate social and economic interests.

A "HEADS-UP"

I'm quite aware that the preference for political conservatism that many people-in-the-pews in the US have is also induced by factors besides their Christian beliefs. There are specific cultural, economic, geographical, historical, educational, and psychological factors that also contribute to the tidal pull toward political conservatism. For instance, studies show that both political and religious conservatives reliably score low on openness to experience and on ambiguity tolerance. Low openness to experience means that, generally speaking, political and religious conservatives become ideologically isolated and don't know what it's like to live differently or have different beliefs than the ones they have. Consequently, everything unlike them is feared for not being understood. Low tolerance means they need certainty and black and white standards. They can't accept nuance, complexity, or uncertainty.[10]

CHAPTER SUMMARY

In answer to the question raised in Lux's article, "How Do Christians Become Conservative?," I described how the two share a number of important perspectives and that they complement one another in effective, if not always seemly, ways. The upshot is that, even after at least five decades of canoodling, the hookup between conservative Christianity and political

---

8. Woodward, "$1 Million Habit."

9. For a satirical humorous expression of this critique see Franken, "Gospel of Supply Side Jesus."

10. See Gerber et al., "Big Five Personality Traits"; Nilsson and Jost, "Authoritarian-Conservatism Nexus"; and Entringer et al., "Big Five Personality and Religiosity."

conservatism continues hot and heavy. Will their relationship endure? I'm not sure. Their troths are now so tightly plighted, that I doubt either could survive well without the other. They appear to be codependently stuck with one another. My fervent hope is that, even if the relationship persists, in due course it will become irrelevant as humanity eventually moves ahead by leaving both behind. Just sayin'.

Chapter 13: A Novel Defense of Objective Ethics Without Christianity or Any Religion

Preview

Christians frequently claim that one of the definitive criticisms of atheism is that it is incompatible with objective morality. This chapter aims to respond to that claim by showing how an objective theory of ethics can be set out and defended with no reference to Christianity or any other religion. I call this objective theory of ethics "Ethical Rationalism." Ethical Rationalism is a two-principle moral code: (1) don't harm others and (2) help them whenever feasible. I argue that Ethical Rationalism and, hence, objective morality, is justified on the basis of the fact that, all other things being equal, all moral agents would have a greater chance of achieving more of their highest goal of experiencing a long and fulfilling life if they lived in a society that followed Ethical Rationalism than if they lived in a society that followed any other moral code.

INTRODUCTION

Most Christians believe that a powerful argument for the existence of God and, therefore, the falsity of atheism, can be generated from the supposed fact that only the existence of a suitably powerful, morally perfect supernatural being can provide a proper objective foundation for ethical behavior. In other words, they believe that without the existence of God there can be no objective morality. This belief helps to explain a number of facts, some disturbing, about contemporary American society. For example, polls show that Americans hold atheists in lower esteem than they do members of any other major social group.[1] In addition, not surprisingly, it is very difficult for an avowed atheist to win election to any American public office. Many Christians are firmly convinced that objective ethics works in their favor. This chapter will challenge that contention.

ARGUMENT FOR GOD'S EXISTENCE FROM THE OBJECTIVITY OF ETHICS

1. Ethical judgments are objective, that is, they are true or false independently of what anyone may think about them.[2]
2. The only way to account for ethical objectivity is to posit the existence of a suitably credentialed supernatural being, God, who grounds ethical objectivity.
3. Therefore, God exists and atheism is false.

Some atheists have challenged the soundness of the argument for God's existence from the objectivity of ethics by challenging the truth of premise 1. Other atheists, myself included, have instead challenged the truth of premise 2.[3] In the remainder of this chapter I will explain and defend the contention that there is a justified moral code, that is, a justified set of objective ethical principles that I call "Ethical Rationalism" which doesn't require the existence of any supernatural being.

ETHICAL RATIONALISM

Starting Point: A Fulfilling Life

My starting point is simple. All moral agents[4] want to live a fulfilling life. You do. I do. Everyone does. Each person's notion of what constitutes a fulfilling

---

1. See "Atheists Remain Most Disliked."
2. For example, it is objectively true that raping, torturing, and murdering a child is immoral regardless of what anyone might believe about it.
3. See, for example, Carrier, "Moral Facts Naturally," 333–64; also in two of Carrier's blogs, see "Real Basis" and "Your Own Moral Reasoning."
4. A moral agent is a being that has enough intelligence to understand the difference

life for him or her will be as unique as is each person's desires, needs, talents, and environment. Spelling out what constitutes a fulfilling life for oneself may be as specific as carefully listing and ranking one's desires, interests, opportunities, and resources in some detail, followed by evaluating specific strategies to achieve these. For example, a fulfilling life for one particular person might include things like the following: work summers in a local bank if possible; graduate from college with a major in business; join the Lions Club; apply for a scholarship to get an MBA; marry only after getting an MBA; have two children; run one's own business by age thirty; etc. In some cases, the notion of a fulfilling life may be much less detailed. Perhaps simply an implicit recognition that life as it is now going is more or less fine, and that you will work to try to keep it that way. Note that one's idea of what constitutes a fulfilling life for oneself need not be a static blueprint for future action. A rational person will frequently revise and update her idea of what constitutes a fulfilling life for her, as the person herself, her environment, or the knowledge available to her changes.

A freely chosen fulfilling life and the process of trying to achieve it give life its meaning (see chapter 6 section entitled "Meaning Of Life—Proposed"), purpose, direction, and zest. Most people judge their life to be worth living when they're satisfied with the progress already made, and likely to be made, in achieving their fulfilling life. The most satisfying moments of our lives are milestones on the road to realizing our fulfilling life, such as births, graduations, marriage, promotions, etc. On the other hand, whenever the pursuit of a fulfilling life is stymied due to pain or adverse social, political, or economic conditions, our *joie de vivre* (joy of living) suffers. Sometimes unfortunately, when conditions are foreseeably and unremittingly dire, life is no longer a blessing but a curse.

Connection between a Fulfilling Life and a Universally Correct Moral Code

Given the importance of achieving a fulfilling life, it makes sense to try to connect living a morally correct life with living a fulfilling life. More specifically, our following the universally correct moral code should be able to be shown to better contribute to our achieving our fulfilling life than would our following any other or no moral code. That Ethical Rationalism

---

between right and wrong and has free will to choose between them.

can do this will be defended after I have explained its core principles, to which I now turn.

Ethical Rationalism's Two Principles

No-Harm Principle

As its name suggests, this principle mandates in general that we refrain from harming others in terms of life, limb, or property. As such, it includes the following more specific prohibitions.

- Don't cause unjustified bodily or psychological harm to others.
- Don't treat others unfairly.
- Don't lie or dissemble inappropriately.
- Don't take or damage the legitimate property of others.
- Don't violate the autonomy of others, except if their expression of autonomy violates the previous prohibitions of this principle or the next principle to be described.

Some kinds of pain, suffering, and harm that are *not* immoral under the no-harm principle would include the following.

- Pain, suffering, and harm that comes as a consequence of certain voluntary activities such as medical treatments, sports activities, involvement in certain social relationships.
- Pain, suffering, and harm that comes from just punishment or protecting the innocent.
- Pain, suffering, and harm that occurs as the result of nonvoluntary actions of others or from actions that could not have been reasonably foreseen.

Principle of Assistance

According to this principle, capable people have a moral obligation under certain circumstances to help those in need. Although it's difficult to specify in detail what such circumstances are, here follow some useful guidelines.

PART TWO: CHRISTIANITY AND ETHICS

Factors Affecting the Moral Requirement to Assist the Needy

- Our moral obligation to assist others increases in proportion to the severity of their need—life-threatening circumstances, of course, give rise to the greatest severity of need.

- Our moral obligation to assist others decreases in proportion to the degree that our assistance would adversely hinder our own or others' serious well-being. For example, people are not generally morally required to risk their lives to assist others except under certain circumstances such as when it is a previously accepted duty, as, for example, the duties of police, fire, first responders, and military personnel.

- Our moral obligation to assist others decreases in proportion to the likelihood that the assistance could be rendered by others. For instance, you may not have to assist your brother to study for his math test, if he can easily get someone else to give him that assistance instead.

Although it may sometimes be difficult to specify whether a *sufficient* severity of need or *significant* hindrance to one's well-being exists, such difficulties don't render the principle of assistance unworkable. Examples at the extremes of the spectrum of need and hindrance can be identified easily enough. For example, one would have a moral obligation to wade into a shallow pond to prevent a young child from drowning, even if this required ruining an expensive pair of shoes (high need of another/low well-being hindrance for the assister), assuming no one else could render the assistance. On the other hand, one would not have a moral obligation to race into a burning building in imminent danger of collapse in order to rescue someone's wedding album (low need of another/high well-being hindrance for the assister). Between such extremes, we must apply the general guidelines laid out above as judiciously as possible in order to satisfy the principle of assistance.

Additional Comments on Ethical Rationalism's Moral Code

First, Ethical Rationalism's moral code can be boiled down to the following summary principle/definition.

> *Don't hinder others but, whenever feasible, help them to achieve their fulfilling lives.*

Second, in order to judge the moral status of any human action under Ethical Rationalism, one must apply its two principles as follows.

a. An action is *immoral* if doing it would violate either of Ethical Rationalism's two principles (for example—lying).

b. An action is *morally required* if not doing the action would violate either of Ethical Rationalism's principles (for example—paying one's debts).

c. An action is *nonmoral* if neither doing nor not doing it would violate the principles (for example—wearing a green shirt on Tuesday).

d. An action is *supererogatory* if doing the action is not morally required but is morally praiseworthy. In other words, a supererogatory action is one that is above and beyond what is morally required (for example—putting one's life in danger to save the life of another person).

Third, under Ethical Rationalism, one has no moral obligations to oneself. This follows from Ethical Rationalism's view that morality's function is to fairly judge *interpersonal* competition among moral agents for goods needed or wanted for the achievement of a fulfilling life.

Fourth, Ethical Rationalism does not make value judgements about the content of anyone's notion of what a fulfilling life is for them, except to mandate that the contents may not violate either principle of Ethical Rationalism. This is a positive aspect of ethical rationalism because it allows people to decide for themselves nonmoral matters of personal taste, thus supporting personal autonomy. For example, I don't need a moral code looking over my shoulder telling me, under pain of moral sanction, that I should watch opera and not cartoons. Watching either in most circumstances is nonmoral in that it would not violate either principle of Ethical Rationalism. However, given that ethical rationalism is a moral code based on reason, it certainly encourages people to investigate alternatives in order to make an informed decision about which choice of action would likely more fully contribute to their fulfilling life.

Fifth, each principle of Ethical Rationalism gives people certain rights as well as certain corresponding duties. Each principle of Ethical Rationalism is attractive in that it helps our efforts to achieve our fulfilling life by giving people certain *rights* that they can legitimately expect other moral agents to respect. For example, the no-harm principle gives me the right to be secure in my person and property from any unjustified infliction of pain, suffering, or harm by other moral agents. The Principle of Assistance gives me the *right* to expect help from other moral agents when my need is significant and the effort required to address that need is, at most, modest. At the same time, each principle of Ethical Rationalism also gives moral agents *duties* owed to others that correspond to each of one's own Ethical Rationalism-conferred rights. If I have a right to be secure from predation by others and to have them assist me in appropriate circumstances, then I incur the corresponding duties to refrain from being predatory toward them and to assist them under appropriate circumstances. We should never lose sight of the rights/duties symmetry embedded in each principle. This is akin to the rationale behind the venerable Golden Rule (do unto others as you would have them do unto you). I want to stress that a key advantage of Ethical Rationalism is that the value of the rights a moral agent gets by adhering to its two principles more than compensates for the obligations incurred to earn those rights. This is the crucial fact that puts the "rational" in Ethical Rationalism.

In sum, Ethical Rationalism matches up well with most people's views about how human beings generally ought to behave in a moral fashion (don't lie, cheat, steal, kill, etc., and help when you can). Its value is to be found less in the claim to have *discovered* new moral principles, than in being able to *justify* those principles. Let's turn now to see how this most important claim of justification is accomplished.

Justification of Ethical Rationalism

Ethical Rationalism is justified by showing that following its two principles is *necessary* and *sufficient* for giving all moral agents the best chance of living a fulfilling life, compared to the chance they would get if they followed some other moral code. Let's see first why following Ethical Rationalism's two principles is necessary for that.

Following Ethical Rationalism's Two Principles Is Necessary for Living a Fulfilling Life

Consider the following hypothetical thought experiment. Imagine there is a moral agent, M, who has some concept of a fulfilling life for himself. Imagine, further, that M has to choose either to try to achieve his notion of a fulfilling life in one of two possible societies: society A or society

B. (See table 12.1 below.) Assume that M has to make the choice under what is called the "veil of ignorance."[5] When choosing under the veil of ignorance, M does not know his

- age, gender, race, ethnicity, nationality, social or economic status, time or place in which he is living;
- talents, interests, strengths, weaknesses, abilities; or
- social, political, or religious beliefs.

Assume further that societies A and B are equivalent to one another in all aspects but one. All the people in society A endorse and strive to live up to the No-Harm Principle, whereas not all people in society B do. (See table 12.1 below.) The question is this: In which society would it be rational for M to choose to live? I think the answer is clear. M would be rational to choose to live in society A. In society B, in which not all moral agents endorse and try to follow the No-Harm Principle, the life and physical safety of M, obviously important for trying to achieve his fulfilling life, would be less well protected than they would be in society A, in which all moral agents endorse and aspire to follow the No-Harm Principle.

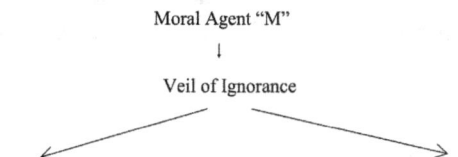

Society A (follows the No Harm Principle)   or   Society B (doesn't follow the No Harm Principle)

Table 12.1

Next, imagine a second similar thought experiment where M has to choose between trying to achieve his fulfilling life in society C, in which all moral agents endorse and try to follow the Principle of Assistance, and society D, in which not all moral agents endorse and try to follow the Principle of Assistance. Otherwise societies C and D are identical, or at least relevantly comparable. (See table 12.2 below.) The rational choice for M would be to opt to live in society C because it would be more advantageous for M to live in a society that would provide him assistance than

5. Rawls, *A Theory of Justice*, 136.

to live in one in which such assistance was not the standard. Remember that the obligation to render assistance under the Principle of Assistance is mitigated to the extent that rendering it would not significantly hinder the assister's own legitimate well-being.

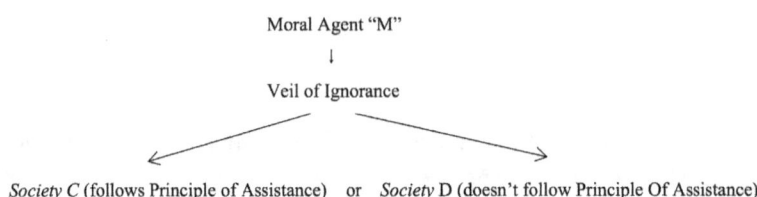

Table 12.2

The takeaway from these two thought experiments is that they show that M would be more rational living in a society that endorsed and tried to follow Ethical Rationalism's two principles than in any society that lacked one of the two. The protections that the two principles give to M's trying to achieve his fulfilling life are protections that it would be irrational for him to reject if he wants the best chance to achieve a fulfilling life. In short, each of Ethical Rationalism's two principles is necessary for M to have that best chance.

Following Ethical Rationalism's Two Principles Is Sufficient for Living a Fulfilling Life

Let's next see why Ethical Rationalism's two principles are also sufficient, that is, no other principles are needed, for giving all moral agents the best chance of living a fulfilling life, compared to the chance they would get if they followed some other moral code.

Imagine that a critic says that Ethical Rationalism is *not* sufficient because it lacks an important moral principle, say, the principle of clapping. In other words, the universally correct moral code is actually not ethical rationalism's two principles, but rather those two principles plus a third, the principle of clapping. This principle stipulates that all moral agents have a moral obligation to clap their hands three times when they enter someone's house. Sounds screwy, I know. However, I'll use the thought experiment approach again to show that ethical rationalism is sufficient without this proposed additional principle. (See table 12.3 below.)

We can ask whether moral agent, M, would be rational to choose to try to achieve her fulfilling life by living in society E, which follows Ethical Rationalism's two principles, or in society F, which follows Ethical Rationalism's two principles plus the principle of clapping. I think the answer is clear. It would *not* be rational for M to choose Society F, since having to clap your hands three times when entering someone's house would be a nuisance that would not assist anyone's efforts to achieve a fulfilling life.

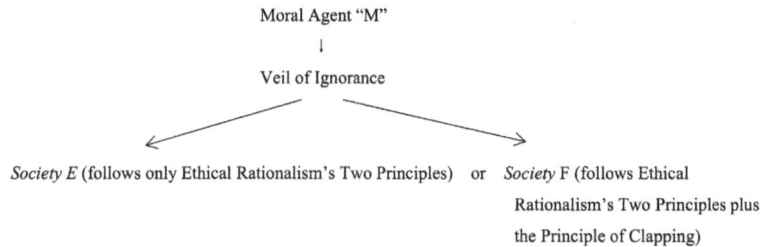

Table 12.3

So, unless a critic can propose an additional principle to add to Ethical Rationalism's two principles that would further the efforts of moral agents to achieve their fulfilling lives, I will continue to maintain that Ethical Rationalism's two principles are additively sufficient. Note that if a critic were to propose an additional principle that did give additional assistance to all moral agents in their efforts to achieve their fulfilling lives, then all I would need to do would be to add that principle to Ethical Rationalism.

Justification Argument for Ethical Rationalism

I'll now layout and defend a justification argument for Ethical Rationalism. Note that the justification for each step in the justification argument is given in italics.

1. All moral agents want to live a fulfilling life (*self-evident*).
2. If all moral agents want to live a fulfilling life, then it would be rational for them to follow all and only Ethical Rationalism's two principles (*ethical rationalism's two principles were shown above to be*

necessary and sufficient for giving all moral agents the best chance of living a fulfilling life).

3. Therefore, it would be rational for all moral agents to follow all and only Ethical Rationalism's two principles (*follows from 1 and 2 and the rule of inference called* modus ponens).

4. If it would be rational for all moral agents to follow all and only ethical rationalism's two principles, then all and only Ethical Rationalism's two principles constitute the universally correct moral code (*by definition, a moral code is the universally correct moral code if and only if it is the one and only moral code that would be rational for all moral agents to follow*).

5. Therefore, all and only Ethical Rationalism's two principles constitute the universally correct moral code. (*follows from 3 and 4 and the rule of inference called* modus ponens)

Beyond Ethical Rationalism's Moral Code

Importance of Moderation and Variety of Intrinsic Goods in One's Fulfilling Life

Given the definition of a fulfilling life, it follows that it is to each person's advantage to select a fulfilling life which will maximize his or her satisfaction in life. The key to such a maximization is to be found in the notion of *intrinsic goods*, those things which are held to be good in and of themselves and not simply because they lead to or facilitate other things we may desire. Examples of intrinsic goods would be experiences comprising physical pleasure, ecstatic and meditative experiences, relationships of intimacy, aesthetic enjoyment, personal achievement and creativity, and possession of certain kinds of knowledge. By their definition, it's clear that intrinsic goods should be woven, more rather than less, into one's fulfilling life. The difficult question is this: What amounts of which intrinsic goods and when? The appropriate mix for any particular person is impossible to specify in the abstract. Too much depends on the contingencies of personality and circumstances.

However, the experiences of many thoughtful and sensitive people throughout history in many different cultures have suggested that variety and moderation with respect to intrinsic goods are the cornerstones of living the "good life." An unbalanced pursuit of any one intrinsic good, say, physical pleasure, has often been found to lead to a less satisfactory and rewarding life than would be given by a fulfilling life with a more balanced inclusion of intrinsic goods. Nevertheless, if one were to do otherwise and no principles of Ethical Rationalism were thereby violated, such an unbalanced pursuit of certain intrinsic goods would not be immoral, though it might be unwise.

The Most Valuable Kinds of Intrinsic Goods for Most People

The evidence of past experience not only suggests the advantages of the general strategies of moderation and variety, but also yields more specific recommendations with respect to which kinds of intrinsic goods one might be wise to pursue in one's fulfilling life. The consensus of experience points to the greater and longer term satisfactions of intrinsic goods associated with intellect, the arts, and affection. These have the potential for furnishing deep enjoyment throughout one's life. Ethical Rationalism certainly does not devalue the significant satisfactions associated, say, with physical pleasure, but it does take into consideration the verdicts of those who have experienced all types of intrinsic good. I think it's worth reiterating (from the end of chapter 6) what I reported that American writer Bessie Stanley said about the nature of a fulfilling life:

> To laugh often and love much; to win the respect of intelligent persons and the affection of children; to earn the approbation of honest citizens and endure the betrayal of false friends; to appreciate beauty; to find the best in others; to give of one's self; to leave the world a bit better, whether by a healthy child, a garden patch or a redeemed social condition; to have played and laughed with enthusiasm and sung with exultation; to know even one life has breathed easier because you have lived—this is to have succeeded.[6]

---

6. Stanley, "Success." Bessie A. Stanley was responding to a contest held in 1906 by the *Emporia* (Kansas) *Gazette*, which put its readers to the task of defining success. People loved it and recycled it, and by 1951 Stanley's winning paragraph was being misattributed to Ralph Waldo Emerson in a syndicated newspaper column by Midwestern journalist Albert Edward Wiggam. From here it was off to the races. You'll find that paragraph attributed to Emerson in books (like *The Real Meaning of Success* by Helen Exley or *1001 Ways to Stop Overeating, End Boredom, and Just Have Fun* by Tracie Johansen), on T-shirts you can order from Etsy, and on Facebook pages galore. Hanlon, "On Fake Emerson Quotes."

Once again, if for some reason your own inclinations do not line up with these suggestions, then Ethical Rationalism says by all means feel free to follow them, of course, within the parameters specified by Ethical Rationalism's two principles.

CONCLUSION

Recall that I started this chapter by giving the argument for God's existence from the objectivity of ethics. Here it is repeated.

Argument for God's Existence from the Objectivity of Ethics Revisited

1. Ethical judgments are objective, that is, they are true or false independently of what anyone may think about them.
2. The only way to account for ethical objectivity is to suppose the existence of a suitably credentialed supernatural being, God, who grounds ethical objectivity.
3. Therefore, God exists and atheism is false.

I stated earlier in the chapter that I would challenge the soundness of this argument by challenging the truth of its premise (2). If my argument that Ethical Rationalism's two principles constitute objectively correct morality is sound, then premise 2 of the argument for God's existence from the objectivity of ethics is false and, thereby, the argument, itself, is unsound and does not demonstrate that atheism is false.

Part Three: **Christianity And Atheism**

Chapter 14: The Christian God Doesn't Exist Because of Unfair Human Experiences

Chapter 15: The Christian God Doesn't Exist Because of Unfair Salvation Opportunities

Chapter 16: The Christian God Doesn't Exist Because if He Did, He Would Be an Absentee Father

Chapter 17: The Christian God Doesn't Exist Because of the Quantity of Apparently Unjustified Suffering

Chapter 18: The Christian God Doesn't Exist Because This World Does

> *Note*: for readers interested in relatively recent books presenting other arguments for the nonexistence of God than the ones presented here, I recommend Lataster, *The Case Against Theism: Why the Evidence Disproves God's Existence*; Pearce, *30 Arguments against the Existence of God*; Philipse, *God in the Age of Science? A Critique of Religious Reason*; Martin, *Atheism: A Philosophical Justification*; and Everitt, *The Nonexistence of God*.

Chapter 14: The Christian God Doesn't Exist Because of Unfair Human Experiences

Preview

This chapter lays out and defends an atheological (atheistic) argument in which the what-we-wouldn't-have-expected-in-our-experience-of-the-world-if-the-Christian-God-existed is the existence of invidious divinely originated discrimination against certain innocent humans.

INTRODUCTION

Many atheists, agnostics, and even Christians agree that the most pressing intellectual difficulty involved in justifying belief in God is what is known as the problem of evil. That is, why do bad things (including horrendous pain, suffering, and harm) happen to good people if there exists a maximally powerful, knowledgeable, and morally good deity who could, and presumably would want to, prevent it? Christians, of course, postulate that God is such a deity. If so, then this world must be God's perfect creation. As such, it should contain no gratuitous (unjustified) pain, suffering, or harm. In other words, as philosopher Jonathan M. S. Pearce puts it, "So if this world is perfect, it has to have the perfect optimal amount of suffering in some manner."[1] He adds this:

1. Pearce, *30 Arguments*, 24.

Which is to say that if you stub your toe tomorrow, or if a baby gets cancer, or if another tsunami kills a further 230,000 people (as the 2004 tsunami in the Indonesia area did), those examples of suffering are necessary, and there cannot be one less unit of pain or *suffering* than there would or should be. Whatever suffering the (Christian) theist observes of the world around them, it must be necessarily perfect or optimal.[2]

As you might imagine, the cogency of such a Christian view concerning pain, suffering, and harm has been vigorously challenged by atheists and agnostics. In this chapter I don't intend to directly challenge the cogency of the Christian view that Pearce and others describe. Rather, instead of citing *the amount, extent, and intensity* of pain, suffering, and harm in our world as adequate evidence that very likely God doesn't exist, I'll cite *the uneven and unfair distribution* of said pain, suffering, and harm as comprising adequate evidence that it's very likely that God doesn't exist. I'll do that by setting out what I call the "argument for God's nonexistence from the existence of unfair human experiences." Since the focal point of the argument is divinely sourced unfairness, I'll start by defining "unfairness."

DEFINITION OF UNFAIRNESS

Assume that P, A, and B are persons or groups of persons, and that O is a non-immoral outcome desired by both A and B.

> *Definition of Unfairness*: P acts unfairly towards B in comparison to how P acts toward A with regard to O if and only if, without sufficient reason, either P intentionally treats A in a manner that P knows will assist A in getting O in a way that P does not so assist B, or P intentionally treats B in a manner that P knows will hinder B from getting O in a way that P does not so hinder A.

This formal definition is a mouthful but it tracks well with our commonsense notion that unfairness occurs when someone *arbitrarily* advances or hinders the interests of one party in contrast to another party with regard to an outcome that's important to both parties. For example, imagine that a teacher tells her class that they will have a test tomorrow and she gives out a helpful study guide sheet only to students whose last name has an even number of letters. I don't think you need to

---

2. Pearce, *30 Arguments*, 25.

be a professional philosopher to have your intuitive unfairness detector flashing red at this point. The problem is not just that the teacher gave the study sheet to one group but not the other. The unfairness registers because the criterion of distribution of the helpful study guide was totally arbitrary from a teaching-learning standpoint.

One potential objection that might be raised to the definition of unfairness is the following. Consider a situation in which there is a set of persons, S, with similar levels of need. Assume that P has the resources to assist only one member of S. The question is this. According to the definition of unfairness, if P assists only one member of S, would P be acting unfairly toward the members of S that she did not assist? I would say no, as long as the method of the selection of the member to be assisted would not itself violate the definition of unfairness. The most common way that could be done would be by some form of random selection.

ARGUMENT FOR GOD'S NONEXISTENCE FROM THE EXISTENCE OF UNFAIR HUMAN EXPERIENCES

As a hypothetical example of what I will argue would be divine arbitrariness in distributing instances of pain, suffering, and harm in our world, I offer the following thought experiment (TE) example.

Thought Experiment TE

> A baby, B1, is buried alive by an earthquake. She dies alone after seventy-two hours of horrendous suffering. B2, her twin, is also buried by the earthquake a few feet away from B1 but she dies instantly and painlessly. The entire population of their small village also perishes in the earthquake. No bodies are ever recovered. In fact, no specific evidence of the earthquake event ever comes to light.[3]

Being twins, B1 and B2 would have had very similar life experiences with the important exception that B1 experienced seventy-two hours of horrendous pain and suffering that B2 did not. According to many, if not most, Christian theologies, God would grant B1 and B2 the *summum bonum* of heavenly eternal salvation. To do otherwise would contravene

---

3. In all probability, scenarios like TE likely have, alas, occurred among the 117 billion or so humans who have existed since our species arose some three hundred thousand years ago.

God's omnibenevolence. So, they both will have essentially the same postmortem experiences.

The moral problem that TE gives rise to is that, according to the definition of unfairness given above, God would act unfairly toward B1 in causing/permitting her to linger in agony for three days while causing/permitting B2 to die instantly and painlessly. If so, then that divine unfairness would compromise God's omnibenevolence which, in turn, would constitute compelling evidence for his nonexistence. The formal layout for the argument for God's nonexistence from the existence of unfair human experiences is as follows. Note that the justification for each line in the argument follows the line and is in italics within parentheses.

ARGUMENT FOR GOD'S NONEXISTENCE FROM THE EXISTENCE OF UNFAIR HUMAN EXPERIENCES FORMATTED

1. If God acts unfairly, then he has a moral deficiency.
   (*Acting unfairly is, by definition, a moral deficiency.*)
2. It is likely that God acts unfairly.
   (*This will be shown below by using TE.*)
3. Therefore, God has a moral deficiency.
   (*This follows from 1 and 2 via the logical rule of reasoning called* modus ponens.)
4. If God exists, then he has no moral deficiencies.
   (*This follows from the definition of "God."*)
5. Therefore, it is not the case that God exists.
   (*This follows from 3 and 4 via the logical rule of reasoning called* modus tollens.)

The argument for God's nonexistence from the existence of unfair human experiences is clearly formally valid. Its soundness, however, requires that premise 2 be shown to be true. In the remainder of the chapter, I'll argue that there are adequate reasons supporting the truth of premise 2 and, therefore, adequate reasons to hold that the argument for God's nonexistence from the existence of unfair human experiences is sound.

To start with, if we assess God's behavior in TE, namely, his differential treatment of B1 vis-à-vis B2, in terms of the definition of unfairness, it's pretty clear that his behavior must be judged as being unfair to B1. Which is to say that, without sufficient reason, God treats B2 in a manner that he knows will assist B2 to get O, namely, postmortem supreme happiness *without any suffering beforehand*, in a way that God does not so assist B1. In other words, God makes it that both B1 and B2 get to go to heaven. However, it seems that there are no sufficient reasons why God makes it the case that only B1 has to suffer horribly before getting there.

RETORTS TO OBJECTIONS TO THE ARGUMENT FOR GOD'S NONEXISTENCE FROM THE EXISTENCE OF UNFAIR HUMAN EXPERIENCES

The key phrase in the application of the definition of unfairness to TE is clearly "without sufficient reason." Here follow some explanations that Christians might offer to justify their claim that God could have sufficient reasons which would justify his discriminatory differential treatment of B1 vis-à-vis B2.

First Christian Objection

Christians might contend that God's absolute sovereignty as an omnipotent being who created humans would justify his decision to require B1 but not B2 to suffer horribly before being given heavenly salvation as a result of TE. In other words, God is morally justified in determining when any human comes into earthly existence and when and how they go out of such existence.

Non-Christian Retort

Christians believe that God is omnibenevolent as well as omnipotent. As such, his sovereignty, which is to say, his permissible range of action, must be in accord with his omnibenevolent nature. However, as described above, God's treatment of B1 vis-à-vis B2 would not be in accord with his omnibenevolence because, according to the definition of unfairness, his treatment of B1 would be unfair. For example, imagine a father who lets one of his twin baby children, but not the other, suffer terribly for no apparent reason when he could have done otherwise, and then rewards both identically and lavishly afterward. I would think that no morally competent person would think that the father's parental sovereignty and subsequent lavish reward would morally justify the father's discriminatory actions.

Second Christian Objection

Christians could argue that the fact that B1, postmortem, receives the gift of the greatest possible human happiness would neutralize the charge that God would violate his omnibenevolence by causing/permitting B1's suffering.

Non-Christian Retort

The supporter of the argument for God's nonexistence from the existence of unfair human experiences could respond that God's compensating B1 for harming her does not suffice to justify his harming her in the first place, especially given that B2 was not so harmed and yet received the same eternal, maximal postmortem happiness. For example, a person cannot morally justify raping someone by simply paying them off after the fact. Compensation is not the same as justification.

Let me here reiterate that the argument for God's nonexistence from the existence of unfair human experiences is not, strictly speaking, just a version of the argument from evil, which claims that God can be said to not exist because the innocent suffer.[4] The main focal point of this chapter's unfairness argument is not simply the fact that an innocent person (B1) suffered horribly, it is also the fact that there was a divine "thumb on the scale of fairness," as it were, against B1. After all, being babies, both were totally innocent, despite what the doctrine of original sin says. Yet God caused/permitted B1, but not B2, to experience horrendous suffering. Why? How can that not be unfair?

---

4. Nevertheless, I do think that the argument from evil also does apply to B1's suffering in TE since that horrendous suffering would be unjustified.

Third Christian Objection

Christians could maintain that B1's suffering could be said to be justified because it would entitle her to receive some sort of a higher measure of compensatory postmortem reward in heaven than her twin would receive.

Non-Christian Retort

The supporter of the argument for God's nonexistence from the existence of unfair human experiences could counter by noting that there cannot be any greater happiness than the greatest possible happiness that any human being can experience, namely, the happiness associated with eternal heavenly existence. Another way of putting it is that no human being experiencing the *summum bonum* of heaven can be said to be any more or less happy and fulfilled than any other human being experiencing the *summum bonum*. When it comes to the latter, there are no gradations of "*summum*-ness." It's like pregnancy. Either you have the *summum bonum* or you don't, full stop.

Fourth Christian Objection

A Christian could contend that, due to human cognitive limitations, we may simply not be able to understand what God's morally sufficient reasons are for his differential treatment of B1 and B2. Perhaps, in ways we can't see, that differential treatment somehow would bring about some greater compensating good or the prohibition of an evil greater than B1's suffering that could not otherwise have been prevented without that suffering. It's simply beyond our limited comprehension to be certain that God couldn't have sufficient moral justification. This Christian response is another instance of the Christian apologetical defense known as skeptical theism that we will see again in subsequent chapters.

Non-Christian Retort

Whatever constitutes the beyond-our-knowledge sufficient reason that skeptical theists may be referring to in order to justify God's discriminatory treatment of B1 vis-à-vis B2, it can't be associated with some greater good (or prevented evil) for B1 in this life because B1 ends up being deceased. It also can't be properly associated with some greater good (or prevented evil) for B1 in the afterlife since B1 "automatically" receives the highest good possible in the afterlife by being admitted to heaven. Nor could B1's being given that *summum bonum* somehow *require* her three days of horrendous suffering since, recall, B1's twin, B2, who is virtually identical to B1 from ethical and other perspectives, receives the same postmortem good as B1 without having to experience three days of horrendous suffering. Finally, given the details of TE, it's highly implausible, even if logically possible in some fashion, that B1's differential treatment would bring about a greater good or avoid a greater evil for anyone else. Keep in mind that mere *possibility* doesn't entail actual *plausibility*. It may be logically possible for me now to bench press three hundred pounds, but that alone would not make it plausible that I could do so.

In short, I conclude that Christian objections to premise 2 are without merit. If so, then the soundness of the unfairness argument is adequately defended.

Chapter 15: Christian God Doesn't Exist Because of Unfair Salvific Opportunities

> *There is no faith, therefore, where the Gospel is not heard; and where there is no faith, there is no salvation.*[1]
>
> —Charles Hodge

Preview

As with the previous chapter, this chapter focuses on a claim of divine unfairness to construct an argument for God's nonexistence. I term this the "argument for God's nonexistence from the existence of unfair salvific (having to do with salvation) opportunities." The what-we-wouldn't-have-expected-in-our-experience-of-the-world-if-the-Christian-God-existed in this argument is the inherent unfairness of the opportunities available to humans for experiencing their *summum bonum* or highest good, namely, eternal salvation in heaven. The chapter's aim is to show that the general doctrine of salvation found in Christianity is not cogent because its implementation unavoidably involves unfair salvific opportunities. The existence of the unfair opportunities are defended against the most challenging Christian retorts and are finally made the grist for establishing the soundness of the argument from unfair salvific opportunities that concludes that God very likely does not exist.

---

1. Hodge, *Systematic Theology*, 648.

DEFINITION OF UNFAIRNESS

I will use the same definition of "unfairness" that I introduced in the previous chapter. I repeat it here. Assume that P, A, and B are persons or groups of persons, and that O is a non-immoral outcome desired by both A and B.

> *Definition of Unfairness*: P acts unfairly towards B in comparison to how P acts toward A with regard to O if and only if, without sufficient reason, either P intentionally treats A in a manner that P knows will assist A in getting O in a way that P does not so assist B, or P intentionally treats B in a manner that P knows will hinder B from getting O in a way that P does not so hinder A.

This formal definition is a mouthful but it tracks well with our commonsense notion that unfairness occurs when someone *arbitrarily* advances or hinders the interests of one party in contrast to another party with regard to an outcome that's important to both parties.

GENERAL CHRISTIAN DOCTRINE OF SALVATION

The general Christian doctrine of salvation (henceforth just "doctrine of salvation") sets out the necessary and sufficient requirements that must be met by humans if they are to experience the *summum bonum* for themselves, that is, in more common parlance, eternal heavenly salvation.

One of the most nettlesome problems associated with the doctrine of salvation is that there are many versions of it on offer and no clear means for determining which is the correct one. For example, there is the Roman Catholic version, the Lutheran version, the Church of Latter Day saints version, the Eastern Orthodox version, and many others. Fortunately, for the purpose of showing unfairness in the opportunities to satisfy the doctrine of salvation, we need not delve into the differences among the many versions or which, if any, is the correct version. It will suffice to note that all major versions of the doctrine of salvation have roughly the same general outline, namely, God reveals to humans a set of beliefs and behaviors, the holding and practicing of which is necessary and sufficient for any human to be gifted the experience of the *summum bonum*, that is, to be saved.[2] Christian salvation is most commonly construed as experi-

---

2. The Calvinist (Reformed) tradition, which is a distinct minority view in Christianity, holds that salvation (election) is determined directly by God and that therefore there are no necessary and sufficient beliefs and behaviors required for it. As non-Calvinist

encing postmortem, maximal, eternal, happiness in the form of the most intimate loving relationship with God in heaven. Most Christians endorse the view that if persons do not satisfy the proper revealed requirements of the doctrine of salvation, they will not experience the *summum bonum*.[3] Instead, as Christian scholar Charles Hodge, quoted at the beginning of the chapter, alluded, they will experience eternal separation from God, which many Christians maintain includes eternal conscious torment in hell (see chapter 4 for more about God and hell).

ARGUMENT FOR GOD'S NONEXISTENCE FROM THE EXISTENCE OF UNFAIR SALVIFIC OPPORTUNITIES

For the sake of argument, I will assume that there is a correct doctrine of salvation, though we don't need to know what comprises it. My general contention in the argument for God's nonexistence from the existence of unfair salvific opportunities is that the existence of unfair salvific opportunities to identify and satisfy the correct doctrine of salvation, whatever it may be, supports the conclusion that the Christian God does not exist. The formal presentation of this argument is laid out next.

ARGUMENT FOR GOD'S NONEXISTENCE FROM EXISTENCE OF UNFAIR SALVIFIC OPPORTUNITIES FORMATTED

The justification for each statement is given in italics in the parentheses following the statement.

1. If God exists, then he is omnibenevolent
   (*follows from the definition of "God"*).

2. If God acts unfairly, then he's not omnibenevolent
   (*follows from the definitions of "unfairness" and "omnibenevolence"*).

3. It's likely that God does act unfairly (*to be shown below*).

Christians have amply argued, this view has significant problems. I won't delve into them here.

3. See John 3:18.

4. Therefore, it's likely that God isn't omnibenevolent
   (*follows from lines 2, 3, and the rule of correct reasoning, modus ponens*).

5. Therefore, it's likely that God doesn't exist
   (*follows from lines 1, 4, and the rule of correct reasoning, modus tollens*).

The argument for God's nonexistence from the existence of unfair salvific opportunities is logically *valid*, meaning that *if* the premises (1, 2, and 3) are all true, then the conclusions (4 and 5) must be true as well. The question is whether the argument is *sound*, that is, besides being logically valid, whether all its premises are, in fact, true. As it turns out, premise 3 is the only arguable premise. In the following section I will defend the argument's soundness by defending the truth of its premise 3.

DEFENSE OF PREMISE 3 THAT IT'S LIKELY THAT GOD ACTS UNFAIRLY

"Unables" and "Ables" Groups of Humans

I start by dividing all humans who have ever lived into two groups: the unables and the ables. The unables are those who are or were unable to satisfy the salvific requirements of the correct doctrine of salvation *due to reasons beyond their control*. The ables are those who are or were not unables. The unables can be divided into the following four classes.

Class I unables are humans who die in utero due to miscarriages or induced abortions. As I pointed out in chapter 1, recent studies have shown that less than 30 percent of all human conceptions are born alive.[4] Assuming that personhood begins at conception, as most Christians hold, it follows that class I unables account for about 72 percent of all the human persons who have ever existed. If 72 percent is a reasonable estimate, then, of course 28 percent *do* survive to be born alive. Demographers estimate that about 117 billion human beings have lived in the three hundred thousand year history of our species,[5] If so, then simple math tells us that there have been

---

4. Kavanagh, "Most Human Embryos," para. 7. See also: Benagiano, "Fate of Fertilized Human Oocytes," 732–43; Berger, *Developing Person*, 94; Ord, "Scourge," 12–19; Vaquero, "Diagnostic Evaluation," 79–84; Zinaman, "Estimates of Human Fertility," 503–9.

5. Routley, "How Many Humans," para. 10.

about 418 billion conceptions (117 billion divided by .28 = 418 billion). Therefore, there have been some 301 billion human persons who were not born alive (418 – 117 = 301). Obviously, none of the 301 billion (class I unables) who died in utero could have satisfied the salvific requirements (whatever they might be) of the correct doctrine of salvation.

Class II unables are those who are born but who either die before reaching the age of moral accountability, perhaps something like seven or eight, or have cognitive handicaps sufficient to preclude them ever reaching the age of accountability. Clearly, none of the class II unables would be able to satisfy the salvific requirements of the correct doctrine of salvation.

Class III unables are those who died before the doctrine of salvation was revealed in history some two thousand years ago. Class III unables could not be expected to satisfy a doctrine that had not yet been revealed.

Class IV unables are those who lived in parts of the world where Christianity and the correct doctrine of salvation were unknown, or not a part of mainstream acceptance, or not correctly or fully explained. Examples would be an Australian aborigine living a thousand years ago or someone born in the heartland of some religious tradition other than Christianity, for example, in Mecca. A class IV unable might also be someone who is captured by some ideology that was not in accord with Christianity. An example of this possibility was given by noted Christian apologist, William Lane Craig, when he remarked, "Had I been born in Nazi Germany, I might have been an ardent member of the Hitler Jugend and maybe even participated in atrocities."[6] Notice that Craig is tacitly admitting that salvation for him and, by extension, for all persons, is in part an accident of birth. This is already strong supporting evidence for the soundness of the argument for God's nonexistence from the existence of unfair salvific Opportunities. Class IV unables cannot be expected to satisfy a doctrine that had not been promulgated in any locale anywhere near their habitat or had been rendered unpalatable by social circumstances or poor presentations.

Summary Tally of Unables

1. 418 billion = the number of total human conceptions[7]

---

6. Craig, "Middle Knowledge," para. 11.
7. See section entitled "Important Relevant Data about Prenatal Mortality" in chapter 1.

2. 117 billion = the number of humans born alive[8]

3. 301 billion = the number of human conceptions that were not born alive (418 billion − 117 billion) (these are the class I unables)

4. 55 billion = the number of humans who lived before a Christian salvific message was first given in history (these are the class III unables)[9]

5. 356 billion = (301 billion + 55 billion) = the number of human conceptions that were not born alive plus the number of humans who lived before the Christian salvific message was first given in history (these are the class I plus the class III unables)

6. 62 billion = (117 billion − 55 billion) the number of humans who lived after a Christian salvific message first appeared in history

7. 50 billion = the number of humans who lived after a Christian salvific message first appeared in history and who either never heard it at all, or never heard it properly, or were cognitively unable to comprehend it (these are the class IV plus class II unables)[10]

8. 12 billion = the number of humans who lived after a Christian salvific message first appeared in history and heard such a message. They comprise only about 2.9 percent (12 billion out of 418 billion) of all humans who ever lived

Actually, even among the twelve or so billion persons (again, only about 2.9 percent of all humans who ever lived) who *did* hear some sort of Christian salvific message, there has been no consensus about what the "correct" Christian salvific doctrine is (assuming, for the sake of argument,

---

8. Routley, "How Many Humans," para. 10.

9. Kaneda and Haub, "How Many People," table 1, line 4.

10. The fifty billion is 80 percent of the sixty-two billion who lived after the Christian message first appeared in history. I think this is a reasonable estimate because, until European countries began bringing Christianity to the Western Hemisphere, Sub-Saharan Africa, Australasia, and East and South Asia, starting after 1500, Christianity was largely unknown in those regions which comprised a significant majority of the estimated half a billion people on the planet in 1500. Even for a number of centuries after that Christianity was still largely unknown to a large majority of the peoples in those areas. Moreover, factored into the 80 percent are those who were born but who either died before reaching the age of moral accountability, perhaps something like seven or eight, or had cognitive handicaps sufficient to preclude their ever reaching the age of accountability. For most of human history it has been estimated that the mortality rate for children was around 50 percent. See Roser, "Mortality in the Past," 1.

that there is one). This means that, of the twelve billion or so Christians who have ever lived, some considerable percentage of them (at least half, if there was no consensus) must have not accepted the correct Christian salvific doctrine. This truncated group of Christians would comprise, at most, no more than 1.5 percent or some six billion persons. Moreover, if satisfying the correct Christian salvation doctrine is a necessary condition for salvation, a view that most professed Christians seem to have accepted,[11] then the number of Christians who could have possibly been saved would be around the six billion/1.5 percent figure of all persons who ever lived! One would not expect that a perfectly powerful, knowledgeable, and, especially, a perfectly good and all-loving deity, who wants all persons to be saved (1 Tim 2:3–4), would have actualized this world we inhabit. We will see the one he would have actualized in chapter 18.

Let me next describe two types of unfairness and then evaluate Christian objections to charges of salvific unfairness.

TWO TYPES OF UNFAIRNESS ASSOCIATED WITH THE CHRISTIAN DOCTRINE OF SALVATION

1. Unables vis-à-vis ables *inter*group unfairness
2. Ables vis-à-vis ables *intra*group unfairness

UNABLES VIS-À-VIS ABLES INTERGROUP UNFAIRNESS DESCRIBED AND EVALUATED

As I pointed out earlier in the chapter, recent research has shown that it's likely that about 97 percent of all humans who have ever lived, some 406 billion out of 418 billion, have been unables. As such, for reasons beyond their control, they would not have had an opportunity to learn about or satisfy the requirements of the correct doctrine of salvation. Consequently, according to many versions of Christianity, they would be unable to experience the *summum bonum* of salvation. (For example, see

---

11. If one were to hold that satisfying the "correct" Christian doctrine of salvation is *not* a necessary condition for salvation, then that would prompt two difficult questions. What *are* the necessary conditions for salvation and why wouldn't God simply have revealed them instead of permitting the proliferation of a cacophony of competing Christian salvific doctrines throughout the history of Christianity? I would say that there are no good answers to these questions.

the comment of Charles Hodge at the beginning of this chapter.) According to the definition of "unfairness" given at the beginning of this chapter, the lack of proper salvific opportunity for unables to experience the *summum bonum* vis-à-vis the opportunity that the ables have would clearly be unfair to the unables. If so, then the truth of premise 3 (*it's likely that God acts unfairly*) is established and, thereby, so is the soundness of the argument for God's nonexistence from the existence of unfair salvific opportunities. This unfairness prompts the following question. Why would God, the most perfect being possible who is all-loving, actualize this world in which 97 percent of his highest creations, whom he wanted to know him and love him, would be unable to do so for reasons beyond their control? I see no reasonable answer to that question.

Evaluation of Five Christian Retorts to the Conclusion That the Correct Doctrine of Salvation Involves Invidious Discrimination against Unables

First Christian Retort: Class III and IV Unables Have Sufficient Salvific Knowledge; The General Revelation Defense.

Some Christians, especially conservative evangelical Christians, as well as the apostle Paul (Rom 1:18–25), hold and have held that what I call class III and IV unables are, in fact, morally culpable for not satisfying the correct doctrine of salvation. They argue that these unables have, in fact, been made aware of God's existence, his moral law, their own sinfulness, and the need to seek forgiveness for their sins. This awareness comes from what Christians call *general revelation*. It's given to humans in two ways. The first is via humans' reflections on certain aspects of nature, such as its beauty, awesomeness, regularity, etc. The second way is via humans experiencing the inner witness of the Holy Spirit in their consciences. That being the case, class III and IV unables who don't acknowledge their sinfulness, don't seek God's forgiveness, don't turn away from idolatry, and don't work to satisfy God's moral law as a part of the correct doctrine of salvation are morally culpable for not doing so. Therefore, God's excluding these culpable class III and IV unables from experiencing the *summum bonum* of salvation is morally justified. In a recent article, Rhyne Putnam, associate vice president for academic affairs at Williams Baptist University, gives voice to this view, as follows.

Paul seems to anticipate the objection to God's judgment on Gentiles who never receive the law when he states, "The wrath of God is being revealed from heaven against all the godlessness and wickedness of people, who suppress the truth by their wickedness" (Rom. 1:18). God is right to judge even those pagans who have never received the law because what can be known about God was clearly impressed on them through *creation* and *conscience*. They still rejected God and turned to idols. . . . They had the . . . opportunity to return praise to the God who made them [emphasis added].[12]

Rebuttal to the Claim That Class III and IV Unables Have Sufficient Salvific Knowledge through Their Reflections on Nature

To begin with, this Christian retort would not apply to the largest class of unables, class I unables (those who die in utero), comprising some 301 billion "persons." They wouldn't be able to reflect on anything, let alone come to the conclusion that God exists. So, already here Paul's claim that *all* humans have received the necessary salvific knowledge from general revelation is disconfirmed. Also, due to the cognitive limitations of class II unables, their coming to reflective beliefs about salvific issues would not be possible for most, if not all, of them. This is more disconfirmation of Paul's claims.

With respect to class III and IV unables, there are a number of reasons to doubt the claims that Paul makes with respect to general revelation through reflections on nature.

First, the main problem is that those making those claims have never provided adequate evidence for them. Clearly, Paul was aware of only a very small part of the inhabited world of his time. Even in the part that he was familiar with no sufficient historical or anthropological evidence for any general revelation through nature has ever been found.

Some Christians might invoke the claim of biblical inerrancy to defend Paul's claims. That is, they might argue that since Paul, as God's primary early Christian spokesman, claimed that general revelation through nature was factual, then general revelation through nature must be factual because the Bible cannot contain any errors. One major flaw in

---

12. Putnam, "Will My Lost Neighbor," para. 15.

this reasoning is that the claim of Biblical inerrancy is itself fraught with controversy, even among some Christians.

Second, we know through oral and written testimonies that many class III and IV unables apparently saw too much to believe too much that nature was the benign product of a benevolent, human-loving creator. On the contrary, nature seemed to many class III and IV unables to be less like what Paul claimed about it and more like something "red in tooth and claw" that produces a human existence that for many is "poor, nasty, brutish, and short."[13]

My thought is that, contrary to what Paul claimed, it wasn't some sort of culpable spiritual hardness of heart that resulted in class III and IV unables rejecting God's putative messaging to them through nature. What seems much more likely is that they never really concerned themselves with such abstract thoughts in any meaningful or sustained way. They were, understandably I would think, much more concerned with issues of survival and flourishment.

In sum, there's simply no adequate evidence that any significant number of class III or IV unables ever concluded on the basis of their experience with nature that there existed a human-loving supernatural creator who is also the source of proper moral behavior and to whom they should pledge exclusive worship.

Third, we would expect that God would have wanted, and been able, to communicate important facts about the proper salvation requirements to class III and IV unables in a more direct and convincing manner than through a general revelation through nature that, by the way, God would have known would not be very effective. In fact, Christians believe that there *is* a more effective form of divine communication, namely, what is called *special revelation*, comprising theophanies (divine appearances), dreams, visions, heavenly messengers etc. Noted Christian apologist William Lane Craig admitted as much when he stated that "those who find salvation through General Revelation, if any, are relatively rare, the Gospel [special revelation] is a much more powerful revelation of God's truth that attracts even those who reject General Revelation."[14] God would certainly have been capable of using special revelation to make all humans directly aware of extremely important Christian truths that he wanted them to know, including,

---

13. Tennyson, *Complete Poetical Works of Tennyson*, 162; Hobbes, "Nasty, Brutish, and Short."

14. Craig, "Fate of Those," para. 10.

truths about the correct doctrine of salvation. Yet, specific claims of special revelation being given to class III and IV unables have been rare and factually questionable. Furthermore, if special revelation *were* to occur to only a few class III and IV unables, that itself could be considered a form of unfair salvific assistance to those very select few.

Fourth, if the preaching of Paul et al. about general revelation through nature were true, then it would follow that the one billion or so professed atheists and agnostics[15] in the world today are all really lying or deluded about their nonbelief. However, there's no sufficient evidence that that's true and much sufficient evidence that it's not true.

Rebuttal to the Claim That Unables Have Sufficient Salvific Knowledge through Their Reflections on the Content of Their Consciences Influenced by the Holy Spirit

As mentioned for general revelation through nature, it's hard to see how any class I or II unables could reasonably be said to have come to any knowledge of Christianity and proper morality through the inner witness of the Holy Spirit, given the nonexistent or deficient cognitive statuses of the class I and II unables.

Furthermore, as was also the case with general revelation via reflections on nature, there's no sufficient evidence that any class III or IV unables had any awareness of the truth of Christianity or a divinely sourced morality stemming from the workings of a Holy Spirit somehow through their consciences.[16] If such truths were passed on to any class III or IV unables, it would be difficult to explain why there isn't greater agreement today among Christians on what constitutes the "correct" understanding of the contours of Christianity.

Nevertheless, Paul's claim that class III and IV unables know the contours of Christianity and God's moral rules by means of their awareness of, and reflection on, the workings of the Holy Spirit on their consciences has been echoed by many Christian commentators today, such as, once again, the noted Christian apologist, William Lane Craig. It's

---

15. Those who neither believe nor disbelieve that God exists because they believe there is insufficient evidence to say otherwise.

16. I would also argue that there's insufficient evidence even for the existence of a Holy Spirit. However, I won't pursue that point here.

worth reiterating here Craig's views in this regard that I first set out in this book's introduction.

> Therefore, when a person refuses to come to Christ, it is never just because of lack of evidence or because of intellectual difficulties: at root, he refuses to come because he willingly ignores and rejects the drawing of God's Spirit on his heart. No one in the final analysis really fails to become a Christian because of lack of arguments; he fails to become a Christian because he loves darkness rather than light and wants nothing to do with God. But anyone who responds to the drawing of God's Spirit with an open mind and an open heart can know with assurance that Christianity is true, because God's Spirit will convict him that it is.[17]

The following hypothetical example illustrates the problem associated with putting forth such extravagant claims about the alleged workings of the Holy Spirit on class III and IV unables.

> A man is born in 580 BCE in China into an average rural family. He grows to help around the farm and play happily with his brothers and sisters. He is good-natured and interested in the things around him. He gains a reputation for honesty, bravery, curiosity, and gentleness. He loves to sit during quiet moments and contemplate nature and teaches himself simple artwork for pleasure. When he is older he dutifully marries a bride who is chosen for him according to local tradition and is a thoughtful and considerate husband, for which his wife grows to love and respect him. Their marriage prospers. Although never more than an ordinary farmer, he is a hard worker and reliable neighbor, gladly helping the needy in his community, occasionally being sought out for the wisdom and fairness of his judgement. He is a kind and patient father, and his children admire him. He struggles through many difficulties and manages to remain at peace with himself and others. In his old age he pursues his artwork, creating delicate paintings and teaching his grandchildren both the skills he taught himself and the appreciation of beauty that inspired them. He dies at a very old age content with his life, surrounded by the people he loved, counted by those who knew him as a good, loving, and virtuous man. This hypothetical man had no religion per se—no belief in any god, let alone the Christian God, no mystical experiences, no encounters with the divine, no personal relationship with Jesus, no enlightening raptures and, in fact, very little concern with spiritual matters. Although he

---

17. Craig, *Reasonable Faith*, 47

frequently discussed and contemplated such issues, he eventually came to the conclusion that they were not likely to be true and not likely to be important, and never found good reason to change his mind about that. He would have classified himself as an atheist or metaphysical naturalist, had he been familiar with the terms.[18]

Although the above example is hypothetical, I surmise that throughout history there have been countless relevantly similar morally benign lives of class III and IV unables unconnected to any purported workings of a Christian Holy Spirit. Such lives present a serious challenge to the claims of Paul, Craig, and other likeminded Christians that class III and IV unables are, in fact, morally blameworthy for not embracing Christianish notions; and that God is thereby morally justified in withholding the *summum bonum* of eternal salvation from them, including even possibly sending them to eternal perdition.

Some Christians might cite the near universal acceptance throughout history of what has been called the "common moral decencies" as proof that the Holy Spirit has acted on the consciences of at least some class III and IV unables. These "decencies" include such precepts as don't steal, cheat, lie, harm, kill, etc. that have been staples in virtually all societies. However, such precepts were frequently relativized by context, culture, and contingencies, and were rarely, if ever, held to apply much outside an inner group such as family, clan, tribe, etc. It's likely that such moral precepts eventually attained a near universal acceptance in large part, not because they were divinely sourced, but because, through a form of moral natural selection, groups that successfully applied them tended to flourish more than those that did not as successfully do so.

Second Christian Retort to the Claim of Invidious Discrimination against the Unables Vis-à-Vis the Ables: The Salvation-for-All-Unables Defense.

This retort, which is probably the most common pushback to the charge of unfairness towards unables, construes God as graciously gifting all unables with the *summum bonum* of salvation. The reason for this is that "ought" implies "can." That is, since, for reasons over which they have no control, unables cannot identify and satisfy the correct doctrine of

---

18. sastra@excel.net, post on "Return of the Hypothetical Chinaman," godexist (message board), n.d.

salvation, they, therefore, cannot be said to have *ought* to have done so. Accordingly, God, being omnibenevolent, does not deprive unables of the *summum bonum* of salvation, as that would represent invidious discrimination by him against the unables vis-à-vis the ables. In this way, the charge of divine unfairness toward unables would be vacated.

Rebuttal to the Salvation-for-All-Unables Defense

If God were to guarantee salvation to all unables, the problem of the unfairness of salvific opportunity would not disappear. It would simply be shifted from unfairness toward the unables to unfairness toward the ables. This would be so because all the unables would now be *guaranteed* to experience the *summum bonum* of salvation, while none of the ables would have such a guarantee. In order for the ables to be saved they would first have to discern the correct version of the doctrine of salvation, no easy task, given the large number of options on offer. Then they would have to struggle to satisfy its salvific requirements, again, no easy task. In fact, the Gospels say that many ables will end up not satisfying the requirements of the correct doctrine of salvation (See Mark 4:11–13; Matt 7:13–14; and Luke 13:23–24). If so, then, to reiterate, under this Christian defense there would still be significant divine invidious discrimination, only now it would be directed toward the ables rather than the unables.

Third Christian Retort to the Claim of Divine Invidious Discrimination against the Unables Vis-à-Vis the Ables: The Salvific Universalism Defense

To counteract the charge of divine unfairness toward the ables just described, Christians could claim that the correct doctrine of salvation involves salvific universalism, which specifies that all humans, unables and ables alike, will be saved eventually. In that case, there would be no invidious salvific discrimination by God against either unables or ables.

Rebuttal to the Salvific Universalism Defense

First, universalism is very much a minority view among Christians. There is much scriptural attestation and revered traditional Christian thinking that runs counter to it. In fact, the Catholic Church condemned it at the regional council of Orange in 543. Biblical scholar Richard Bauckham, professor of New Testament studies at the University of St. Andrews, has written,

> Until the nineteenth century almost all Christian theologians taught the reality of eternal torment in hell. Here and there, outside the theological mainstream, were some who believed that the wicked would be finally annihilated. . . . Even fewer were the advocates of universal salvation.[19]

Second, if Christians were to adopt salvific universalism, they would have to admit that, with respect to one of Christianity's most venerable doctrines, namely, the correct doctrine of salvation, Christians had it very wrong for two thousand years. That would constitute an admission of a serious deficiency for Christianity, given that if God existed and Christianity is true, it would be expected that he would not let error of such magnitude for such an important doctrine persist for such a long period of time.

Fourth Christian Retort to the Claim of Divine Invidious Discrimination against the Unables vis-à-vis the Ables: The Middle Knowledge Defense

Middle knowledge is a concept that holds that God has omniscient awareness of what would happen if certain circumstances were to occur, even if they, in actuality, never do occur. God's awareness includes knowledge of the free, uncoerced choices of humans in those circumstances. So, for example, using his middle knowledge, God would know whether, say, Joan would take a job as supervisor at her company if it were offered to her under such and such circumstances, even if it were never *actually* offered to her. More pertinently, some Christians maintain that God could use his middle knowledge to determine whether a particular unable person, say U1, would freely accept and satisfy the salvific requirements of the correct doctrine of salvation in some set of circumstances which philosophers typically call a "possible world,"[20] if those requirements would have been properly explained and offered to U1 in that world. If, by using his middle knowledge, God knows that that would be the case, then he could justifiably

---

19. Bauckham, "Universalism," 47.

20. A possible world is a complete and consistent way the world is or could have been. The actual world we live in is one of the countless possible worlds.

gift U1 with the *summum bonum* of salvation in *this* world. On the other hand, if God knows through his middle knowledge that, under certain circumstances, another unable, U2, would freely reject the salvific requirements of the correct doctrine of salvation in some possible world, then God would be justified in withholding the *summum bonum* from U2 in *this* world. In this way, God cannot be said to have treated unables unfairly. In effect, they reaped what they would have freely sown, salvation from acceptance of the correct doctrine of salvation in some possible world, and non-salvation from rejection of it in some possible world.

Rebuttal to the Middle Knowledge Defense of God's Salvific Treatment of Unables

First, there's a robust dispute among Christians about whether God even *has* middle knowledge,[21] based in part on the fact that it has questionable scriptural attestation.

Second, some Christians have objected to the middle knowledge defense because it specifies that unables are saved, not on the basis of what they actually consciously chose and did, but on what they have never chosen or done, nor will ever choose or do. Christian theologian James Beilby expresses this view with the following comparison.

> Suppose I am offered the congressional Medal of Honor. When I ask how I achieved this honor (since I have never served in the military), I am told that God knows that if I would have served in the military and been placed in a particular difficult situation, I would have acted in a way to warrant receiving the Medal of Honor. Even if the idea that God has knowledge of counterfactual situations makes perfect sense to me, would I feel like I earned the medal? Would I wear it proudly? I think the answer is no. For similar reasons, it is far better that a person's final destination be decided by a decision that they consciously and explicitly make, not by decisions that they would have made.[22]

---

21. For critiques of middle knowledge, see: Adams, "Middle Knowledge," 109–17; Kenny, *God of the Philosophers*, 61–71; Hacker, "Refutation of Middle Knowledge," 545–57, expanded in Hacker, *God, Time, and Knowledge*; and Hunt, "Middle Knowledge," 1–24.

22. Beilby, *Postmortem Opportunity*, 94.

Christian apologist William Lane Craig concurs with Beilby. In answer to a question about whether God would use his middle knowledge to determine the salvific fate of people who die as infants. Craig says the following. (We saw part of this comment earlier in this chapter.)

> It would be immoral to judge a person, not for things he has done, but for things that he would have done under different circumstances. Had I been born in Nazi Germany, I might have been an ardent member of the Hitler Jugend and maybe even participated in atrocities. Under other circumstances, I might have been a thief or a terrorist. Am I therefore morally culpable for such acts? Well, of course not, for I never committed them! . . . So God will judge people on the basis of what they actually do . . . . Matt 11:20–24.[23]

Christians, such as Beilby and Craig, who don't accept the middle knowledge defense, hold that Scripture makes it clear that in order to be saved, humans must make a free, conscious, knowledgeable, and personal decision to accept the strictures of the correct doctrine of salvation. As Christian theologian Rhyne Putnam put it, "Most within our ranks embrace exclusivism, claiming that those who die without placing conscious, personal faith in Christ face eternal separation from God in hell."[24] Critics maintain that the Middle Knowledge Defense is flawed because it allows salvation even though the saved person never makes a free, conscious, knowledgeable, and actual affirmation of a personal faith in Christ.

Third, if one holds that God has middle knowledge, then there is a confounding difficulty surrounding Christianity's very important doctrine of the original sin of Adam and Eve. Presumably, through middle knowledge God would have known before actualizing this world containing Adam and Eve that they would commit the Original Sin and thereby bring about untold amounts of pain, suffering, and death to their more than four hundred billion descendants and to untold numbers of sentient animals. God would also know that their sin would produce a debilitating legacy of hundreds of billions of deformed, sin-inclined human natures estranged from him.[25] Given those terrible outcomes, it is not impertinent to ask why God would have actualized our world when he could have easily used his middle knowledge to actualize a better one instead. Call it World*. In World* the primal couple would not commit an original sin.

23. Craig, "Middle Knowledge," para. 11.
24. Putnam, "Will My Lost Neighbor," para. 2.
25. For more on problems with the doctrine of original sin, see chapter 1 of this book.

Presumably, World* would not be plagued with the many terrible horrendous shortcomings which plague this world. Moreover, World* would be much more in concert with God's omnibenevolent nature as a maximally loving Father to his human children.[26]

Fourth, given that there is a myriad of possible worlds, it's very likely that all, or at least most, unables would accept the correct doctrine of salvation in some possible worlds and reject it in others. William Lane Craig responded as follows to a questioner who asked about the suitability of the Middle Knowledge Defense for what I call class I and II unables.

> The difficulty with your solution (the Middle Knowledge Defense) becomes especially evident when you reflect that a person who died in infancy would have done different things under different circumstances. . . . Under some circumstances those who died in infancy might have grown up to become wonderful Christians; under other circumstances, they might have joined the Internet Infidels. So how could God [justly] judge them for the different things they would have done under various circumstances?[27]

Craig's answer is that God couldn't. If so, then the Middle Knowledge Defense crumbles with respect to justifying the salvific fate of unables, who, recall, comprise about 97 percent of all the human persons who have ever been conceived in this world.

Fifth Christian Retort to the Claim of Invidious Discrimination Against the Unables Vis-à-Vis the Ables: All Unables Are Lost to Hell Because of Their "Transworld Damnation"

Dr. William Lane Craig holds that "if there were anyone who would have responded to the gospel, if he had heard it, then God in his love would have brought the gospel to such a person."[28] In other words, Craig is saying that those who do not hear the gospel in this world, those I call unables, suffer from what Craig calls "transworld damnation." That is, there is no possible world in which the unables would have ever accepted the gospel if it had been offered to them. Moreover, Craig believes that God has providentially ordered the world so that "anybody who never hears the gospel [namely,

26. For more on middle knowledge and original sin see chapter 1 section entitled "Doctrine of Original Sin's Knowledge Problem."

27. Craig, "Middle Knowledge," para. 11.

28. Craig, "No Other Name," 185.

the unables] and is lost would have rejected the gospel and would have been lost even if he had heard it."[29] In effect, all the unables suffer from this transworld damnation thing. If so, then God is not acting unfairly in consigning all unables to hell. It's what the unables deserve for their transworld damnation that they brought on themselves by their free choices they would make in all other possible worlds they could live in.

Rebuttal to the Claim That All Unables Are Lost to Hell Because of Their "Transworld Damnation"

Given the enormous number of possible worlds (millions? Or more?) that any unable could exist in, the likelihood of there being even one unable who would be transworld damned would seem to be vanishingly small. Assume, for the sake of argument, that there are only fifty possible worlds (rather than the much more likely number of millions or more) that each of the 406 billion unables in this world could exist in where they have the choice of accepting the gospel presented to them or rejecting it. This would mean that there would be 406 billion times fifty, or 20.3 trillion (20,300,000,000,000) choices made by the 406 billion unables in those fifty possible worlds. According to Craig's view, every one of those 20.3 trillion choices would be to reject the gospel. So, the final tally would be 20.3 trillion no-to-the-gospel choices and *zero* yes-to-the-gospel choices. That seems wildly improbable, to say the least. Of course, that implausible scenario would be even more implausible if there were more than just fifty possible worlds, like, for example, millions of possible worlds that the 406 billion unables could exist in, as almost certainly there would be.

Sixth Christian Retort to the Claim of Invidious Discrimination against the Unables Vis-à-Vis the Ables: The Postmortem Opportunity Defense

Christian theologian James Beilby has produced the most recent articulation and defense of what has been termed "postmortem opportunity."[30] According to the latter, at some point after death, perhaps at the last judgment, unables will come into the presence of God and be given the

---

29. Craig, "Politically Incorrect Salvation," 93.
30. Beilby, *Postmortem Opportunity*.

opportunity they didn't have while alive on earth, namely, to come to know the correct doctrine of salvation and then freely and explicitly decide whether or not to satisfy its requirements.[31] According to postmortem opportunity, everyone, the unables postmortem and the ables premortem, would have the opportunity to explicitly and freely embrace or not the requirements of the correct doctrine of salvation. Postmortem opportunity defense advocates contend that it would eliminate the salvific unfairness toward unables without discriminating against the ables and without invoking an ad hoc salvific universalism.

Rebuttal to the Postmortem Opportunity Defense of God's Actions toward Unables

First, even those who promulgate it acknowledge that it's very much a minority view among Christians. For example, Beilby himself has written:

> The theory of Postmortem Opportunity is currently *not* the dominant answer to the question of the destiny of the unevangelized. In fact, it has largely fallen off the church's radar for much of the last 1500 years. And the primary factor keeping Postmortem Opportunity off the radar screen for most contemporary Christians is the belief that there are decisive reasons to believe that a Postmortem Opportunity is impossible—namely that it runs contrary to scripture [emphasis in the original].[32]

Second, as with salvific universalism, if Christians were to affirm the correctness of the postmortem opportunity defense, they would have to admit that a large majority of them did not recognize that postmortem opportunity is a crucial element in the correct doctrine of salvation for more than two thousand years. They would also find it very difficult to explain why God would have permitted such an omission to persist for that long stretch of time concerning one of his most important doctrines. Such an admission would also prompt this question: What other Christian doctrines today are we mistaken about?

---

31. There is a related view which might be called at-the-moment-of-death opportunity that is similar to postmortem opportunity but which occurs at the moment of death, not postmortem. The problems for postmortem opportunity to be described presently would apply, *mutatis mutandum*, to at-the-moment-of-death opportunity.

32. Beilby, *Postmortem Opportunity*, 107.

Third, as part of the implementation of postmortem opportunity, unables would get a salvific advantage over ables by having incontrovertible postmortem evidence that there is a correct doctrine of salvation and what it is before they would choose whether to accept it or not. Most ables would not get that during their earthly existence. As per the definition of unfairness, that would represent unfairness directed toward ables.

Fourth, it's difficult to imagine that any unable person in postmortem opportunity would reject the offered correct doctrine of salvation postmortem. Such a rejection would amount to a highly implausible situation in which a fully informed, impartial, sane person opts in person to God to eternally experience the highest form of unhappiness and very possibly torment involving never-ending pain and suffering, rather than to opt for the eternal, maximal goodness associated with the *summum bonum* of heavenly salvation. If so, then postmortem opportunity would satisfy the definition of unfairness toward ables by giving unables a much easier path to the *summum bonum* compared to what ables would have.

Fifth, in postmortem opportunity any unable would only have to make a simple onetime postmortem acceptance of the correct offer of salvation. Presumably, immediately after that acceptance, the unable in question would begin experiencing the *summum bonum* straight away. That would be in sharp contrast to the situations of the ables, all of whom, assuming that they were able to identify and accept the correct doctrine of salvation, would still have to scrupulously live up to its requirements throughout the course of an adult lifetime, during which time, according to many versions of Christianity, they could apostatize (give up the faith), and many have, and thereby lose the *summum bonum* of salvation. This contrasts sharply with the situation obtaining for postmortem unables and would represent an unfair discrimination against ables.

Section Summary

The assessment of unable vis-à-vis able unfairness in the foregoing section supports the truth of premise 3 (*it's likely that God acts unfairly*) and, thereby, the soundness of the argument for God's nonexistence from the existence of unfair salvific opportunities.

ABLES INTRAGROUP UNFAIRNESS EVALUATED

So far, in defending premise 3 (*it is likely that God acts unfairly*) of the argument from unfair salvific opportunities, I have demonstrated that there would be unavoidable *inter*group invidious discrimination against either unables or ables, depending on how the correct doctrine of salvation is understood. In this section I'll explain and evaluate a second type of serious unfairness with respect to the correct doctrine of salvation, namely, ables *intra*group unfairness.

As I mentioned earlier, when it comes to the correct doctrine of salvation, it's not enough to simply acknowledge its correctness, one must summon up and sustain the pious righteousness to actually satisfy its requirements over a potentially long period of a morally accountable life. This can be a formidable challenge. The unfairness problem here is that many ables, call them "disadvantaged ables," face significant obstacles relative to other ables, call them "non-disadvantaged ables," in attempting to satisfy the requirements of the correct doctrine of salvation over the course of their morally accountable lives. Most of the obstacles—of a social, historical, geographical, economic, cultural, or psychological nature—are beyond the control of the disadvantaged ables, thereby rendering the disadvantaged ables nonculpable for being disadvantaged. English philosopher Jonathan M. S. Pearce elaborated the following list of potential disadvantage-making elements affecting those I call disadvantaged ables.[33]

1. Their genetic inheritance.
2. Their life in the womb, shaping their genetic self.
3. Their time and place at birth.
4. Their parents, relatives, race, and gender; their nurture and experiences in infancy and childhood.
5. Their mutations in their brain and body throughout life; and other purely random events.
6. Their natural physical stature, looks, smile, and voice; intelligence; sexual drive and proclivities; personality and wit; and natural ability in sports, music, and dance.
7. Their religious training; economic circumstances; cultural influences; political and civil rights; the prevailing customs of their times.

33. Pearce, *30 Arguments*, 165–6.

8. The blizzard of experiences throughout life, not chosen by them but which happened to them.

More specifically, contrast the following situations for two ables: A1 and A2. A1 is correct doctrine of salvation advantaged and A2 is correct doctrine of salvation disadvantaged. A1 is raised in a stable, flourishing family that loves and nurtures him. Moreover, his family assists and encourages him to understand, appreciate, and satisfy the correct doctrine of salvation requirements. In contrast, A2 is raised in a dysfunctional family in which she is abused, neglected, and not raised to understand, appreciate, or satisfy the correct doctrine of salvation. All other things being equal, the likelihood that A1 will ultimately attain the *summum bonum* by satisfying the salvific requirements of the correct doctrine of salvation would be considerably greater in comparison with A2's chances. The major cause of the different salvific outcomes for A1 and A2 would be sheer luck having to do with accidents of birth, genetics, fortune, environment, or other contingent circumstances as articulated above in Jonathan M. S. Pearce's list. Yet, no version of the doctrine of salvation makes any allowance for such factors. In fact, given that God is the creator and sustainer of those factors, it would follow that he would be ultimately responsible for the fact that far fewer disadvantaged ables, than non-disadvantaged ables, would succeed in ultimately experiencing the *summum bonum* of salvation. Apropos the definition of unfairness, that would amount to invidious discrimination against the disadvantaged ables vis-à-vis the non-disadvantaged ables. Such discrimination would constitute additional substantive evidence for the truth of premise 3 (*it's likely that God acts unfairly*) and, thereby, for the soundness of the argument from unfair salvific opportunity.

EVALUATION OF THE SKEPTICAL THEISM CHALLENGE TO PREMISE 3 OF THE ARGUMENT FOR GOD'S EXISTENCE FROM THE EXISTENCE OF UNFAIR SALVIFIC OPPORTUNITIES

At the close of his review of James Beilby's book *Postmortem Opportunity* in the magazine *Christianity Today*, Rhyne Putnam voices what some Christians would consider to be the decisive defense against the charge that God acts unfairly in salvific matters, namely, skeptical theism. Putnam writes,

> As to resolving the tension created by the destiny of the unevangelized—whether God is right or good in condemning those who never heard the gospel—I fall back on the words of my dad: "We can always count on God to do the right thing, no matter what." We take comfort in knowing God's righteousness surpasses our ignorance.[34]

As we have seen earlier in this book, skeptical theists are theists (believers in an all-powerful, all-knowing, all-good personal, supernatural, creator deity) who maintain that, due to the vast knowledge gap between us and God, we should be skeptical about our ability to know what God's reasons are for at least some of the things he does or does not do. More pertinently, given the topic at hand, skeptical theists emphasize that we should be skeptical about our ability to know what God's reasons are for treating people discriminatively with respect to salvific opportunities. Skeptical theists emphasize that the epistemic (knowledge) gap between us and God is so vast that it could prevent us from seeing how God's discriminatory salvific treatment of humans could be morally justified on the basis that, although we can't see how, the discriminatory salvific treatment brings about a greater good than the harm caused by it. Skeptical theists would emphasize that our inability to specify what that greater good could be would not underwrite the conclusion that such a good doesn't exist. If so, then the truth of premise 3 (*it's likely that God acts unfairly*) and the soundness of the argument for God's nonexistence from the existence of unfair salvific opportunities would be undermined.

Response to the Skeptical Theism Challenge to Premise 3 of the Argument for God's Nonexistence from the Existence of Unfair Salvific Opportunities.

I already argued above that unables, numbering some 406 billion, around 97 percent of all humans who ever lived, would be unfairly denied access to salvific opportunities through no fault of their own. Now we must add a certain nontrivial number of disadvantaged ables, who would be unfairly denied access to salvific opportunities through no fault of their own, to that 406 billion number. Fortunately, the 406 billion number of unables is already so large that we needn't precisely estimate how much that number would be augmented by the addition of the numbers of disadvantaged

---

34. Putnam, "Will My Lost Neighbor," para. 18.

abels. We can say, with some confidence, that the augmentation, refer to it as 406+ billion, would be more than trivial.

In sum, we can safely say that having 406+ billion human persons denied the *summum bonum* of eternal salvation would constitute an enormous loss of the highest good, such that it is difficult to imagine how losing that amount of *summum bonum* due to salvific unfairness could conceivably be compensated for, offset, or justified in way, as the skeptical theism challenge claims.

Thus, I judge that the skeptical theism challenge to the truth of premise 3 (*it's likely that God acts unfairly*) and, thereby, to the soundness of the argument for God's nonexistence from the existence of unfair salvific opportunities is unsuccessful.

SUMMARY AND CONCLUSION

The challenge that the argument for God's nonexistence from the existence of unfair salvific opportunities brings to Christianity is that, if God exists and loves humans maximally, then we shouldn't expect to see the kinds and amounts of salvific unfairness that we see in the world. I strove to show that the existence of such unfairness is demonstrable and unavoidable, and that, therefore, there is sufficient reason to hold that premise 3 (*it's likely that God acts unfairly*) of the argument for God's nonexistence from the existence of unfair salvific opportunities is true and that, therefore, the argument is sound. If so, then its conclusion that very likely God does not exist is upheld.

Chapter 16: Christian God Doesn't Exist Because If He Did, He'd Be an Absentee Father

Preview

I present a somewhat novel version of the atheistic argument from divine hiddenness. I say "somewhat novel" in that the argument in this chapter focuses on an interesting and important instance of divine hiddenness that I haven't seen highlighted by atheists heretofore. In this argument, the what-we-wouldn't-have-expected-in-our-experience-of-the-world-if-God-existed is that for more than 296,000 years of our species's existence, God's existence, laws, and relationship with humans were unknown to all the humans living during that time. I refer to this absence as the divine temporal gap, or just the gap. I contend, in what I call the "argument for God's nonexistence from the existence of a divine temporal gap," that the existence of the gap constitutes convincing evidence for the nonexistence of God.

ARGUMENT FOR GOD'S NONEXISTENCE FROM THE EXISTENCE OF A DIVINE TEMPORAL GAP

The formal layout for the argument for God's nonexistence from the existence of a divine temporal gap is as follows. Note that the justification for each line in the argument follows the line and is in italics within parentheses.

IF HE DID, HE'D BE AN ABSENTEE FATHER

1. If God exists, then he's omnibenevolent.
   (*This is based on the definition of "God."*)

2. If God absented himself (the gap) from scores of millions of humans during the whole of their lives, then God harmed them.
   (*God's absence would deprive his human children of having a loving relationship with him, their Father. In effect, God would have been an absentee Father.*)

3. God did absent himself from scores of millions of humans during the whole of their lives.
   (*See section below in this chapter entitled, "The Gap."*)

4. Therefore, God harmed scores of millions of humans.
   (*Follows from 2 and 3 plus the rule of correct reasoning called* modus ponens.)

5. If God harmed scores of millions of humans, then he is not omnibenevolent. (*Follows* from *the definitions of "harm" and "omnibenevolent."*)

6. Therefore, God is not omnibenevolent.
   (*Follows from lines 4 and 5 by the rule of correct reasoning called* modus ponens.)

7. Therefore, God does not exist. (*Follows from lines 1 and 6 plus the rule of correct reasoning called* modus tollens.)

The argument for God's nonexistence from the existence of a divine temporal gap is logically *valid*, meaning that, if the premises (1, 2, 3 and 5) are all true, then, by the laws of logic, conclusions (4, 6, and 7) must be true as well. The important question is whether the argument for the nonexistence of God from the existence of a divine temporal gap is *sound*. That is, besides being logically valid, are all its premises, in fact, true? Premises 1, 2, and 5 are all true by noncontroversial definitions of their constituent terms. Premise 3 is the controversial premise that needs to be argued for. To that task I now turn.

PART THREE: CHRISTIANITY AND ATHEISM

DEFENSE OF THE SOUNDNESS OF THE ARGUMENT FOR GOD'S NONEXISTENCE FROM THE EXISTENCE OF A DIVINE TEMPORAL GAP

The Gap

Some Christians are young Earth creationists (YECs) and others are old Earth creationists (OECs). The YECs, most often biblical fundamentalists or literalists, believe that the age of the universe and the Earth is less than ten thousand years. The OECs accept the standard cosmological view that the universe is about 13.8 billion years old and the Earth some 4.5 billion years old. In defending the argument for the nonexistence of God from the existence of a divine temporal gap, I'm going to concentrate on Christian old Earth creationism since young Earth creationism is made extremely implausible by an overwhelming scientific consensus based on a prodigious amount of evidence in favor of the 13.8/4.5-billion-year ages of the universe/Earth.

The most recent trustworthy estimate of when our species, *Homo sapiens*, emerged is that it was at least three hundred thousand years ago.[1] Most Christians believe that there was a primal human pair (Adam and Eve) from whom all humans who have ever been conceived are descended. Christian OECs are rather vague on the details, but most hold that God selected the primal pair out of a population of already existing hominins[2] and ensouled them in some manner. OEC Christians further maintain that the primal pair failed a test of obedience given to them by God. Most Christians call this failure the original sin which resulted in what is called "the fall (from God's grace)." Because of the original sin/fall, the primal pair and all their descendants have been severely punished. For the purpose of defending the argument for the nonexistence of God from the existence of a divine temporal gap, I don't need to critique the cogency of the doctrine of original sin/fall here. For that, see chapter 1 of this volume. My concern here is with the timeline associated with the existence of Adam and Eve in light of the three hundred thousand year history of *Homo sapiens*. More specifically, the heart of my argument is that, assuming, as most OECs do, that Gen 1–11 is what Christian apologist William Lane Craig calls "mytho-history"[3] and

---

1. See Handwerk, "Evolutionary Timeline of Homo Sapiens."

2. "Hominin" is a term given to humans and all of our extinct bipedal ancestors–those who walked upright on two feet.

3. Craig, *In Quest*, 132. Craig holds that mytho-history is not meant to be a

not a blow-by-blow factual history, God doesn't reveal his existence, nature, or laws to humans nor does he develop any relationship with them until, at best, the time of the patriarch, Abraham, around 2,000 BCE.[4]

For the sake of argument, I'll assume that there really was an Abraham living at that time, whom the Old Testament references. If so, then that means that God has interacted with humans for only the last four thousand years or so, the time from Abraham to the present, out of the three hundred thousand years of humans' existence. In other words, God has been AWOL from his human children for more than 98 percent of the time that our species has existed. It has been estimated that more than ten billion humans lived during that period,[5] knowing nothing about God. I call that 296,000-year period the gap (from Adam to Abraham). Those 296,000 years comprise almost twelve thousand generations[6] of humans who knew virtually nothing about God. Even at the time of Abraham, if one assumes that God exists and revealed himself, it was only to a very small percentage of humans living in the Near East of Western Asia. In fact, even some 3,400 years later, say, fourteen hundred CE, no humans in the entire western hemisphere, Australia, Indonesia, or the Pacific Islands knew anything about God, nor did the vast majority of humans in East Asia and sub-Saharan Africa.

The existence of the gap is strange and unexpected, especially if, as Christians maintain, we are indeed the crowning glory of God's creation and he is our loving Father who wants us to reciprocate his love. You can't reciprocate someone's love if you have no idea that that someone exists. This prompts the question of why God would have been AWOL from the human race for nearly twelve thousand generations. Some possible answers that Christians might offer include the following.

---

blow-by-blow recitation of events that actually occurred, but rather to serve other informational purposes.

4. Parrot, "Abraham."
5. Kaneda and Haub, "How Many People," table 1, line 2.
6. More specifically, given the numbers used above, 11,780 generations over the course of two hundred ninety-six thousand years, assuming twenty-five years per generation.

Young Earth Defense of the Gap

Christians could try to explain the gap by adopting a young Earth timeline, that is, they could hold that the Earth (and the whole universe) is only six thousand to ten thousand years old.

Response

As I noted above, young Earth creationism brings Christianity into serious conflict with the overwhelming scientific consensus about the age of the universe (13.8 billion years), Earth (4.5 billion years), and of our species (at least three hundred thousand years).[7]

Skeptical Theism Defense of the Gap

A skeptical theist could argue that, because of the vast knowledge difference between God and humans, we are unable to figure out what God's morally sufficient reasons are for the gap. However, that inability would not necessarily show that God had no morally sufficient reasons for the gap.

Response

The problem with the skeptical theism defense is that the gap would have resulted in more than ten billion humans[8] living during the gap period being deprived of the opportunity to experience the *summum bonum* (greatest good) of eternal heavenly salvation. The reason being that during the gap period humans would not have known that God existed, that they needed to be reconciled with him, and what is required of them in order that they be so reconciled. If the skeptical theism defense were true, then God's beyond-our-knowledge reasons for the gap would have had to have produced enough good to compensate for the loss of all the *summum bonum* of salvation of more than ten billion gap humans. But, since that loss would have been the loss of the *greatest* human good for all the gap humans, it's hard to

---

7. As I will explain below in this chapter's section entitled "Coda: William Lane Craig on the Historicity of Adam and Eve," prominent Christian apologist William Lane Craig has also pointed out that young Earth creationism has a significantly flawed low estimate for the age of the universe.

8. Kaneda and Haub, "How Many People," table 1, line 4.

see how there could be any good that could have adequately compensated for the loss of so much greatest good during the gap time.

Thus, I conclude that the skeptical theism defense for the gap fails.

Paul of Tarsus Defense: There Was No Gap

Recall from chapter 15 that Paul claimed that all humans, including those who lived before God revealed his two Testaments, knew, on the basis of their experience of God's creation and the testimony of the Holy Spirit in their consciences, that God existed and what comprised the general outline of his moral law.

Response

I won't repeat my criticisms from chapter 15 of Paul's claims here. The reader can read them in the section entitled "Rebuttal to the Claim That Class III and IV Unables Have Sufficient Salvific Knowledge Through Their Reflections on Nature" in chapter 15. I will, however, remind the reader that many have found Paul's claims there to be highly implausible.

CONCLUSION

All the most likely Christian explanations for the existence of the gap are unconvincing. If so, then the truth of premise 3 of the argument for God's monexistence from the existence of a divine temporal gap is sustained and, thereby, so is the soundness of the argument itself.

CODA: WILLIAM LANE CRAIG ON THE HISTORICITY OF ADAM AND EVE

As I mentioned a number of times, William Lane Craig is arguably the most visible, effective, and credentialed Christian apologist in the world today. He has recently published a book entitled *In Quest of the Historical Adam: A Biblical and Scientific Exploration*.[9] In which he somewhat surprisingly concludes that there was an historical Adam who most likely lived, not about three hundred thousand years ago when our species emerged, but

9. Craig, *In Quest*.

about seven hundred and fifty thousand years ago and was probably a part of the hominin species, *Homo heidelbergensis*.[10] I won't comment here on the plausibility or not of Craig's quite unorthodox (from a conservative Christian perspective) conclusion about Adam and Eve being part of *Homo heidelbergensis*. However, I do note that if his timeline for Adam and Eve is accepted, then the evidence for the argument for God's nonexistence from a divine temporal gap would be significantly strengthened and the likelihood of its soundness commensurately enhanced. The reason is that, given Craig's Adam and Eve timeline, the Gap would now be some 746,000 years, more than two and a half times as large as the 296,000-year estimate used in the argument for God's nonexistence from a divine temporal gap. That would amount to a divine gap involving thirty thousand rather than twelve thousand generations! Clearly, this would make God's absence even more inscrutable and would make the soundness of the argument for God's nonexistence from a divine temporal gap even more likely.

---

10. Craig, *In Quest*, 330.

Chapter 17: The Christian God Doesn't Exist Because of the Quantity of Apparently Unjustified Suffering

Preview

For the sake of clarity and economy of presentation, I'll abbreviate the expression "apparently unjustified suffering" as AUS, and the expression "genuinely unjustified suffering" as GUS. In this chapter, the what-we-wouldn't-have-expected-in-our-experience-of-the-world-if-God-existed is the unimaginable amount of AUS of humans and animals in the past and continuing today. I aim to show that this immense quantity of AUS experienced by sentient beings over the course of the hundreds of millions of years that they have existed is sufficient evidence to show that it is likely that there has also been some GUS. If so, then the existence of the Christian God is very unlikely.

INTRODUCTION

I define "an instance of GUS" as "any instance of acute suffering or premature death experienced by a sentient being,[1] human or animal, for which suffering there exists no *genuine* adequate moral justification." I define "an instance of AUS" as "any instance of acute suffering or premature death experienced by a sentient being, human or animal, for which suffering

---

1. I take sentience to include the ability to suffer and feel pain.

there exists no *apparent* adequate moral justification." Examples of instances of AUS would include a fawn suffering a slow, painful death as a result of being burned in a forest fire started by a lightning strike, and the rape, torture, and murder of a child.

Christians don't deny that there have been instances of AUS. What they deny is that there has ever been an instance of GUS. For Christians, the justification for that denial is the fact that God exists and that his nature ensures that he would never cause or permit any instance of GUS. Upholding this claim is important for Christians because, if there were ever even one instance of GUS, then God could not reasonably be said to exist because such GUS would be inconsistent with his nature, especially his omnibenevolence.

In what follows I will show that it's very likely that one or more instances of GUS has occurred in the five hundred million year history of sentient beings on this planet. To this end, I offer an argument that I call the argument for the nonexistence of God from the quantity of apparently unjustified suffering (another mouthful!). The argument cites the existence of a staggering amount of AUS as sufficient evidence to soundly conclude that it's likely that there's been one or more instances of GUS. If so, then it's likely that God does not exist.

In the following section I set out the argument for the nonexistence of God from the quantity of apparently unjustified suffering, and then in the next section following that I defend the argument's soundness.

FORMATTED ARGUMENT FOR GOD'S NONEXISTENCE FROM THE QUANTITY OF APPARENTLY UNJUSTIFIED SUFFERING

1. It is likely that there have been more than 7 quadrillion (7,000,000,000,000,000) instances of AUS in the history of sentient beings.

2. If it is likely that there have been more than 7 quadrillion (7,000,000,000,000,000) instances of AUS in the history of sentient beings, then it is likely that there has been at least one instance of GUS in the history of sentient beings.

3. Therefore, it is likely that there has been at least one instance of GUS in the history of sentient beings.

4. If it is likely that there has been at least one instance of GUS in the history of sentient beings, then it is likely that God does not exist

5. Therefore, it is likely that God does not exist.

ARGUMENT FOR GOD'S NONEXISTENCE FROM THE QUANTITY OF APPARENTLY UNJUSTIFIED SUFFERING DEFENDED

The argument for the nonexistence of God from the quantity of apparently unjustified suffering is clearly valid. Which is to say, *if* all of its premises 1, 2, and 4 are true, then its conclusion must be true as well. The most important question for evaluating any argument is whether it is a *sound* argument, that is, whether, in addition to being valid, all its premises are, in fact, true. So, I now turn to defending the truth of premises 1, 2, and 4.

Defense of the Truth of Premise 1

(It is likely that there have been more than 7 quadrillion [7,000,000,000,000,000] instances of AUS in the history of sentient beings.)

Estimation of the Quantity of AUS Experienced by Humans

The most common demographic estimate is that about 117 billion humans have been born[2] since our species emerged some three hundred thousand years ago.[3] It doesn't seem at all unreasonable to stipulate that the median human lifespan during that time has been about twenty years. Furthermore, it also doesn't seem unreasonable to estimate that each human experienced at least one instance of AUS during each year of their life. Thus, the median number of instances of AUS experienced in a human lifetime would be around twenty. Finally, the total number of instances of AUS experienced by all humans would then be twenty times 117 billion (the total number of humans who have ever been born alive) or about 2.34 trillion (2,340,000,000,000) or, rounding down, 2 trillion (2,000,000,000,000) and of course this number grows every day.

2. Routley, "How Many Humans," para. 10.
3. Handwerk, "Evolutionary Timeline of Homo Sapiens."

PART THREE: CHRISTIANITY AND ATHEISM

Estimation of Quantity of AUS Experienced by Sentient Animals

Since there have been many more species of sentient animals (henceforth just "animals") than species of humans, and since most animals evolved millions, tens of millions, or even hundreds of millions of years before humans, we can safely estimate that, minimally, there have been ten thousand times as many animals as humans. That means that, conservatively speaking, at least 1.17 quadrillion (1,170,000,000,000,000) animals have lived. Let's assume a median three year life span and that each animal experiences two instances of AUS each year. If so, then each animal would experience, on average, about six instances of AUS in its lifetime. Thus, the number of animal AUS sums to a stunning total of about 7.02 quadrillion (7,020,000,000,000,000), or rounding down, 7 quadrillion (7,000,000,000,000,000) instances of animal AUS over the approximate five hundred million year history of animals, and that number also grows every day.[4]

Total Amount of Animal and Human AUS

Summing up the number of instances of animal and human AUS yields the astronomical number of more than 7.02 quadrillion (7,020,000,000,000,000) instances to date. For the sake of convenience, I'll henceforth round this number down to 7 quadrillion (7,00,000,000,000,000). Of course, the estimates of the number of instances of AUS of animals and humans are only of a back-of-the-envelope quality. However, I venture to say that these estimates are at least in the ballpark, so to speak.[5] If so, then I conclude that premise (1) is true.

Defense of the Truth of Premise 2

(If it is likely that there have been more than 7 quadrillion [7,00,000,000,000,000] instances of AUS in the history of sentient beings, then it is likely that there has been at least one instance of GUS in the history of sentient beings.)

---

4. For definitive rebuttals to Christian attempts (see, for example, Murray, *Nature Red in Truth*) to defend God from being responsible for the existence of such gargantuan amounts of animal suffering, see Loftus, "Darwinian Problem of Evil," and SKYDIVE-PHIL, "Can Animals Suffer?" The latter YouTube reference comprises the responses of eminent and relevant scientists who hold that the evidence that animals do experience pain is compelling.

5. I'd venture to say that these estimates are low.

All other things being equal, it would seem to be extremely unlikely that out of more than 7 quadrillion instances of AUS in the history of sentient beings, there was not one instance of GUS. But a Christian might say that all other things are not equal. It's possible that God has morally sufficient reasons for causing or permitting such a huge amount of AUS, which reasons humans, with their limited intellectual abilities compared to God, are simply unable to fathom. Sound familiar? It should. It's another instance of that Christian apologetic standby, skeptical theism. If the skeptical theism challenge is sound, then, the truth of premise 2 and the soundness of the argument for the nonexistence of God from the quantity of apparently unjustified suffering cannot be adequately supported.

Response to the Skeptical Theism Challenge to Premise 2

I would start by asking the Christian proponent of skeptical theism against premise 2 this question: Would you accept that the following situation would constitute adequate evidence that probably some GUS existed? The situation is that all 808 billion (henceforth rounded down to 800 billion) sentient beings on our planet[6] suffer horrendously and die tomorrow. Imagine the Christian maintains that that situation would not constitute adequate evidence that some GUS exists because, a la skeptical theism, God could still have morally sufficient reason for causing even that catastrophic amount of pain, suffering, and death tomorrow. If so, then I would charge that holding that position would render the skeptical theism challenge unfalsifiable. That is, there would be no evidence that the Christian would accept that could show that the skeptical theism hypothesis would be false. After all, think about it, if the horrendous pain, suffering, and premature death of every sentient being on this planet would be insufficient to show that it's likely that some GUS exists, then what evidence *could* possibly be sufficient?

The problem is, it's widely accepted that positing an unfalsifiable hypothesis is logically problematic. As John Messerly, former professor of philosophy and computer science at the University of Texas at Austin,

---

6. There are currently about eight billion humans on the planet now. Assume that there are about a hundred times as many sentient animals as humans existing today. That would mean that there are some 800 billion sentient animals alive now. So, in sum, under the above modest numerical assumptions, there are about 808 billion sentient beings on earth.

bluntly put it, "So if a hypothesis is in principle incapable of being falsified—no matter what evidence I produce—then that hypothesis or belief is just vacuous nonsense."[7]

Alternatively, in order to avoid the charge of unfalsifiability, a Christian might admit that the enormous amount of horrendous pain, suffering, and premature death happening to every sentient being tomorrow on our planet *would* adequately support the belief that some GUS likely existed.[8] But, the Christian could add, clearly no such amount of horrendous pain, suffering, and premature death has ever existed, nor is there any reason to think that it would ever exist in a God-actualized world. Thus, the Christian could claim that the skeptical theism challenge to premise 2 still stands.

In response, I would note that, as I indicated earlier in the chapter, over the last five hundred million years or so at least 1.17 quadrillion (1,170,000,000,000,000) sentient animals and humans have lived, compared to the approximately 800 billion sentient animals and humans alive today. Furthermore, as I calculated above, it's very likely that those 1.17 quadrillion sentient beings would likely have collectively experienced more than 7 quadrillion (7,000,000,000,000,000) instances of horrendous pain, suffering, and premature death during their lifetimes. That enormous amount of horrendous pain, suffering, and premature death would be more than 8,750 times the amount of the horrendous pain, suffering, and premature death experienced by all of today's 800 billion sentient animals and humans, were they all to suffer horrendously and die tomorrow. So, if a Christian were to admit that the cumulative horrendous pain, suffering, and premature death of 800 billion sentient beings would be sufficient to elicit the acknowledgement that some GUS likely exists, then, *a fortiori* (even more so), the existence of more than 8,750 times that amount of horrendous pain, suffering, and premature death should elicit the same acknowledgement that likely some GUS has occurred.

A Christian might try to defend the skeptical theism claim by citing the following dissimilarity. Assume, for the sake of argument, that the horrendous pain, suffering, and premature death experienced by sentient beings over the last five hundred million years is 8,750 times more than what would be experienced if every sentient being alive were to suffer horrendously and

---

7. "Why Non-Falsifiable Beliefs," para. 6.

8. This would be the case because the Christian accepts that God, being omnipotent, omniscient, and omnibenevolent, would have the means, method, and motivation to prevent such an enormous amount of pain, suffering, and harm in a world that he actualized and presided over.

die tomorrow. That former amount of suffering and death occurred over a period of five hundred million years, whereas the latter amount of suffering and death of all of today's sentient beings is postulated to happen essentially all at one time (tomorrow). The Christian could claim that such a time difference would undercut the atheist's attempt to defang the skeptical theism hypothesis which challenges the truth of premise 2.

I respond that, with respect to assessing the gravity of an immoral act, the relevant fact is the total quantity and acuteness of the pain, suffering, and harm experienced by the victims, not the period of time over which those experiences occurred. For example, we wouldn't say that someone who murdered fifty people over the course of fifty years would be less morally culpable than if he had murdered all fifty victims at one time. In terms of assessing the moral gravity of murdering fifty people, the time element is irrelevant.

To sum up: on the one hand, if the horrendous pain, suffering, and premature death of every sentient being on earth tomorrow were claimed to be insufficient for establishing that some GUS likely existed, then I'd argue that the skeptical theism hypothesis supporting that insufficiency would be unfalsifiable. If so, it would be ineffective for disproving premise 2 and for challenging the soundness of the argument for the nonexistence of God from the quantity of apparently unjustified suffering. On the other hand, if the Christian were to acknowledge that the horrendous pain, suffering, and premature death of all sentient beings on earth tomorrow *would be* sufficient for establishing the likelihood that some GUS existed, then they would have a hard time denying that *the actual historical existence* of some 8,750 times as much horrendous pain, suffering, and premature death over the last five hundred million years would not be sufficient for showing that some GUS likely existed. If some GUS does likely exist, then premise 2 of the argument for the nonexistence of God from the quantity of apparently unjustified suffering would be adequately defended and, thereby, so would the soundness of the argument itself.

Bayesian Calculations Defending the Truth of Premise 2

Let's now generate a reasonable numerical estimate of the probability that God doesn't exist, given the evidence of their being 7 quadrillion instances of AUS in the history of sentient beings, as posited in the argument for the nonexistence of God from the quantity of apparently unjustified suffering.

We can do this by using something called Bayes' Theorem, named after an eighteenth-century Englishman Thomas Bayes. We don't need to get too deep into the weeds here and, if you choose, you can skip the details of the following calculations of the probability of the hypothesis that God doesn't exist using Bayes' Theorem and the amount of AUS. Do note, however, the result that the use of Bayes' Theorem gives at the end of this section.

Explanation of the Terms Used in Bayes' Theorem

P = probability that something stated is true

h = hypothesis being tested, in our case here, it is that *God doesn't exist*

$\sim h$ = negation of h, namely, *God exists*

e = all the evidence directly relevant to the truth of h, namely, in our case here, 7 quadrillion instances of AUS in the history of sentient beings

b = total background knowledge, that is, all available knowledge about anything and everything

$P(h|b)$ = the *prior probability* that h is true, given only our knowledge of b (that is, if we knew nothing about the e)

$P(h|e.b)$ = the *posterior probability* that h is true, given all the available e and b

$P(e|h.b)$ = the probability that all the e we have would exist, if h and b were true

$P(\sim h|b)$ = the probability that $\sim h$ is true, if all we know is b. This = $[1 - P(h|b)]$.

$P(e|\sim h.b)$ = the probability that all the e we have would exist, if $\sim h$ and b were true

Bayes' Theorem

$$P(h|e.b) = \frac{P(h|b) \times P(e|h.b)}{[P(h|b) \times P(e|h.b)] + [P(\sim h|b) \times P(e|\sim h.b)]}$$

Application of Bayes' Theorem to the Nonexistence of God, Given the Argument from the Quantity of Apparently Unjustified Suffering

$$P(\text{God doesn't exist}|e.b) = \frac{P(\text{God doesn't exist}|b) \times P(e \text{ exists}|\text{God doesn't exist}.b)}{[P(\text{God doesn't exist}|b) \times P(e \text{ exists}|\text{God doesn't exist}.b)] + [P(\text{God exists}|b) \times P(e|\text{God exists}.b)]}$$

Now, to fill in plausible numbers—

P(God doesn't exist|b) = for the sake of argument I will set it as P(.5), that is, a 50 percent chance

P(God does exist|b) = likewise, for the sake of argument I will set it as P(.5), that is, a 50 percent chance

P(e exists|God doesn't exist.b) = P(.9), that is, a 90 percent chance that there would be 7 quadrillion instances of AUS if God doesn't exist.[9]

P(e|God exists.b) = P(.1), that is, there is a 10 percent chance that there would be 7 quadrillion instances of AUS if God exists.[10]

$$P(\text{God doesn't exist}|e.b) = \frac{P(.5) \times P(.9)}{[P(.5) \times P(.9)] + [P(.5) \times P(.1)]}$$

$$P(\text{God doesn't exist}|e.b) = \frac{.45}{[.45] + [.05]} = .9 = 90 \text{ percent chance that h (God doesn't exist) is true}$$

In English, the above calculation says that the (posterior) probability that God doesn't exist is .9 (90 percent), given that there is only a .1 (10 percent) chance that all the evidence we have, namely, 7 quadrillion instances of AUS in the history of sentient beings, would exist if God existed. In effect, I defended the reasonableness of the 10 percent assessment by defending premise 2 of the argument for the nonexistence of God from the quantity of apparently unjustified suffering starting above in the section of this chapter entitled "Total Amount of Animal and Human AUS." To briefly sum up that defense: in order to avoid the criticism that skeptical theism is an unfalsifiable hypothesis, a Christian would have to accept the conclusion that the horrendous suffering and death of all 808 billion sentient beings alive now

---

9. I actually think this rather low.
10. I actually think this is rather high.

would suffice to falsify the skeptical theism hypothesis. However, if the horrendous suffering and death of 808 billion sentient beings suffices to falsify the skeptical theism hypothesis, then, even more so, the horrendous suffering and death of 1,250 times that number of sentient beings (namely, 1 quadrillion sentient beings who ever lived) should suffice for postulating only a 10 percent chance that all the evidence we have would exist if God existed [P(e|God exists.b)]. The following list shows the probabilities for the hypothesis that God doesn't exist for other values of the probability that all the evidence we have would exist if God existed [P(e|God exists.b)].

If P(e|God exists.b) = .2, then P(God doesn't exist|e.b) = 82 percent

If P(e|God exists.b) = .3, then P(God doesn't exist|e.b) = 75 percent

If P(e|God exists.b) = .4, then P(God doesn't exist|e.b) = 69 percent

If P(e|God exists.b) = .5, then P(God doesn't exist|e.b) = 64 percent

If P(e|God exists.b) = .6, then P(God doesn't exist|e.b) = 60 percent

If P(e|God exists.b) = .7, then P(God doesn't exist|e.b) = 56 percent

If P(e|God exists.b) = .8, then P(God doesn't exist|e.b) = 53 percent

If P(e|God exists.b) = .9, then P(God doesn't exist|e.b) = 50 percent

If P(e|God exists.b) = .93, then P(God doesn't exist|e.b) = 49 percent

Notice that the probability that God doesn't exist, given all the evidence we have, namely, the likely 7 quadrillion instances of AUS in the history of sentient beings doesn't fall below 50 percent until the probability of there being 7 quadrillion instances of AUS in the history of sentient beings if God exists is 93 percent, that is, until P(e|God exists.b) = .93 (93 percent). Since .93 or 93 percent is an unreasonably high estimate, I conclude that the probability of God's not existing is considerably above the reasonable threshold for believing that he doesn't exist. If so, then the challenge to the truth of premise 2 would be unsuccessful according to the above application of Bayes' theorem.

Defense of the Truth of Premise 4

(If it is likely that there has been at least one instance of GUS in the history of sentient beings, then God does not exist.)

By definition, an omnibenevolent being could never cause or permit even one instance of GUS, as any instance of unjustified suffering would be inconsistent with the being's omnibenevolence.

CHAPTER CONCLUSION

I argued that the argument for the nonexistence of God from the quantity of apparently unjustified suffering is sound because it is valid and its three premises, 1, 2, and 4, are all true. Thus, the conclusion of the argument, namely, that it is likely that God does not exist, is sustained.[11]

---

11. Complimenting the argument presented and defended in this chapter, one of the best and most comprehensive critiques of Christian attempts to show that the argument from evil (unjust suffering) is unsound is found in Sterba, *Is a Good God*.

Chapter 18: Christian God Doesn't Exist Because This World Does

Preview

Two of the most important beliefs that most Christians hold are (1) God is maximally good, which includes having maximal love for human beings, and (2) the eternal postmortem experience of the beatific vision of God in heaven is the highest good for all human beings. In light of these two foundational beliefs, the what-we-wouldn't-have-expected-in-our-experience-of-the-world-if-God-existed in this chapter is God creating this world we inhabit. I'll argue that we would have expected that he would have created a world, unlike the world we now inhabit, in which humans are created and then immediately and directly offered the option of eternally experiencing the highest good of the beatific vision of him in heaven. This alternative world, which I call "heaven world," would not have the pain, suffering, and confusion that permeate the world that we exist in. If so, then I conclude that the fact that heaven world does not exist constitutes adequate evidence that God does not exist either.

INTRODUCTION

So far, in chapters 14, 15, 16, and 17 of part III, we evaluated four atheistic arguments based on four different kinds of what-we-wouldn't-have-expected-in-our-experience-of-the-world-if-God-existed. To review: in chapter 14 it was the existence of unfair human experiences; in chapter 15 it was the existence of unfair salvific opportunities; in chapter 16 it was the existence of an inexplicable twelve thousand or thirty thousand generations absence of God's presence to humans; and in chapter 17 it was the existence of an enormous quantity of apparently unjustified horrendous suffering of humans and animals. In this chapter the what-we-wouldn't-have-expected-in-our-experience-of-the-world-if-God-existed is the very existence of this world itself. I will argue that the existence of the world we inhabit constitutes adequate evidence that God does not exist.

Philosopher Richard La Croix argued that since God, in addition to being omnipotent and omniscient, is also wholly free and the greatest possible good, he would have freely chosen not to create any world at all.[1] La Croix claimed that this follows because creating any world, especially one like ours containing vast amounts of suffering of the innocent, could not possibly result overall in a greater good than the greatest possible good already in existence before creation, namely, God himself. Thus, La Croix concludes that the existence of God is inconsistent with the creation and existence of any created world, especially one containing suffering of the innocent. But, since such a world does exist, he concluded that God does not and cannot exist. I'm not going to do a evaluation of La Croix's argument here, except to say that I found it persuasive. What I will do in this chapter is to show that even if LaCroix's argument were to be judged to be unsound and that God would be justified in creating a world, it wouldn't be this world that we inhabit. It would be what below I call "heaven world."

HEAVEN WORLD (HW)

The argument to be developed here rests on the claim that if God existed and actualized a material world, he would have shown his maximal goodness, including his maximal love for humans, by actualizing a different world than this world we live in. I will call this alternative world "heaven world" and will abbreviate it as HW. I will abbreviate the name for the world we inhabit as TW (standing for "this world"). In relevant outline, HW would include God's creating humans and endowing all of them with free will, rationality, moral agency, a clear and comprehensive knowledge of their creator and creation circumstances, and a clear and comprehensive understanding of what options they have concerning their existence.

---

1. La Croix, "Unjustified Evil," 20–28. LaCroix's article is reprinted in Martin and Monnier, *Impossibility of God*, 116–24.

For our purposes, the most important difference between HW and TW is that upon creating humans in HW, God would immediately and directly offer each human the beatific vision of God in heaven. The Beatific Vision is the *summum bonum*, or greatest good, for humans. It consists of people directly experiencing the most sublime bliss stemming from a freely chosen, intimate, loving, direct union with God forever in heaven. The *Catechism of the Catholic Church*, for instance, says that heaven (comprising the beatific vision) is the state of supreme and definitive happiness, the goal of the deepest longing of humanity.[2] The theme in the second part of medieval Christian theologian, (Saint) Thomas Aquinas's work *Summa Theologica* is human beings' striving after their last (highest) end, which is the blessedness of the *beatific vision*. Christian philosopher Shawn Floyd elaborates on the importance that Aquinas placed on the experience of the beatific vision.

> Thus he [Aquinas] says that human beings "attain their last end by knowing and loving God" (*Summa Theologica* IaIIae 1.8). Aquinas refers to this last end—the state in which perfect happiness consists—as the Beatific Vision. The Beatific Vision is a supernatural union with God, the enjoyment of which surpasses the satisfaction afforded by those goods people sometimes associate with the last end.[3]

It's important to note that God's creating and then directly offering humans immediate access to the beatific vision in HW is similar to what Christians claim actually happens to some humans in TW. Let me explain. As was mentioned several times earlier in this volume,[4] research has shown that some 72 percent of human conceptions, about 301 billion in the history of our species, have died in utero. From here on, I'll refer to this 72 percent as the "short-lived." Given that the most prevalent Christian belief about when personhood begins is that it is at conception, we must assume that in this world (TW) God would immediately and directly offer every postmortem short-lived the option of experiencing the beatific vision, since any other course of action with respect to them after they die in utero would compromise God's omnibenevolence and maximal love for humans. God's direct postmortem offer of the beatific

2. See Maggiolini, "Heaven," sec. 2014.
3. Floyd, "Thomas Aquinas," para. 17.
4. See section entitled "Important Relevant Data about Prenatal Mortality" in chapter 1.

vision to the short-lived in TW would be similar to what I envision he would offer to *all* humans upon his creating them in HW.[5] I shall have more to say about the short-lived later in the chapter.

HW ARGUMENT FOR THE NONEXISTENCE OF GOD

I aim to show that, from ethical and human flourishing considerations, HW would be superior to TW and, as I shall show later in the chapter, to any other possible world[6] as well. That being the case, in accordance with his maximally good and loving nature, God would have actualized HW rather than TW, or any other possible world. Since HW does not exist, I conclude that God does not either. The formal presentation of this reasoning, called the heaven world argument, follows.

HEAVEN WORLD ARGUMENT FOR THE NONEXISTENCE OF GOD FORMATTED

1. There are numerous important ethical and human flourishing advantages that HW has over TW, and no disadvantages.
2. If there are numerous important ethical and human flourishing advantages that HW has over TW, and no disadvantages, then if God exists, he would have actualized HW rather than TW.
3. Therefore, if God exists, he would have actualized HW rather than TW.
4. It is not the case that God actualized HW rather than TW.
5. Therefore, it is not the case that God exists.

---

5. Recall that in chapter 15 I argued that such a divine offer to what I called there class I unables and what I call in this chapter the short-lived would be unfair in comparison to how God treats all other human persons.
6. A possible world is a complete and consistent way the world is or could have been. The actual world we live in is one of the countless possible worlds. Another possible world might be one in which Abraham Lincoln is not assassinated in 1865.

HEAVEN WORLD ARGUMENT FOR THE NONEXISTENCE OF GOD EVALUATED

The argument is valid, that is, if all the premises 1, 2, and 4 are true, then the conclusions 3 and 5 would be true as well. Premise 4 is obviously true. I will now defend the truth of the remaining two premises, 1 and 2. If an argument is valid and all the premises are true, then we say the argument is sound. As I've noted a number of times earlier in the book, soundness is the gold standard for the logical worth of an argument. I will eventually show that the HW argument for the nonexistence of God is indeed sound.

Defense of Premise 1

(*There are numerous important ethical and human flourishing advantages that HW has over TW, and no disadvantages.*)

First, the most important advantage of HW over TW would be that in HW, unlike in TW, virtually all humans would be saved, that is, they would experience the *summum bonum* of the beatific vision. I do not mean to say that it would be logically impossible for a HW person to reject God's invitation to experience the beatific vision, only that it would be extremely unlikely, given the nature of what is being offered (the highest good for humans), the nature of the person extending the offer (God), the nature of how it is being offered (face-to-face by God), and the status of the humans being offered the experience of the beatific vision (having free will and being rational and fully informed). This very likely universal salvation in HW would much better satisfy God's desire that all people be saved (1 Tim 2:4) than what happens with respect to salvation in TW. At the same time, in accepting God's invitation to experience the beatific vision, HW people would thereby eliminate their chance of suffering eternal damnation. This is significant because, as I noted a number of times, according to the Bible, in TW many people are not saved. They don't attain the highest good of the beatific vision. Rather, they experience eternal separation from God and, perhaps, eternal torment as well. That is, they end up in hell (Luke 13:23–24; Matt 7:13–14).

Second, as is the case in TW's heaven, in HW there would be no human or animal suffering from natural causes (called natural evil) such as what results from disease, animal predation, accidents, fires, floods earthquakes, etc. In addition, no one would suffer harm from any free will choices of humans (called moral evil). This would be so because HW people, like the humans and angels in TW's heaven, would not choose to do evil since their attention and inclinations would be so firmly, completely, and eternally fixed on the magnetic, joyous, loving, awe-inspiring, and all-consuming experience of the beatific vision. Also, it's not clear that anyone experiencing the beatific vision *could* suffer from anything.

Third, Christians claim that God created humans for a number of purposes, namely, to have them freely come to know and love him and share in his blessed life,[7] to glorify and enjoy him forever,[8] and to worship him. These purposes would be far better realized in HW because all humans there would experience the highest good of the beatific vision, which experience, by definition, would entail the maximal realization of God's aforementioned purposes.

Fourth, for HW people, unlike for TW people, there would be no decision obstructions (see next three sections) of a knowledge-related, atheism-related, sociological-related, or psychological-related nature involving the acceptance of the existence of God and the truth and value of his invitation to experience the beatific vision. The absence of such obstructing decision factors that abound in TW would assure that the choices of HW people would be free and properly informed. Let's examine more closely how HW would not have any of these decision obstructions.

Knowledge-Related Obstructing Decision Factors

Many people in TW have never had a live option to acknowledge God's existence or to accept his invitation to experience the *summum bonum* of the beatific vision because they died in utero, or were born but died before they were able to make an informed morally accountable decision, or never developed the mental capacities to make an informed free choice, or lived in times before Christianity was known or where it was never clearly, fully, or properly explained or understood. In chapter 15 I showed how only about 12 billion humans out of a total of 418 billion humans (less than 3 percent) who have ever lived could have heard the Christian gospel.[9] In addition, some people who were cognizant of claims about God's existence and his offer of salvation judged the claims to be implausible due

---

7. Maggiolini, "Life of Man."
8. Westminster Confession, "Confession Chapter 4."
9. See the section in chapter 15 entitled "Summary Tally of Unables."

to insufficient evidence. As per the definition of HW, these obstructing lack-of-knowledge factors would not exist in HW.

Atheism-Related Obstructing Decision Factors

In TW, these factors include the existence of massive amounts of horrendous human and animal suffering (see material in the section entitled "Total Amount of Animal and Human AUS" in chapter 17), the hiddenness of God—why hasn't there been more evidence for his existence (see chapter 16)—and the unfairness associated with unfair salvation opportunities to attain the beatific vision of the *summum* bonum (see chapter 15). With respect to the unfairness associated with opportunities for receiving the *summum bonum*, presumably the shortlived (those who die before the age of moral accountability) are automatically guaranteed it, while all others are not. These three atheistic-related challenges to Christian belief, particularly the first two (pointless suffering and divine hiddenness), have spawned large numbers of atheists and agnostics,[10] especially in recent times. These obstructing decision factors would not exist in HW because in that world there would be no suffering, God would not be hidden since he would treat directly with humans, and there would be no unfairness in attaining the beatific vision, as it would be offered to all in an identical manner.

Sociological and Psychological Obstructing Decision Factors

Many people's decisions about God's existence and offer of salvation have been warped by sociological or psychological influences such as personal misfortune, flawed upbringing, geographical location, e.g., living in Mecca versus Mississippi, inferior education, lack of relevant factual information, poor role models, economic disadvantage, human predation, or psychological handicaps. Given the description of HW, these obstructive decision factors would not be present there (see more on this in the section entitled "Ables Intragroup Unfairness Evaluated" in chapter 15).

---

10. Those who think there is insufficient evidence to be justified in either believing or disbelieving in God.

Defense of Premise 2

(If there are numerous important ethical and human flourishing advantages that HW has over TW, and no disadvantages, then if God exists, he would have actualized HW rather than TW.)

The truth of—*there are numerous important ethical and human flourishing advantages that HW has over TW, and no disadvantages*—in premise 2 was addressed in defending premise 1. The justification of—*if God exists, he would have actualized HW rather than TW*—in premise 2 would seem to be a fairly straightforward matter. A maximally good creator would not actualize a world, TW, containing massive amounts of suffering that results in only *some* humans attaining the *summum bonum* of salvation and only *some* humans satisfying the creator's purposes for creating humans. Instead he would have actualized a world, HW, in which it would be very likely that *all* humans would attain the beatific vision and freely satisfy God's purposes for their creation, and all this without any unwarranted horrendous suffering being required. If so, then the suffering in TW can be deemed to be unwarranted. Moreover, given that, by definition, an omnibenevolent God would not cause or permit any unwarranted suffering, it can be soundly concluded that God would have actualized HW rather than TW.

RESPONSES TO CHRISTIAN CHALLENGES TO THE HW ARGUMENT FOR THE NONEXISTENCE OF GOD

First Christian Challenge to the HW Argument: In HW humans would have to forego the Great Good of Having a Conscious, Embodied Earthly Life

Responses

First, while it is true that most embodied conscious humans in TW experience some happiness and satisfaction, human earthly existence is certainly not an unalloyed good. Almost all embodied, conscious humans also experience considerable amounts of acute suffering, some of it horrendous, which, of course, they would not experience in HW.

Second, the Gospel of Mark (8:36 KJV) says, "For what shall it profit a man, if he shall gain the whole world, and lose his own soul?" Whatever happiness and satisfaction humans may experience in TW pales into insignificance when compared to the experience of the beatific vision, for which all in HW can directly opt.

Third, if having a conscious, embodied existence were as great a good as the critics of HW might say it is, it would be difficult to explain why an omnibenevolent God would deny it to more than 70 percent (301 billion) of humans, namely, the short-lived.

Second Christian Challenge to the HW Argument: In HW humans Would Have to Forego the Value Associated with God's Keeping His Epistemic (Knowledge of Him) Distance from Them

Christians tell us that God wants humans to freely enter into an intimate and loving relationship with him. However, he doesn't want to force them to do so by overriding their free will or otherwise coercing them. To this end he keeps an appropriate epistemic distance from them in TW. This would not be possible in HW where God treats directly with persons.

Responses

First, when HW people parley directly with God, they would obviously thereby get sufficient reasons to believe that he exists and has invited them to experience the beatific vision. Furthermore, if a person takes on a belief as a result of receiving clear and adequate evidence for the belief from an unimpeachable source, that would not necessitate any loss of the person's free will or her being the subject of improper coercion. If a credentialed physician gives me important information about my health which I subsequently act upon, my so acting would not be an instance of my free will being abrogated by a coercive physician. God would have the means, method, and motivation to present to HW people the facts of his existence and his offer of the beatific vision in noncoercive terms that would not override their free will.

Second, according to Christianity, God has in fact dropped his epistemic distance with many persons, ostensibly without compromising their free will or unduly coercing them, as, for example, with the disciple Paul. Also, God presumably does not keep his epistemic distance from the postmortem short-lived in the course of extending to them an invitation to experience the *summum bonum* of salvation. This is pertinent because, recall, the short-lived comprise a substantial majority (about 72 percent) of the persons who have ever lived in TW and their postmortem status is similar to what the status of all people in HW would be. Many Christians also believe that many humans during their lifetimes, including such well known figures as Abraham, Moses, Paul, Peter, Mary the mother of Jesus, Joseph Smith, and others were given powerful direct or indirect visible manifestations of God which involved an absence of divine distance. Christians do not believe that any of those cases involved improper coercion, annulment of free will, or the creation of any other negative consequences. On the contrary, those individuals are considered to have been privileged and to be righteous archetypes of their faith.

Third Christian Challenge to the HW Argument: In HW Humans Would not Experience the Value of Soul-Making

This challenge is associated with Christian philosopher John Hick's theory of soul-making as a plausible divine justification for the suffering in TW.[11] Christian critics of the HW argument for the nonexistence of God, in the spirit of Hick, could claim that God actualized TW with its ethical and human flourishing shortcomings in order to create an environment in which humans could develop a higher level of goodness than they could bring about in a world like HW. In short, God's actualization of TW makes soul-making possible, and, thereby, makes possible the development of important positive human character traits and virtues such as courage, compassion, and heroism. Hick summarized his view as follows.

> The value-judgement that is implicitly being invoked here is that one who has attained to goodness by meeting and eventually mastering temptation, and thus by rightly making responsible choices in concrete situations [as in TW], is good in a richer and more valuable sense than would be one created *ab initio* in a state either of innocence or of virtue [as in HW]. In the former case, which is that of the actual axiological [ethical] achievements of mankind, the individual's goodness has within it the strength of temptations overcome, a stability based upon an accumulation of right choices,

---

11. Hick, *Evil and the God*.

and a positive and responsible character that comes from the investment of costly personal effort.[12]

Catholic priest Philip Dion put it this way.

> St. Augustine said, "There would be no martyrs if there were no tyrannical persecutions." Hence, it is by the wickedness He permits in some men, that God stimulates others to goodness and virtue and sanctity. For example, God willed to permit the evil of guilt in Hitler and so many Nazis and communists who ran the concentration camps in World War II . . . . Because of that suffering, many victims are saints before the throne of God today who would not be there had God not permitted the evil will and sin of their persecutors.[13]

According to Hick and, presumably, Fr. Dion as well, God makes certain that the attainment of such character-enhancing goods associated with soul-making more than compensates for the ethical and human flourishing detriments that make soul-making possible. The attainment of those character-enhancing goods, then, justifies God's actualizing TW rather than HW.

Responses

There have been many retorts to Hick's views. However, I'll limit mine to those which are most relevant to the HW Argument.

First, keep in mind that HW people would be able to make free will decisions as well as can people in TW. However, since it would be very likely that there would be no suffering in HW, HW people would not need to make moral decisions occasioned by horrendous suffering. That fact would in no way render human existence in TW preferable to existence in HW from the perspective of humans or an omnibenevolent God. Given the many ethical and human flourishing advantages that HW has over TW cited earlier in this chapter, especially the avoidance of the almost unimaginable amount of acute animal and human suffering in TW through the ages, it's difficult to see how any human or omnibenevolent deity would prefer TW over the alternative of HW. Contrary to what Hick and Fr. Dion claimed, an omnibenevolent God would not prefer a world in which

---

12. Hick, *Evil and the God*, 255–56.
13. Dion, "Does God Will It," 19.

humans use free will to murder a million children (as in the Holocaust) so that some persons could show moral fortitude in trying to stop those murders. Rather, God would prefer a world, HW, in which all humans would freely choose to enjoy the *summum bonum* and to use their free will to maximally love him, themselves, and all other persons.

Second, if Christians were to hold that God would actualize TW over HW because TW allows some humans to build their souls by making morally exemplary free will decisions, they would have to explain why that actualization would not jeopardize God's omnibenevolent character in terms of unfairness. (See chapters 14 and 15 for more on divine unfairness.) Actualizing TW would result in God acting unfairly toward the short-lived who again, remember, comprise a robust majority (72 percent) of all humans who have ever lived in TW. By definition, the short-lived are unable to make any free will decisions in TW. Thus, they would be arbitrarily deprived of an opportunity to gain the great good of moral righteousness resulting from a morally virtuous free will response to horrendous events to build their souls. That would amount to immoral discrimination toward the short-lived which would be inconsistent with the character of an omnibenevolent being. Of course, such discrimination would not occur in HW.

Third, under the soul-making defense of God's actualizing TW rather than HW, God would be treating some innocent people, through their suffering, often horrendous, as mere means for making it possible for another group of people, to have the possibility of soul-making. This would be a serious violation of what many philosophers would hold to be at the core of proper morality, namely, that people should be treated as ends in themselves and not merely as a means to some ends. That being the case, people like John Hick and Fr. Dion would have to be judged wrong in claiming that God was morally justified in permitting, for example, the Nazi program of genocide to proceed because the vast suffering that that program inflicted on millions of innocent victims generated some moral heroes. To many critics, myself included, that view is morally offensive. Better to have no genocide and fewer moral heroes. By the way, true moral heroes would be the first to agree with that assessment.

Fourth, soul-making in TW could not bring about as much aggregate goodness as would be brought about by the experience of the highest good of the *summum bonum* in HW by all humans. Furthermore, many of those who experience horrendous suffering, or who know those who do, or learn about the level of horrendous suffering being experienced in TW have apostatized (renounced a religious belief) and, as a result, presumably have lost the *summum bonum* of salvation. Such losses would diminish even further the likelihood that soul-making in TW would justify the horrendous suffering often required for it, especially when virtually all in HW would experience the *summum bonum* without there being any horrendous suffering.

Fifth, soul-making by means of suffering and adversity is either necessary for attaining the *summum bonum* or it's not. If it's necessary, then, once again, since the short-lived could never experience it, they would thereby be unfairly debarred from attaining the summum bonum. This unfairness would weaken or demolish the ethical justification of God's actualization of TW. On the other hand, if soul-making is not necessary for attaining the *summum bonum*, then its usefulness as a defense of God's actualizing TW would be minimal at best.

Sixth, soul-making by means of suffering and adversity is useful only for rational beings who have not yet reached the perfection of their natures. Those who have already reached that point have no need for it. Their souls are already "made," as it were. For example, Adam and Eve before their sin in the garden of Eden, the short-lived, including those who died without ever being morally accountable, and supernatural persons, such as God and angels, all never underwent any soul-making through suffering and adversity because they didn't need to. They were, or are, at perfection relative to their natures. Likewise, HW people wouldn't need soul-making through suffering and adversity either since they would attain the perfection of their natures by accepting God's offer to experience the *summum bonum* of the beatific vision.

Once again, Shawn Floyd's encapsulation of Thomas Aquinas's view that the beatific vision is the final perfection of humans is apropos here.

> What is it, then, in which our last end really consists or is realized? For Aquinas, the last end of happiness can *only* consist in that which is perfectly good, which is God. Because God is perfect goodness, he is the only one capable of fulfilling our heart's deepest longing and facilitating the perfection at which we aim. Thus he says that human beings "attain their last end by knowing and loving God" (*Summa Theologica* IaIIae 1.8). Aquinas refers to this last end—the state in which perfect happiness consists—as the Beatific Vision. The Beatific Vision is a supernatural union with

God, the enjoyment of which surpasses the satisfaction afforded by those goods people sometimes associate with the last end.[14]

As Aquinas puts it, the beatific vision brings about the final end and perfection of a human being's nature, that is, a made soul. God's desire for humans to experience this end or goal of perfection would be fully realized in HW when humans therein accept God's invitation to join him in a free, personal, intimate, eternal, loving relationship via the beatific vision. Most importantly, once again, this perfection of human nature would not only come to all in HW, versus coming to considerably less than all in TW, but it would also come about without the massive suffering required for it in TW.

Some Christians, such as Hick, however, have asserted that God doesn't want soul-making to simply be the product of accepting a divine invitation, as it would be in HW; rather, they claim that God wants it to be earned, as Hick put it, by "the investment of costly personal effort," as in TW. However, this claim is challenged by the fact that Adam and Eve in the garden of Eden, angels ostensibly, and, most relevantly, the short-lived who experience the *summum bonum* of the beatific vision in TW's heaven because they died without ever being morally accountable, all received perfected soul-made natures by divine largess, not by "the investment of costly personal effort." Nor is there any indication that this manner of reaching soul-perfected natures tarnishes or diminishes the goodness or happiness associated with the beatific vision.

Fourth Christian Challenge to the HW Argument: Actualizing TW Involved No Moral Deficiencies on God's Part

Christian philosopher Robert Adams has argued that God's actualization of a "less perfect world" (like TW) than one he could have actualized (like HW) would not involve any defect in God's character.[15] Adams claims that, on the one hand, people with whom God would have populated a better world than TW (like HW, for example) have never existed because God never actualized their world. Thus, God cannot be said to have harmed such nonexistent beings by not having created HW. On the other hand, Adams claims that God cannot be said to have harmed the people in TW either because his creating them was a gracious manifestation of

---

14. Floyd, "Thomas Aquinas," para. 17.
15. See Adams, "Must God Create the Best?," 276–82.

his divine love that gave them the precious gifts of existence and God's unconditional grace that they otherwise would not have had if he didn't create them in TW. Thus, Adams concludes that since God didn't harm anyone in the world he actualized (TW) and didn't harm anyone in the worlds that he did not actualize (like HW), then he cannot be said to have acted in a morally deficient manner by actualizing a less perfect world than he could have actualized, like TW.

Response

Assume that Adams is correct that no one is harmed by God's actualizing TW.[16] Following an insight by Christian philosopher Philip Quinn,[17] atheist philosopher William Rowe charged that there is still a case to be made that God's actualizing a less perfect world, like TW, than one he could have actualized instead, like HW, could be said to manifest a pertinent moral deficiency on God's part. Rowe says,

> Following Philip Quinn, I'm inclined to think that if an all-powerful, all-knowing being creates some world other than the best world it can create, then it is possible there should exist a being morally better than it is. Quinn remarks: "An omnipotent moral agent can actualise any actualisable world. If he actualises one than which there is a morally better, he does not do the best he can, morally speaking, and so it is possible that there is an agent morally better than he is, namely an omnipotent moral agent who actualises one of those morally better worlds."[18]

Rowe adds that Quinn's "omnipotent moral agent (whom I will call 'God+') who actualizes one of those morally better worlds" could be understood to do so as a supererogatory (more than what is normally morally expected) act.[19] Moreover, given that it is morally virtuous to perform supererogatory acts, God+ would thereby be morally superior to God. If so, then God could not be said to be unsurpassably good. But, since being

---

16. For the sake of argument, I will accept Adams's claim that no members of TW could or would be members of HW. If they could have been members of HW, then one could construct a strong argument that they would have been harmed by being created in TW rather than in HW.
17. Quinn, "God, Axiological Perfection," 213.
18. Rowe, *Can God Be Free?* 81.
19. Rowe, *Can God Be Free?* 82.

unsurpassably good is a necessary property of being God, then any being that is not unsurpassably good can't be God. Thus we would have expected God to have created HW so as to avoid this objection.

Christian "No Best World" Retort

Christians, in turn, could claim that Rowe's and Quinn's reasoning is vulnerable to the "no best world" retort. A number of prominent Christian philosophers[20] has argued that there is an infinite hierarchy of increasingly better worlds that would be better than any world that God could have chosen to actualize. If so, then God+ could be surpassed in goodness by an omnipotent creator, God++, who could, in a supererogatory manner, actualize a better world than the one actualized by God+. But then, God++ could, in turn, be surpassed in goodness by God+++ in the same way as God+ could have been surpassed by God++, and so on ad infinitum. If there is no best possible world that God could have actualized, then God cannot be said to have compromised his omnibenevolence by actualizing TW. Adams, gives voice to this conclusion when he says, "If there is no maximum degree of perfection among possible worlds, it would be unreasonable to blame God, or think less highly of His goodness, because He created a world less excellent than he could have created."[21] Other Christian philosophers concur.[22]

Response

For it to be the case that God should have actualized HW over TW, and all other possible worlds (AOPW) for that matter, as the HW argument for the nonexistence of God requires, it isn't necessary that HW be the best possible world, simply speaking, that is, the best without any qualifications.[23] God's decision to actualize a world would include, among other

20. Plantinga, *God, Freedom, and Evil*, 61; Schlesinger, *Religion and Scientific Method*; Swinburne, *Existence of God*, 114–15.

21. Adams, "Must God Create the Best?," 275.

22. See Howard-Synder and Howard-Snyder, "How an Unsurpassable Being," 260–68; O'Connor, *Theism and Ultimate Explanation*, 111–29; Langtry, *God, the Best*, 74–78.

23. It might be held that there could be a best possible world simpliciter if God could actualize a world containing an infinite number of good-making components. If such an actualization is possible, then the theist's objection here would still be unhorsed since it would be expected that God would have created that best possible world simpliciter rather than TW.

things, a decision about the numbers, N, and kinds, K, of persons the actualized world would comprise. Once N and K values are set, it then becomes feasible to determine a *relativized* best possible world among worlds that have the same N and K values.

Identifying a population-equalized best possible world would involve comparing the ethical and human flourishing values associated with TW, HW, and members of AOPW (all other possible worlds) when all the compared worlds have the same N and K values. TW with specific N and K values can be represented as *TW-with-NK*. HW with specific N and K values can be represented as *HW-with-NK*. Finally, members of AOPW with specific N and K values can be represented as *AOPW-with-NK*.

The rationale behind the N and K population caveats for making cross-world value comparisons is to avoid making such comparisons mainly a function of the mere extrinsic numbers and kinds of inhabitants, rather than a function of intrinsic ethical and human flourishing values of the compared worlds, such as those spelled out earlier in this chapter in the section entitled "Defense of Premise 1 (There are numerous important ethical and human flourishing advantages that HW has over TW, and no disadvantages)." In light of that section's value factors favoring HW, and the population caveats just described, *HW-with-NK* would be superior to *TW-with-NK* as well as superior to *AOPW-with-NK* in so far as there could not be any member of *AOPW-with-NK*, including *TW-with-NK*, that could be superior to *HW-with-NK* in ethical and human flourishing terms. This would be so because only in *HW-with-NK* would virtually *all* persons enjoy the *summum bonum* of experiencing the beatific vision. Therefore, neither *TW-with-NK* nor any member world of *AOPW-with-NK* could contain more good than the greatest good for all beings who could experience good, as would be the case in *HW-with-NK*.

Furthermore, neither *TW-with-NK* nor any member of *AOPW-with-NK* could contain *as much* good as would be in *HW-with-NK*. If it did, it would not be essentially different from *HW-with-NK*; in fact, it would *be* *HW-with-NK*, namely, the only NK-populated world in which *all* persons experience the *summum bonum* of the beatific vision. So, I conclude that there *is* a best possible world among worlds having the same N and K values, namely, *HW-with-NK*, which, according to the HW argument for the nonexistence of God, God, if he really existed, would have actualized rather than *TW-with-NK*.

Fifth Challenge to the HW Argument: God's Reasons for Actualizing TW Rather Than HW May be Impossible to Understand (Skeptical Theism—Yet Again!)

Christians could argue that even if the previous five theistic challenges to the HW argument are deemed to be unsuccessful and that we are unable to determine a justification for God's actualizing TW rather than HW, that alone would not suffice for us to reasonably conclude that God would have no justification. His justification could simply be beyond our ability to know it. This sort of defense, which we've encountered multiple times earlier in this volume, would be an application of the increasingly employed Christian apologetic known as skeptical theism. Recall that it holds that humans, given their significant cognitive limitations compared to God, should be skeptical about their ability to comprehend God's reasons for his actions, such as why he actualized TW rather than HW. In effect, skeptical theism is just a more formal elaboration of such expressions as "God's ways are not our ways" or "God acts in mysterious ways."

Responses

First, if skeptical theists maintain that God does not reveal his reasons for actualizing TW rather than HW because humans could not understand the reasons, then one fairly obvious response is that an omnipotent God could give humans some sort of cognitive assistance so they *could* understand his reasons. Call it a "brain boost," if you like.[24] Such assistance would allow humans to understand God's reasons. It might be comparable to the innate ability of young children to learn their native languages intuitively.

Second, Christians presumably believe that humans in TW's heaven, would know why God actualized TW rather than HW. That being the case, God must be able to give those TW heavenly persons the appropriate comprehension assistance. If so, then it would seem that he could have done something similar for earthly persons in TW.

Third, one would think that God would have wanted to assist humans to understand his reasons for actualizing TW rather than HW, if only to forestall humans experiencing corrosive doubts about whether God exists due to an inability to understand why God actualized TW rather than HW.

---

24. Drange, *Nonbelief and Evil*, 206.

Those doubts could frustrate the purposes mentioned earlier for which Christians say that God created humans in the first place.

Sixth Challenge to the HW Argument: More Skeptical Theism

God does not reveal his reasons for actualizing TW rather than HW because not revealing them produces greater goods or prevents greater harms (both hidden to us now) than what would result from his giving us his reasons.

Response

The value of such hidden goods or avoided evils must always be less than the value associated with the *greatest good* of experiencing the *summum bonum* of salvation that *all* HW persons would experience. In this regard, Christian philosopher Marilyn McCord Adams says, "The good of beatific, face-to-face intimacy with God is simply incommensurate with any merely non-transcendent goods or ills a person might experience."[25]

Hence, I conclude that the use of skeptical theism to challenge the HW Argument does not succeed.

Section Summary

In the preceding section I aimed to show that the six Christian challenges to the soundness of the HW argument for the nonexistence of God are unsuccessful. In fact, if I'm correct that Christians have failed to delegitimize the claim that if God existed, he would have actualized HW rather than TW, then Christians, in a manner of speaking, could be said to be "hoist by their own petard (bomb)." The petard here would be the venerable and widely held Christian belief that existence with the beatific vision in TW's heaven is the *summum bonum* for humans. If it is, and if existence in TW's heaven is very similar to existence in HW, then, to deny the ethical and human flourishing superiority of HW over TW would be implicitly, and perhaps heretically, to deny the preferability of heavenly existence in TW to earthly existence in TW, a view which no Christian has ever held.

---

25. Adams, "Horrendous Evils," 218.

CHAPTER SUMMARY AND CONCLUSION

I set out the HW argument for the nonexistence of God which concludes that God does not exist because if he did, he would not have actualized TW but rather HW. I supported that contention by showing that HW would be superior to TW and all other possible worlds for compelling ethical and human flourishing reasons and by pointing out that in HW the purposes for which Christians claim God created humans would be far better realized than they would be in TW or any other possible world. Finally, I argued that the most important Christian challenges to the HW argument for the nonexistence of God are unsuccessful, and that its conclusion that God does not exist is therefore upheld.

CODA FOR PART THREE

The five atheological arguments in the five chapters of part III aimed to show that the most telling error of Christianity is its claim that atheism is false because the Christian God exists. However, it should be noted that, *mutatis mutandum* (with appropriate changes), those five arguments also work to show the nonexistence of other theistic conceptions of deity, for example, those associated with Islam and Judaism.

Bibliography

Ackerman, Andy, dir. "The Foundation." *Seinfeld*, season 8, episode 1. Aired Sep 19, 1996, on NBC.
"Adam, Eve, and Evolution." Catholic Answers, Aug 10, 2004. http://www.catholic.com/library/Adam_Eve_and_Evolution.asp.
Adams, Marilyn McCord. "Horrendous Evils and the Goodness of God." In *The Problem of Evil*, edited by Marilyn McCord Adams and Robert Merrihew Adams, 209–21. Oxford: Oxford University Press, 1990.
Adams, Robert. "Middle Knowledge and the Problem of Evil." *American Philosophical Quarterly* 14 (April 1977) 109–17.
———. "Must God Create the Best?" In *The Problem of Evil: Selected Readings*, edited by Michael Peterson, 275–88. Notre Dame, IN: University of Notre Dame Press 1990, 275–82.
"After IVF." Loma Linda University Center for Fertility and IVF, n.d. https://lomalindafertility.com/resources/what-to-do-with-frozen-embryos/.
"Albigensian Crusade." New World Encyclopedia, last updated Nov 20, 2023. https://www.newworldencyclopedia.org/entry/Albigensian_Crusade.
Alfeyev, Hilarion. "Blessed Are Those Who Have Not Seen and Yet Have Believed." Department for External Church Relations of the Moscow Patriarchate, n.d. http://orthodoxeurope.org/print/19/2/11.aspx.
Andersson, Gerhard. "Chronic Pain and Praying to a Higher power: Useful or Useless?" *Journal of Religion and Health* 47 (September 2007) 176–87. https://pubmed.ncbi.nlm.nih.gov/19105010/.
Arieti, James, and Patrick A. Wilson. *The Scientific and the Divine: Conflict and Reconciliation from Ancient Greece to the Present*. New York: Rowman and Littlefield, 2003.
"Atheists Remain Most Disliked Religious Minority in the U.S." University of Minnesota, Sep 12, 2016. https://twin-cities.umn.edu/news-events/atheists-remain-most-disliked-religious-minority-us.
Augustine, Saint. *The Confessions of St. Augustine*. Translated by Edward Pusey. New York: Macmillan, 1961.
Avalos, Hector. *Fighting Words: The Origins Of Religious Violence*. Amherst, NY: Prometheus, 2005.

BIBLIOGRAPHY

Barker, Dan, and Michael Horner, eds. "Did Jesus Really Rise From The Dead?" The Secular Web, 1996. https://infidels.org/library/modern/dan-barker-barker-horner/.

Bauckham, Richard. "Universalism: A Historical Survey." *Themelios* 4.2 (September 1978) 47–54.

Beilby, James. *Postmortem Opportunity*. Downers Grove, IL: Intervarsity, 2021.

Benagiano, Giuseppe, et al. "Fate of Fertilized Human Oocytes." *Reproductive Medicine Online* 21 (2010) 732–43.

Benson, Herbet, et al. "Study of the Therapeutic Effects of Intercessory Prayer (STEP) in Cardiac Bypass Patients: A Multicenter Randomized Trial of Uncertainty and Certainty of Receiving Intercessory Prayer." American Heart Journal 151.4 (April 2006) 934–42. https://pubmed.ncbi.nlm.nih.gov/16569567/.

Berger, Kathleen Stassen. *The Developing Person through Childhood and Adolescence*. 6th ed. New York: Macmillan, 2003.

Biskupic, Joan. "Scalia Blasts Skeptics Of Christian Beliefs—High-Court Justice Eschews His Brethren's Restraint." *Washington Post*, Apr 10, 1996.

"Bogdan Chmielnicki (1595–1657)." Jewish Virtual Library, 2008. https://www.jewishvirtuallibrary.org/chmielnicki-khmelnitski-bogdan-x00b0.

Broussard, Karlo. "Adam and Eve Were Real People." Catholic Answers, n.d. https://www.catholic.com/qa/adam-and-eve-were-real-people.

"Cambodia." University of Minnesota, n.d. https://cla.umn.edu/chgs/holocaust-genocide-education/resource-guides/cambodia.

Carrier, Richard. "Dear Christian: You Might Be Worshiping the Antichrist." *Richard Carrier* (blog), Nov 27, 2022. https://www.richardcarrier.info/archives/21092.

———. "Moral Facts Naturally Exist (and Science Could Find Them)." In *The End of Christianity*, edited by John Loftus Amherst, 333–64. NY: Prometheus, 2011.

———. "Real Basis for a Moral World." *Richard Carrier* (blog), Nov 12, 2018. https://www.richardcarrier.info/archives/14879.

———. "Your Own Moral Reasoning: Some Things to Consider." *Richard Carrier* (blog), Mar 19, 2018. https://www.richardcarrier.info/archives/13819.

———. "Why Didn't Jesus Tell Us about Germs?" Debunking Christianity, Jan 12, 2014. https://www.debunking-christianity.com/2014/01/why-didnt-jesus-tell-us-about-germs.html?m=1.

Carroll, Sean. *The Big Picture*. New York: Dutton, 2017.

Cherones, Tom, dir. "The Outing." *Seinfeld*, season 4, episode 17. Aired Feb 11, 1993, on NBC.

"Child Mortality and Causes of Death." World Health Organization, n.d. https://www.who.int/data/gho/data/themes/topics/topic-details/GHO/child-mortality-and-causes-of-death.

Christina, Greta. *Why Are You Atheists So Angry? 99 Things That Piss Off the Godless*. Durham, NC: Pitchstone, 2012.

Cliff Notes. "Plot Summary, 'The Better Angels of Our Nature' by Steven Pinker in 5 Minutes—Book Review." YouTube, Nov 19, 2022. https://www.youtube.com/watch?v=yYUurHLMTPc.

Confucius. "Lunyu XIV. 34. (381)." Wengu—Chinese Classics, n.d. http://wengu.tartarie.com/wg/wengu.php?no=381&l=Lunyu.

Craig, William Lane. "The Fate of Those Who Reject Christ." Reasonable Faith, Apr 18, 2021. https://www.reasonablefaith.org/writings/question-answer/the-fate-of-those-who-reject-christ.

———. *In Quest of the Historical Adam: A Biblical and Scientific Exploration*. Grand Rapids: Eerdmans, 2021.

———. "Middle Knowledge." Reasonable Faith, Sep 24, 2007. https://www.reasonablefaith.org/writings/question-answer/middle-knowledge.

———. "'No Other Name': A Middle Knowledge Perspective on the Exclusivity of Salvation Through Christ." *Faith and Philosophy* 6.2 (April 1989) 185.

———. "Politically Incorrect Salvation." In *Christian Apologetics in the Post-Modern World*, edited by T. P. Phillips and D. Ockholm, 75–97. Downer's Grove, IL: InterVarsity, 1995.

———. *Reasonable Faith*. 3rd ed. Wheaton, IL: Crossway, 2008.

Davison, Scott A. "On the Puzzle of Petitionary Prayer." Core, Dec 31, 2010. https://core.ac.uk/download/pdf/153326315.pdf.

———. "Petitionary Prayer." In *The Oxford Handbook of Philosophical Theology*, edited by Thomas P. Flint and Michael Rea, 286–305. Oxford: Oxford University Press, 2009.

Delamontagne, R. Georges. "High Religiosity and Societal Dysfunction in the United States during the First Decade of the Twenty-First Century." *Evolutionary Psychology* 8.4 (October 2010) 617–57. https://journals.sagepub.com/doi/10.1177/147470491000800407.

DellaPergola, Sergio. "Some Fundamentals of Jewish Demographic History." In *Papers in Jewish Demography 1997*, edited by Sergio DellaPergola and Judith Even, 11–33. Jerusalem: The Hebrew University, 2001. https://www.bjpa.org/content/upload/bjpa/dell/DellaPergola%20Some%20Fundamentals.pdf.

Diamant, Jeff, and Besheer Mohamed. "What the Data Says about Abortion in the U.S." Pew Research Center, Jan 11, 2023. https://www.pewresearch.org/short-reads/2023/01/11/what-the-data-says-about-abortion-in-the-u-s-2/.

Diderot, Denis. *Oeuvres Complètes*. Vol. 1. Paris: Garnier Fréres, 1875.

"Discrimination against Atheists." Wikipedia, last updated Dec 6, 2023. https://en.wikipedia.org/wiki/Discrimination_against_atheists.

Dion, Philip. "Does God Will It." *The Priest* (March 1978) 19.

Dolphin, Lambert. "World Population Since Creation." Lambert Dolphin's Place, Jul 31, 2007. https://www.ldolphin.org/popul.html.

Drange, Theodore. *Nonbelief and Evil*. Amherst, NY: Prometheus, 1998.

Entringer, Theresa M., et al. "Big Five Personality and Religiosity: Bidirectional Cross-Lagged Effects and their Moderation by Culture." *Journal of Personality* 91.3 (June 2023) 736–52. https://onlinelibrary.wiley.com/doi/10.1111/jopy.12770?af=R.

Everitt, Nicholas. *The Nonexistence of God*. London: Rutledge Press, 2004.

Find Qualia. "Enlightenment Now (S01EP20)." YouTube, Nov 30, 2022. https://www.youtube.com/watch?v=XB66RfJR5rQ.

Finney, John R. and H. Newton Malony Jr. "Empirical Studies of Christian Prayer: A Review of the Literature." *Journal of Psychology and Theology* 13.2 (June 1985) 104–15. https://journals.sagepub.com/doi/abs/10.1177/009164718501300203.

Floyd, Shawn. "Thomas Aquinas: Moral Philosophy." Internet Encyclopedia of Philosophy, 2018. https://iep.utm.edu/thomasaquinas-moral-philosophy/.

France, R. T. *The Gospel of Matthew*. New International Commentary on the New Testament. Grand Rapids: Eerdmans, 2007.

Franken, Al. "The Gospel of Supply Side Jesus." Beliefnet, 2003. https://www.beliefnet.com/news/2003/09/the-gospel-of-supply-side-jesus.aspx.

BIBLIOGRAPHY

Gerber, Alan S., et al. "The Big Five Personality Traits in the Political Arena." *Annual Review of Political Science* 14 (June 2011) 265–87. https://www.annualreviews.org/doi/10.1146/annurev-polisci-051010-111659.

"Glory." Encyclopedia, last updated May 11, 2018. https://www.encyclopedia.com/philosophy-and-religion/bible/bible-general/glory.

Hacker, William. *God, Time, and Knowledge*. Ithaca: Cornell University Press, 1989.

———. "A Refutation of Middle Knowledge." *Nous* 20 (1986) 545–57.

Hagerty, Barbara Bradley. "Christians Debate: Was Jesus for Small Government?" NPR, Apr 16, 2012. https://www.npr.org/2012/04/16/150568478/christian-conservatives-poverty-not-government-business.

Handwerk, Brian. "An Evolutionary Timeline of Homo Sapiens." *Smithsonian Magazine*, Feb 22, 2021. https://www.smithsonianmag.com/science-nature/essential-timeline-understanding-evolution-homo-sapiens-180976807/.

Hanlon, Chris. "On Fake Emerson Quotes." Avidly, Aug 27, 2019. https://avidly.lareviewofbooks.org/2019/08/27/on-fake-emerson-quotes/.

Harent, Stéphane. "Original Sin." In *The Catholic Encyclopedia*, vol. 11. New York: Robert Appleton Company, 1911. Edited by Sean Hyland. http://www.newadvent.org/cathen/11312a.htm.

Hickel, Jason, and Dylan Sullivan. "Capitalism and Extreme Poverty: A Global Analysis of Real Wages, Human Height, and Mortality Since the Long Sixteenth Century." *World Development* 161 (January 2023). https://www.sciencedirect.com/science/article/pii/S0305750X22002169#section-cited-by.

Hick, John. *Evil and the God of Love*. New York: Harper and Row, 1978.

Hitchens, Christopher. *The Missionary Position: Mother Teresa in Theory and Practice*. London: Verso, 1995.

Hobbes, Thomas. "Nasty, Brutish, and Short." Oxford Reference, n.d. https://www.oxfordreference.com/display/10.1093/oi/authority.20110803100223527.

Hodge, Charles. *Systematic Theology*. Vol. 2. Grand Rapids: Eerdmans, 1940.

Holder, R. Ward. "John Calvin (1509–1564)." Internet Encyclopedia of Philosophy, n.d. https://iep.utm.edu/john-calvin/.

Horn, Trent. "Why Did God Create the World?" Catholic Answers, n.d. https://www.catholic.com/qa/why-did-god-create-the-world.

Howard-Synder, D., and Howard-Synder, F. "How an Unsurpassable Being can Create a Surpassable World." *Faith and Philosophy* 11 (1994) 260–68.

Hunt, David P. "Middle Knowledge: The 'Foreknowledge Defense.'" *International Journal for Philosophy of Religion* 28 (1990) 1–24.

Idahosa, Chizobam. "Love Is a Command: Not a Suggestions." Beautiful in Jesus, n.d. https://beautifulinjesus.com/love-is-a-command/.

"IVF by the Numbers." Penn Medicine, Mar 14, 2018. https://www.pennmedicine.org/updates/blogs/fertility-blog/2018/march/ivf-by-the-numbers.

Johnson, Ian. "Who Killed More: Hitler, Stalin, or Mao?" ChinaFile, Feb 5, 2018. https://www.chinafile.com/library/nyrb-china-archive/who-killed-more-hitler-stalin-or-mao.

Kaneda, Toshiko, and Carl Haub. "How Many People Have Ever Lived on Earth?" PBR, Nov 15, 2022. https://www.prb.org/articles/how-many-people-have-ever-lived-on-earth/.

BIBLIOGRAPHY

Kavanagh, Kathryn. "Most Human Embryos Naturally Die after Conception—Restrictive Abortion Laws Fail to Take This Embryo Loss into Account." The Conversation, Sep 1, 2022. https://theconversation.com/most-human-embryos-naturally-die-after-conception-restrictive-abortion-laws-fail-to-take-this-embryo-loss-into-account-187904.

Kennedy, Bruce P., et al. "Social Capital, Income Inequality, and Firearm Violent Crime." *Social Science and Medicine* 47.1 (1998) 7–17.

Kenny, Anthony. *The God of the Philosophers*. Oxford: Clarendon, 1979.

Kierkegaard, Soren. *Concluding Unscientific Postscript*. Translated by David F. Swenson and Walter Lowrie. Princeton: Princeton University Press, 1941.

Klink, Bart. "The Untenability of Theistic Evolution." The Secular Web, Jan 1, 2009. http://www.infidels.org/library/modern/bart_klink/evolution.html.

La Croix, Richard. "Unjustified Evil and God's Choice." *Sophia* 13.1 (1974) 20–28.

Langtry, Bruce. *God, the Best, and Evil*. Oxford: Oxford University Press, 2008.

Lataster, Raphael. *The Case Against Theism: Why the Evidence Disproves God's Existence*. London: Routledge, 2018.

"The Legal Definition of Genocide." Prevent Genocide International, n.d. http://www.preventgenocide.org/genocide/officialtext-printerfriendly.htm.

Lewis, C. S. *The Problem of Pain*. New York: HarperOne, 1996.

Loftus, John W. "The Darwinian Problem of Evil." In *The Christian Delusion: Why Faith Fails*, edited by John Loftus, 237–70. Amherst, NY: Prometheus, 2010.

———. *The Outsider Test for Faith*. Amherst, NY: Prometheus, 2013.

———. *Why I Became an Atheist*. Amherst, NY: Prometheus, 2008

"Love." Oxford Learner's Dictionary, n.d. https://www.oxfordlearnersdictionaries.com/us/definition/english/love_1.

Luther, Martin. "Tenth Sermon on John 6." In *Luther's Works*, vol. 23, edited by Jaroslav Pelikan, translated by Martin H. Bertram, 80. St. Louis: Concordia, 1959.

Lux, Mike. "How Do Christians Become Conservative?" *HuffPost*, May 10, 2010. https://www.huffpost.com/entry/how-do-christians-become_b_570361.

Maggiolini, Alessandro. "Heaven." In *Catechism of the Catholic Church*, sec. 1023–29. Vatican City: Libreria Editrice Vaticana, 1993. https://www.vatican.va/archive/ENG0015/__P2M.HTM.

———. "The Life of Man—To Know and Love God." In *Catechism of the Catholic Church*, sec. 1–3. Vatican City: Libreria Editrice Vaticana, 1993. https://www.vatican.va/archive/ENG0015/__P2.HTM.

———. "The World Was Created for the Glory Of God." In *Catechism of the Catholic Church*, 2nd ed., sec. 293–94. Washington, DC: United States Catholic Conference, 2011. http://www.scborromeo.org/ccc/p1s2c1p4.htm#293.

Mark, Joshua J. "Thirty Years' War." World History Encyclopedia, Aug 11, 2022. https://www.worldhistory.org/Thirty_Years%27_War/.

Martin, Michael. *Atheism: A Philosophical Justification*. Philadelphia: Temple University Press, 1990.

Martin, Michael, and Ricki Monnier. *The Impossibility of God*. Amherst, NY: Prometheus, 2003.

McDowell, Josh. *Evidence That Demands a Verdict*. San Bernadino, CA: Here's Life, 1979.

McNeill, Jim. "How Many People Were Killed During the French Wars of Religion?" Social History in the Touraine, Sep 12, 2012. https://jimmcneill.wordpress.com/2012/09/12/how-many-people-were-killed-during-the-french-wars-of-religion/.

BIBLIOGRAPHY

McReavy, L. L., and F. X. Meehan. "Pacifism." In *New Catholic Encyclopedia*, vol. 10, 2nd ed., edited by Thomas Carson and Joann Cerrito, 747. Detroit: Gale, 2003.

Messerly, John. "Why Non-Falsifiable Beliefs Are Vacuous." Reason and Meaning, Nov 26, 2020. https://reasonandmeaning.com/2020/11/26/why-non-falsifiable-beliefs-are-absurd/.

Miller, Ed. L., *God and Reason*. New York: MacMillan, 1972.

Mohr, Steven. "Exposing the Myth of Alcoholics Anonymous." *Free Inquiry* 29.3 (April/May 2009) 42–48.

Murray, Michael. *Nature Red in Truth and Claw*. Oxford: University of Oxford Press, 2008.

Narvaez, Darcia, and Daniel K. Lapsley, eds. *Personality, Identity, and Character: Explorations in Moral Psychology*. Cambridge: Cambridge University Press, 2009.

Nilsson, Artur, and John T. Jost. "The Authoritarian-Conservatism Nexus." *Current Opinion in Behavioral Sciences* 34 (August 2020) 148–154. https://www.sciencedirect.com/science/article/abs/pii/S2352154620300401?via%3Dihub.

"On Average, Are Atheists as Moral as Theists?" The Secular Web, n.d. https://infidels.org/library/modern/nontheism-atheism-more-moral/.

O'Connor, Timothy. *Theism and Ultimate Explanation: The Necessary Shape of Contingency*. Oxford: Blackwell, 2008.

O'Neill, Aaron. "Estimated Share of African Slaves Who Did Not Survive the Middle Passage Journey to the Americas Each Year from 1501 to 1866." Jun 21, 2022. https://www.statista.com/statistics/1143458/annual-share-slaves-deaths-during-middle-passage/.

Orchestral Manoeuvres in the Dark. "History of Modern (Part I)." Side 1, track 1 of *History of Modern (Part I)*. Liverpool: The Motor Museum Studio, 2011.

Ord, Toby. "The Scourge: Moral Implications of Natural Embryo Loss." *The American Journal of Bioethics* 8.7 (2008) 12–19.

Ortlund, Gavin. "Did Augustine Read Genesis 1 Literally?" Carl F. H. Henry Center for Theological Understanding, Sep 4, 2017. https://henrycenter.tiu.edu/2017/09/did-augustine-read-genesis-1-literally/.

Parrot, André. "Abraham." Britannica, last updated Nov 19, 2023. https://www.britannica.com/biography/Abraham.

Parsons, Keith. "Hell: Christianity's Most Damnable Doctrine." In *The End of Christianity*, edited by John Loftus, 233–54. Amherst, NY: Prometheus, 2011.

Paul, Gregory S. "The Big Religion Questions Finally Solved." *Free Inquiry* 28.1 (December/January 2008) 24–36.

———. "Theodicy's Problem: A Statistical Look at the Holocaust of the Children, and the Implications of Natural Evil for the Free Will and Best of All Worlds Hypotheses." *Philosophy and Theology* 19.1–2 (2007) 125–49.

PBS NewsHour. "How the World is Getting Better, Not Worse, According to Steven Pinker." YouTube, Feb 22, 2018. https://www.youtube.com/watch?v=tvEiiYfVXnk.

Pearce, Jonathan M. S. *30 Arguments against the Existence of God*. Fareham, UK: Onus, 2022.

Philipse, Herman. *God in the Age of Science? A Critique of Religious Reason*. Oxford: Oxford University Press, 2012.

Pinker, Steven. *The Better Angels of Our Nature*. New York: Penguin, 2012.

———. *Enlightenment Now*. Harlow, UK: Penguin, 2019.

BIBLIOGRAPHY

Piper, John. "Biblical Texts to Show God's Zeal for His Own Glory." *Desiring God*, Nov 24, 2007. https://www.desiringgod.org/articles/biblical-texts-to-show-gods-zeal-for-his-own-glory.

Plantinga, Alvin. *God, Freedom, and Evil*. Grand Rapids: Eerdmans, 1974.

"Punishment." Merriam-Webster, n.d. https://www.merriam-webster.com/dictionary/punishment.

Putnam, Rhyne. "Will My Lost Neighbor Have Another Chance to Receive Jesus After Death?" *Christianity Today*, August 5, 2021. https://christianitytoday.com/ct/2021/august-web-only/postmortem-opportunity-james-beilby-conversion-death.html?utm_medium=widgetsocial.

Quinn, Philip. "God, Axiological Perfection, and Possible Worlds." In *God: The Contemporary Discussion*, edited by F. Sontag and M. Darrol Bryant, 199–215. New York: The Rose of Sharon, 1982.

Raine, Adrian, et al. "High Rates of Violence, Crime, Academic Problems, and Behavioral Problems in Males With Both Early Neuromotor Deficits and Unstable Family Environments." *Archives of General Psychiatry* 53.6 (1996) 544–49.

Rannard, Georgina, and Eve Webster. "Leopold II: Belgium 'Wakes Up' to Its Bloody Colonial Past." BBC, Jun 12, 2020. https://www.bbc.com/news/world-europe-53017188.

Rawls, John. *A Theory of Justice*. Cambridge, MA: Harvard University Press, 1971.

Rose, Patrick A. "Resist Not Evil." *Morning Star New Church*, Aug 1, 2004. http://www.morningstarchapel.org/articles/2004/Resist%20Not%20Evil.html.

Roser, Max. "Mortality in the Past: Every Second Child Died." *Our World in Data*, Apr 11, 2023. https://ourworldindata.org/child-mortality-in-the-past#article-citation.

Routley, Nick. "How Many Humans Have Ever Lived?" *Visual Capitalist*, Mar 25, 2022. https://www.visualcapitalist.com/cp/how-many-humans-have-ever-lived/.

Rowe, William. *Can God Be Free?* Oxford: Clarendon, 2004.

"Rwanda Genocide: 100 Days of Slaughter." BBC, Apr 4, 2019. https://www.bbc.com/news/world-africa-26875506.

Russell, Bertrand. *Why I Am Not a Christian: And Other Essays on Religion and Related Subjects*. Edited by Paul Edwards. New York: Simon and Schuster, 1957.

Saletan, William. "God's Work?" *Slate*, Dec 4, 2014. https://slate.com/technology/2014/12/creationism-poll-how-many-americans-believe-the-bible-is-literal-inerrant-or-symbolic.html.

Schlesinger, G. *Religion and Scientific Method*. Dordrecht: Reidel, 1977.

Shah, Idries. *Reflections*. Baltimore: Penguin, 1970.

Sherlock, Michael A. "The Atheist Atrocities Fallacy—Hitler, Stalin and Pol Pot." *Michael A. Sherlock Author*, Oct 21, 2014. https://michaelsherlockauthor.wordpress.com/2014/10/21/the-atheist-atrocities-fallacy-hitler-stalin-pol-pot-in-memory-of-christopher-hitchens/.

Sinnott-Armstrong, Walter. *Moral Psychology*. Cambridge, MA: MIT Press, 2009.

SKYDIVEPHIL. "Can Animals Suffer? Debunking William Lane Craig and Other Philosophers Who Say No." YouTube, Oct 3, 2012. https://www.youtube.com/watch?v=mLSwRcvX72M&t=1284s.

Slick, Matt. "Do People Send Themselves to Hell or Does God Send Them There?" CARM, Jun 6, 2014. https://carm.org/about-god/do-people-send-themselves-to-hell-or-does-god-send-them-there/.

Slisco, Aila. "Evangelicals Are Now Rejecting 'Liberal' Teachings of Jesus." *Newsweek*, Aug 9, 2023. https://www.newsweek.com/evangelicals-rejecting-jesus-teachings-liberal-talking-points-pastor-1818706.
Spencer, Daniel H. "Evolution, Middle Knowledge, and Theodicy," *Forum Philosophicum* 25.2 (Autumn 2021) 215–33.
Stanley, Bessie Anderson. "Success (Poem)." *Brown Book Magazine*, 1904.
Sterba, James. *Is a Good God Logically Possible?* New York: Palgrave Macmillan, 2019.
Suzuki, Emi, and Haruna Kashiwase. "New UN Estimates Show 14,000 Children Die and 5,000 Babies are Stillborn Every Day Mostly of Preventable Causes." World Bank Blogs, Jan 9, 2023. https://blogs.worldbank.org/opendata/new-un-estimates-show-14000-children-die-and-5000-babies-are-stillborn-every-day-mostly.
Swinburne, Richard. "Does St. Paul Believe in Original Sin? Yeah, but So What?" *Journal of Analytic Theology* 9 (2021) 291–313.
———. *The Existence of God*. 2nd ed. Oxford: Oxford University Press, 2004.
Tarico, Valerie. "God's Emotions: Why the Biblical God Is Hopelessly Human." In *The End of Christianity*, edited by John Loftus, 155–77. Amherst, N.Y.: Prometheus, 2011.
———. "Why Right-Wing Christian Leaders Are Often Indifferent to Needless Suffering." Sep 23, 2015. https://www.alternet.org/2015/09/why-right-wing-christian-leaders-are-often-indifferent-needless-suffering.
Tennyson, Alfred. *The Complete Poetical Works of Tennyson*. Boston: Houghton Mifflin, 1898. https://archive.org/details/completepoeticalootenn/page/n9/mode/2up.
Thomas, Derek. "Why Did Adam's Sin Have Such Terrible Consequences for Humanity and Creation?" Thirdmill, n.d. https://thirdmill.org/answers/answer.asp/file/43142.
Turnbull, H. W., ed. *The Correspondence of Isaac Newton: 1661–1675*. Vol. 1. London: Royal Society at the University Press, 1959.
Vaquero, Elena, et al. "Diagnostic Evaluation of Women Experiencing Repeated in Vitro Fertilization Failure." *European Journal of Obstetrics and Gynecology and Reproductive Biology* 125.1 (2006) 79–84.
Wells, Steve. "How Many Has God Killed? Complete List and Estimated Total (Including Apocryphal Killings)." Dwindling in Unbelief, May 17, 2013. https://dwindlinginunbelief.blogspot.com/2010/04/drunk-with-blood-gods-killings-in-bible.html.
Westminster Confession. "Confession Chapter 4: Of Creation." Reformed Forum, Feb 6, 2008. https://reformedforum.org/podcasts/chapter-4-of-creation/.
Wilson, Ralph F. "Love Your Enemies." JesusWalk Bible Study Series, 2023. https://www.jesuswalk.com/luke/018-enemies.htm.
Wink, Walter. "The Third Way." Chicago Sunday Evening Club, Nov 14, 1993. https://csec.org/csec/sermon/wink_3707.htm.
Woodward, Kenneth L. "A $1 Million Habit." *Newsweek* (September 1980) 35.
Zinaman, Michael J., et al. "Estimates of Human Fertility and Pregnancy Loss." *Fertility and Sterility* 65.3 (1996) 503–9.
Zuckerman, Phil. *Society without God: What the Least Religious Nations Can Tell Us about Contentment*. New York: NYU Press, 2008.
Zuckerman, Phil, et al. *The Nonreligious: Understanding Secular People and Societies*. New York: Oxford Academic, 2016. https://academic.oup.com/book/11828.

About the Author

Richard Schoenig, PhD
Professor of Philosophy (Ret.)
San Antonio College
San Antonio, Texas
bbphiler@gmail.com

I was raised in Bergenfield, New Jersey—a suburb of New York City. I received a BS in chemistry from Fordham University in the Bronx and later a PhD in chemistry from the University of Notre Dame. After a two-year stint as an officer in the US Army Corps of Engineers, I earned an MA and PhD in philosophy from Indiana University, Bloomington. I've published in a variety of chemistry and philosophy journals, am the author of *Exploring Philosophy*, an introductory philosophy textbook, and have written popular articles for magazines such as *The Humanist, The American Rationalist, Free Inquiry*, and *Secular Nation*. I retired after teaching philosophy at San Antonio College in San Antonio, Texas for forty-five years. When not trying to figure out the meaning of life, I can be found grousing about politics, doing crossword puzzles, rooting for the San Antonio Spurs, working on physical fitness, especially playing pick-up basketball, and enjoying the mountains of West Texas (Ft. Davis) and Southwestern Colorado (Silverton).

Index

Abraham, 37, 181, 205
Ackerman, Andy, 84n9
Adam, 3–4, 3n1, 4n2, 5, 6, 7, 8, 8n7, 9, 12, 13, 14, 15, 16, 17, 18, 19, 20, 21, 74, 124, 169, 180, 181, 183, 184, 208, 209
Adams, Marilyn McCord, 214, 214n25
Adams, Robert, 168n21, 209–10, 209n15, 210n16, 211, 211n21
Alfeyev, Hilarion, 73, 74n2
Andersson, Gerhard, 28n1
Apple, Doug, 106–7, 106n9
Aquinas, Thomas, 198, 208–9
Arieti, James, 73n1
Augustine, 5, 31, 57, 57n5, 206
Avalos, Hector, 90n4

Barker, Dan, 47n3
Bauckham, Richard, 167, 167n19
Bayes, Thomas, 192
Beilby, James, 168, 168n22, 169, 171–72, 171n30, 172n32, 175
Benagiano, Giuseppe, 11n10, 156n4
Benson, Herbert, 28n2
Berger, Kathleen Stassen, 11n10, 156n4
Biskupic, Joan, 78n9
Broussard, Karlo, 20n18

Calvin, John, 74
Carrier, Richard, 114, 114n18, 123n3, 126, 126n7, 131n3
Cherones, Tom, 76n7

Chmielnicki, Bogdan (Bohdan Khmelnytsky), 93n13
Christina, Greta, 80n1
Confucius, 104, 104n5
Craig, William Lane, xix, xixn1, 17n15, 38, 38n3, 76, 157, 157n6, 162, 162n14, 163–64, 164n17, 165, 169, 169n23, 170–71, 170nn27–28, 171n29, 180, 180n3, 182n7, 183–84, 183n9, 184n10

Davison, Scott A., 33n8
Dawkins, Richard, 76
Delamontagne, R. Georges, 24n32
DellaPergola, Sergio, 93n12
Dennett, Daniel, 76–77
Diamant, Jeff, 116n1
Diderot, Denis, 9, 9n8, 39, 39n4
Dion, Philip, 31, 31n5, 32, 206, 206n13, 207
Dolphin, Lambert, 91n5
Drange, Theodore, 213n24

Emerson, Ralph Waldo, 72n3, 141n6
Enos, 5
Entringer, Theresa M., 128n10
Eve, 3–4, 3n1, 4n2, 5, 6, 7, 8, 8n7, 9, 12, 13, 14, 15, 16, 17, 18, 19, 20, 21, 74, 124, 169, 180, 184, 208, 209
Exley, Helen, 141n6

Falwell, Jerry, 127, 128

INDEX

Finney, John R., 28n1
Flint, Thomas, 17n15
Floyd, Shawn, 198, 198n3, 208, 209n14
France, R. T., 105–6, 105n7, 106n8, 109, 109nn13–14
Franken, Al, 128n9
Freud, Sigmund, 77

Gerber, Alan S., 128n10

Hacker, William, 168n21
Hagerty, Barbara Bradley, 125n5
Handwerk, Brian, 180n1, 187n3
Hanlon, Chris, 141n6
Harent, Stéphane, 10n9, 12n13
Harris, Sam, 76
Haub, Carl, 158n9, 181n5, 182n8
Heli, 5
Hick, John, 96, 96n19, 205, 205n11, 206, 206n12, 207, 209
Hickel, Jason, 94n17
Hill, Jonathan, 3n1
Hitchens, Christopher, 32n6
Hitler, Adolph, xx, 22, 56, 89, 90, 91, 94, 112–13, 169, 206
Hobbes, Thomas, 162n13
Hodge, Charles, 76, 76n6, 153, 153n1, 155, 160
Holder, R. Ward, 75n4
Horner, Michael, 47, 47n3, 48, 49
Howard-Synder, D., 211n22
Howard-Synder, F., 211n22
Hunt, David P., 168n21

Idahosa, Chizobam, 111n16

Jack the Ripper, 22
Jesus Christ, xx, 5, 19, 20, 25, 30, 33, 37, 38, 41, 43, 47, 54, 57, 58, 70, 74, 76, 77, 99–115, 123, 126, 127, 164
Job, 37
Johansen, Tracie, 141n6
Johnson, Ian, 90, 90n2, 92n8
Joost, John T., 128n10
Joseph (father of Jesus), 5
Judas Iscariot, 30

Kaneda, Toshiko, 158n9, 181n5, 182n8
Kashiwase, Haruna, 41n5
Kavanagh, Kathryn, 11, 11n10, 156n4
Kennedy, Bruce P., 24n31
Kenny, Anthony, 168n21
Kierkegaard, Soren, 41, 41n7, 75, 76n5
Klink, Bart, 5, 5n4

LaCroix, Richard, 197, 197n1
Langtry, Bruce, 211n22
Lapsley, Daniel K., 22n23
Lazarus, 48
Lewis, C. S., 47, 47n2
Lincoln, Abraham, 17, 199n6
Loftus, John W., 42n8, 188n4
Lucifer, 8
Luther, Martin, 10, 12, 38, 38n2, 74, 74n3
Lux, Mike, 122, 122nn1–2, 128

Maggiolini, Alessandro, 81n5, 198n2, 201n7
Malony, H. Newton Jr., 28n1
Mao Zedong, xx, 90, 91
Mark, Joshua J., 92n11
Martin, Michael, 197n1
Mary (mother of Jesus), 205
McDowell, Josh, 77, 77n8
McNeill, Jim, 92n10
McReavy, L. L., 107n11, 108
Meehan, F. X., 107n11, 108
Messerly, John, 189
Miller, Ed. L., 38n1
Mohamed, Besheer, 116n1
Mohr, Steven, 23, 23nn24–25
Monnier, Ricki, 197n1
Montgomery, Peter, 125
Moore, Russell, 125
Moses, 205
Mother Teresa, 32, 33
Murray, Michael, 188n4

Narvaez, Darcia, 22n23
Nilsson, Artur, 128n10
Noah, 37, 91n6

O'Connor, Timothy, 211n22
O'Neill, Aaron, 94n16

INDEX

Ord, Toby, 11n10, 156n4
Ortlund, Gavin, 5n3

Parrot, André, 181n4
Parsons, Keith, 46n1
Pascal, Blaise, 55
Paul, 5, 19, 20, 20n19, 21, 37, 41, 160, 161, 163, 165, 183, 204, 205
Paul, Gregory S., 24n32, 124, 124n4
Pearce, Jonathan M. S., 14, 145–46, 145n1, 146n2, 174–75, 174n33
Peter, 205
Pinker, Steven, 23–24, 24n28
Piper, John, 81–83, 81n6, 83n7, 85
Pius XII, Pope, 19
Plantinga, Alvin, 17n15, 211n20
Pol Pot, xx, 22, 89, 90, 91
Putnam, Rhyne, 160–61, 161n12, 169, 169n24, 175–76, 176n34

Quinn, Philip, 210, 210n17, 211

Raine, Adrian, 24n31
Rand, Ayn, 127
Rannard, Georgina, 94n14
Rawls, John, 137n5
Rose, Patrick A., 104, 105, 105n6, 106
Roser, Max, 158n10
Routley, Nick, 7n6, 11n11, 95n18, 156n5, 158n8, 187n2
Rowe, William, 210, 210nn18–19, 211
Russell, Bertrand, 54, 54n4

Saadi of Shiraz, 102
Saletan, William, 3n1
Salvi, John, 117, 117n2
Scalia, Antonin, 77, 123
Schlesinger, G., 211n20
Seinfeld, Jerry, 76, 84
Seth, 5

Shah, Idries, 102, 102n3
Shakespeare, William, 61
Sherlock, Michael A., 89–90, 89n1
Slick, Matt, 47, 48n4
Slisco, Aila, 126n6
Smith, Joseph, 205
Spencer, Daniel H., 18n17
Stalin, Joseph, xx, 22, 89, 90, 91, 94, 113
Stanley, Bessie Anderson, 72, 72n3, 141, 141n6
Sterba, James, 195n11
Sullivan, Dylan, 94n17
Suzuki, Emi, 41n5
Swinburne, Richard, 18n17, 211n20

Tarico, Valerie, 33, 33n7, 84n10
Tennyson, Alfred, 162n13
Tertullian of Antioch, 37
Thomas (apostle), 37, 76
Thomas, Derek, 15n14
Tiessen, Terrance, 17n15
Turek, Frank, 76

Vaquero, Elena, 11n10, 156n4

Webster, Eve, 94n14
Wells, Steve, 91n7
Wiggam, Albert Edward, 72n3, 141n6
Wilson, Patrick A., 72n1
Wilson, Ralph E., 101–4, 101n2, 102, 103, 103n4
Wink, Walter, 101, 101n1, 108, 108n12, 109
Woodward, Kenneth L., 128n8

Yates, Andrea, 54n3

Zinaman, Michael J., 11n10, 156n4
Zuckerman, Phil, 24n32

www.ingramcontent.com/pod-product-compliance
Lightning Source LLC
Chambersburg PA
CBHW070247230426
43664CB00014B/2424